Uncle John's BRIEFS

Quick Bits
of Fascinating Facts
and Amazing Trivia

D0972954

By the
Bathroom Readers'
Institute

Bathroom Readers' Press
Ashland, Oregon

OUR "REGULAR" READERS RAVE!

"I started reading your books after a colleague, ordinarily not much of a conversationalist, started to get smarter and smarter by the day. We couldn't figure out what was going on until we caught him reading one of your books. I bought my first one that night."

—**Ernie**

"God bless the *Bathroom Reader*. A lavatory without it is like a Pinto without a bumper: You could use it, but who'd want to?"

—**Gregory**

"*Bathroom Readers* are perfect for any occasion. When we needed a housewarming gift, we got an *Uncle John's*. When we needed Christmas presents, we gave *Uncle John's*. We were invited to a birthday party for three men and needed gifts for all three. Not knowing what they liked or needed, we bought three *Bathroom Readers*! The response?... They can't stop talking about it. Thank you."

—**John**

"Just wanted to let you guys know that you are the BEST. I absolutely love your books—I've been reading them since I was ten, and I'm sure I've read all eight or nine in my collection fifteen times each, at least. And, thanks to you, I now have an interesting (albeit annoying) tidbit for every conversation! Many kudos."

—**Kristin**

"I worship your books. They are the best. Congratulations on making the only book I've read in five years that I wasn't forced to read. Rock on!"

—**Vincent**

"You're the best thing to happen to the reading room since indoor plumbing and store-bought tissue (them cornhusks can get mighty rough, you know!) Keep up the good work and Go with the Flow!"

—**Rick**

UNCLE JOHN'S BRIEFS

Articles in this edition have been included from the following books: *Uncle John's Ultimate
Bathroom Reader* © 1996; *Uncle John's Giant 10th Anniversary Bathroom Reader* © 1997;
Uncle John's Great Big Bathroom Reader © 1998; *Uncle John's Absolutely Absorbing Bathroom
Reader* © 1999; *Uncle John's Legendary Lost Bathroom Reader* © 1999; *Uncle John's All-Purpose
Extra Strength Bathroom Reader* © 2000; *Uncle John's Supremely Satisfying Bathroom Reader*
© 2001; *Uncle John's Bathroom Reader Plunges Into History* © 2001; *Uncle John's Ahh-Inspiring
Bathroom Reader* © 2002; *Uncle John's Bathroom Reader Plunges Into the Universe* © 2002;
Uncle John's Bathroom Reader for Kids Only © 2002; *Uncle John's Unstoppable Bathroom Reader*
© 2003; *Uncle John's Bathroom Reader Plunges Into Great Lives* © 2003; *Uncle John's Colossal
Collection of Quotable Quotes* © 2004; *Uncle John's Slightly Irregular Bathroom Reader* © 2004;
Uncle John's Fast-Acting Long-Lasting Bathroom Reader © 2005; *Uncle John's Bathroom Reader
Tees Off on Golf* © 2005; *Uncle John's Bathroom Reader Plunges Into Hollywood* © 2005; *Uncle
John's Curiously Compelling Bathroom Reader* © 2006; *Uncle John's Bathroom Reader Wonderful
World of Odd* © 2006; *Uncle John's Tales to Inspire* © 2006; *Uncle John's Bathroom Reader
Quintessential Collection of Notable Quotables* © 2006; *Uncle John's Bathroom Reader Cat
Lover's Companion* © 2006; *Uncle John's Bathroom Reader Dog Lover's Companion* © 2007;
Uncle John's Bathroom Reader Plunges Into Music © 2007; *Uncle John's Bathroom Reader
Plunges Into National Parks* © 2007; *Uncle John's Triumphant 20th Anniversary Bathroom
Reader* © 2007; *Uncle John's Bathroom Reader Takes a Swing at Baseball* © 2008; *Uncle John's
Unsinkable Bathroom Reader* © 2008; *Uncle John's Bathroom Reader Plunges Into
Pennsylvania* © 2009; *Uncle John's Certified Organic Bathroom Reader* © 2009.

For information, write:
The Bathroom Readers' Institute, P.O. Box 1117, Ashland, OR 97520
www.bathroomreader.com • 888-488-4642

Cover design by Michael Brunsfeld, San Rafael, CA (*Brunsfeldo@comcast.net*)

ISBN-13: 978-1-60710-178-9 / ISBN-10: 1-60710-178-5

Library of Congress Cataloging-in-Publication Data

Uncle John's briefs.
    p. cm.
  ISBN 978-1-60710-178-9 (pbk.)
1. American wit and humor. 2. Curiosities and wonders.
I. Bathroom Readers' Institute (Ashland, Or.) II. Title: Briefs.
  PN6165.U532 2010
  081.02'07—dc22

                        2010019638

                        First Printing
                   1 2 3 4 5 14 13 12 11 10

THANK YOU!

*The Bathroom Readers' Institute sincerely thanks
the people whose advice and assistance
made this book possible.*

Gordon Javna

Amy Miller

Jay Newman

Brian Boone

John Dollison

Thom Little

Michael Brunsfeld

Angela Kern

JoAnn Padgett

Melinda Allman

Sydney Stanley

Monica Maestas

Amy Ly

Lilian Nordland

Ginger Winters

Sarah Rosenberg

David Cully

Mustard Press

Scarab Media

John Javna

Karen Malchow

Publishers Group West

Raincoast Books

The Boxer Rebellion

Long John Silver

Amelia Bloomer

Will Shortz

Porter the Wonder Dog

Thomas Crapper

*…and the many writers,
editors, and other contributors
who have helped make
Uncle John the bathroom
fixture he is today.*

CONTENTS

Because the BRI understands your reading needs, we've divided the contents by length as well as subject.

Short—a quick read
Medium—2 to 3 pages, but still brief

INTRODUCTION

First, a brief history of the Bathroom Readers' Institute: In 1987 a small gaggle of pop-culture aficionados led by Uncle John decided to make a book just for the bathroom. We compiled strange news stories, interesting facts, trivia, history, science, and whatever else we could find to create the very first *Uncle John's Bathroom Reader*. Since then, we've released 22 annual volumes as well as dozens of special editions— kids' books, plus books about pets, states, sports, quotes, science, movies, and much more. All in all, it adds up to nearly 20,000 pages of bathroom reading. (Really? Wow.)

So why *this* book? Most of our *Bathroom Readers* include short, medium, and long articles—and a few extra-long ones for those leg-numbing bathroom experiences. But over the years, a lot of our readers have asked us to put together an edition with all of the best short stuff. So we scoured our entire library to find our all-time favorite 1- and 2-page articles (along with a few absorbing 3-pagers). And voilà—here it is.

Open up *Briefs* to any page, and you're sure to find something you didn't know: an interesting origin, a wise quotation, an obscure bit of history, or something totally random, such as the "Bunga Bunga" hoax (a prankster fools the British Navy), symbolic meanings of dreams, the true story of Mike the Headless Chicken, Irish toasts and curses (our favorite: "Your nose should grow so much hair it strains your soup!"), how to say "mullet" in other languages, the science of farts, and…well, you get the idea.

So turn the page and treat yourself to a few seconds (or hours) of entertainment. Happy reading and, as always…

Go with the Flow!

—Uncle John, the BRI staff,
and Porter the Wonder Dog

YOU'RE MY INSPIRATION

It's always interesting to find out where the architects of pop culture get their ideas. These may surprise you.

CHARLIE AND THE CHOCOLATE FACTORY. In the 1920s, England's two biggest chocolate makers, Cadbury and Rowntree, tried to steal trade secrets by sending spies into each others' factories, posed as employees. Result: Both companies became highly protective of their chocolate-making process. When Roald Dahl was 13, he worked as a taste-tester at Cadbury. The secretive policies and the giant, elaborate machines later inspired him to create chocolatier Willy Wonka.

MARLBORO MAN. Using a cowboy to pitch the cigarette brand was inspired when ad execs saw a 1949 *Life* magazine photo—a close-up of a weather-worn Texas rancher named Clarence Hailey Long, who wore a cowboy hat and had a cigarette in his mouth.

NAPOLEON DYNAMITE. Elvis Costello used it as a pseudonym on his 1986 album *Blood and Chocolate*. Scriptwriter Jared Hess met a street person who said his name was Napoleon Dynamite. Coon liked the name and, unaware of the Costello connection, used it for the lead character in his movie.

THE ODD COUPLE. In 1962 TV writer Danny Simon got divorced and moved in with another divorced man. Simon was a neat freak, while his friend was a slob. Simon's brother, playwright Neil Simon, turned the situation into *The Odd Couple*. (Neil says Danny inspired at least nine other characters in his plays.)

CHARLIE THE TUNA. The Leo Burnett Agency created Charlie for StarKist Tuna in 1961. Ad writer Tom Rogers based him on a beatnik friend of his (that's why he wears a beret) who wanted to be respected for his "good taste."

"I DON'T GET NO RESPECT." After seeing *The Godfather* in 1972, comedian Rodney Dangerfield noticed that all the characters did the bidding of Don Corleone out of respect. Dangerfield just flipped the concept.

WHISKER FACTS

A cat's whiskers are a marvel of form and function. Here are a few facts about them that will have you feline fine.

• On average, cats have 24 cheek whiskers—12 on each side of their face—that are arranged in four horizontal rows.

• Each whisker is rooted in the cat's upper lip, and every root connects to 200 or more nerve endings.

• As a cat moves around an object—a bush or a sofa—air currents create a tiny breeze. The whiskers pick up the changes in air pressure, helping the cat to avoid objects in its path.

• Whiskers also direct hunting cats to their prey. In one experiment, a blindfolded cat was placed in an enclosure with a mouse. When the cat's whiskers touched the mouse, the cat grabbed its prey and delivered a killing bite in one-tenth of a second.

• Once the prey is in the cat's mouth, the whiskers curl forward to sense any movement that might mean the animal is still alive and not safe to eat.

• The width of a cat's outstretched whiskers is usually the same as the width of his body, enabling him to measure whether a hole or opening is wide enough for him to enter. When a cat gains too much weight, though, his whiskers stay the same size. So a fat cat may misjudge the size of his body and get stuck in a hole or cat door.

• Cats also have whiskers on the backs of their front paws, which help him walk over uneven ground without stumbling. Paw whiskers also help cats determine the size and position of captured prey.

• Cats use their whiskers to communicate. Whiskers held out to the side indicate calmness or friendliness. When they're pointed upward, the cat is alert or excited. Backward-pointing: Look out—that's a defensive or angry cat.

• Whiskers are such an important part of a cat's physiology that the feline fetus develops whiskers before any other hairs. And when kittens are born, they're blind and deaf, but the touch sensors on their whiskers are fully operational.

So where *do* they sleep? Ornithologists say birds do not sleep in their nests.

SNAP, CRACKLE…FLOP!

*For every successful cereal like Frosted Flakes or Wheaties, there are
hundreds of bombs like Banana Wackies and Ooboperoos.
Here are a few legendary cereal flops.*

Kellogg's **Kream Crunch (1963).** Frosted-oat loops mixed with cubes of freeze-dried vanilla-orange or strawberry ice cream. According to a Kellogg's exec: "The product kind of melted into gooey ice cream in milk. It just wasn't appetizing."

Sugar Smiles (1953). General Mills' first try at sugar cereal. A bizarre mixture of plain Wheaties and sugar-frosted Kix. Slogan: "You can't help smiling the minute you taste it."

Dinos (early 1990s). After the success of Fruity Pebbles, Post tried naming a cereal after the Flintstones' pet dinosaur. "A question that came up constantly," recalls a Post art director, "was 'We've got Cocoa Pebbles and Fruity Pebbles…so what flavor is Dino?'…It sounds like something Fred would be getting off his lawn instead of something you'd want to be eating."

Day-O (late 1960s). "The world's first calypso-inspired presweetened cereal," from General Mills.

Ooops (early 1970s). General Mills had so many bombs, they came up with a cereal they actually *said* was based on a mistake—jingle: "Ooops, it's a crazy mistake, Ooops, it's a cereal that's great!"

Kellogg's Corn Crackos (1967). The box featured the Waker Upper Bird perched on a bowl of candy-coated twists. An internal company memo said: "It looks like a bird eating worms; who wants worms for breakfast?"

Punch Crunch (1975). A spinoff of Cap'n Crunch. The screaming pink box featured Harry S., an exuberant hippo in a sailor suit, making goo-goo eyes at Cap'n Crunch. Many chain stores perceived the hippo as gay and refused to carry the cereal. Marveled one Quaker salesman: "How that one ever got through, I'll never understand."

To shuffle one's feet while mumbling is to *whittie-whattie*.

REJECTED!

If you gave up every time you failed, you'd never succeed. These people got rejected, but they didn't give up—and the rest of us benefited.

Who wants to copy a document on plain paper?"
This was included in one of the 20 rejection letters Chester Carlson received for his invention—the Xerox machine. After six years of rejections, the Haloid Company bought his idea in 1944. The first copier was sold in 1950, and Carlson made over $150 million in his lifetime.

"The product is worthless."
Bayer Pharmaceuticals' 1897 rejection of Felix Hoffman's formula for aspirin. (They eventually accepted it in 1899.)

"Too different from other juvenile titles on the market to warrant its selling."
One book publisher said this in 1937 about *And to Think That I Saw It on Mulberry Street*, the first children's book by Dr. Seuss. In fact, 27 publishers rejected it before Vanguard Press accepted. Dr. Seuss went on to write over 40 children's books that sold nearly half a billion copies.

"Balding, skinny, can dance a little."
Paramount Pictures made this assessment after an early audition by Fred Astaire. He signed with RKO Studios instead.

"We are not interested in science fiction which deals with negative utopias. They do not sell."
This was said to Stephen King in the early 1970s about his first novel, *Carrie*. The book went on to become the first of dozens of bestsellers for King, the top-selling horror author of all time.

"Hopeless."
A music teacher's opinion of his student's composing ability. The student: Ludwig van Beethoven.

UNCLE JOHN HELPS OUT AROUND THE HOUSE

Impress your family with these strange household tips.

• Having trouble removing a stubborn splinter? Squirt some Elmer's Glue on the area. When it dries, peel it off—the splinter will come off with it.

• To protect fine china from getting scratched, put a coffee filter between each dish or teacup when you stack them.

• Telephone getting grimy? Wipe it down with a soft cloth dipped in rubbing alcohol.

• Lose a contact lens in your carpet? Cover the end of a vacuum hose with a stocking and secure it with a rubber band. Then vacuum, holding the hose about an inch off the carpet. The stocking will prevent the lens from being sucked in.

• In a pinch, olive oil makes an effective (but greasy) substitute for shaving cream.

• Used fabric softener sheets are excellent for wiping dust off computer and TV screens.

• Adding a cup of coarse table salt to a load of wash helps prevent colors from fading.

• You can use Silly Putty to clean the gunk off your computer keyboard (and when you're finished you can use it to remove lint from clothes).

• Spy tip: Mailing a sensitive document? Seal the envelope with egg white—it's nearly impossible to steam open.

• Wash windows on a cloudy day: sunlight makes the cleaner dry more quickly, which can cause streaks.

• Kitty litter is good for soaking up oil and other fluids your car drips on your driveway.

• Spice drops (similar to gum drops) make an effective bait for mousetraps.

• To unclog a metal showerhead, unscrew it, remove the rubber washer, and simmer the showerhead in equal parts water and vinegar for about five minutes. (*Soak*—do not boil—plastic showerheads.)

• If you freeze candles before you use them, they will burn slower and last longer.

...is also known by many doctors as "Stroke Alley."

"DID I SHAVE MY LEGS FOR THIS?"

…and other great—and real—country song titles.

"Mama Get a Hammer (There's a Fly on Papa's Head)"

"Rednecks, White Socks, and Blue Ribbon Beer"

"He Went to Sleep and the Hogs Ate Him"

"Redneck Martians Stole My Baby"

"If Fingerprints Showed Up on Skin, Wonder Whose I'd Find on You"

"It Ain't Love, but It Ain't Bad"

"Flushed from the Bathroom of Your Heart"

"She Feels Like a Brand New Man Tonight"

"She Got the Gold Mine (I Got the Shaft)"

"You're the Reason Our Kids Are Ugly"

"She Dropped Me in Denver (So I Had a Whole Mile to Fall)"

"Thank God and Greyhound She's Gone"

"She Broke My Heart at Walgreens (and I Cried All the Way to Sears)"

"Get Your Tongue Outta My Mouth (Cause I'm Kissing You Goodbye)"

"All My Exes Live in Texas (That's Why I Hang My Hat in Tennessee)"

"I Got in at Two With a Ten and Woke Up at Ten With a Two"

"Touch Me with More Than Your Hands"

"My Wife Left Me for My Girlfriend"

"Get Your Biscuits in the Oven and Your Buns in the Bed"

"Drop-Kick Me, Jesus, Through the Goalposts of Life"

"I'm the Only Hell (My Mama Ever Raised)"

"Too Dumb for New York, Too Ugly for L.A."

"If You See Me Gettin' Smaller, It's 'Cause I'm Leavin' You"

By age 30, the average American has had 7.5 different jobs.

BASEBALL'S DISABLED (AND EMBARRASSED) LIST

Uncle John was supposed to have this article done a month ago, but he broke three of the fingers on his typing hand when he jammed them in the toilet paper dispenser. It turns out he's not the only guy to hurt himself in a way that he'd rather not talk about.

Vince Coleman (St. Louis Cardinals, 1985): Bruised his leg and chipped a bone in his knee when a mechanical tarp at Busch Stadium rolled over him while he was stretching before a playoff game. (He wasn't paying attention.) Coleman ended up missing the rest of the postseason, including the World Series, which the Cardinals lost to the Kansas City Royals in seven games. "That tarp was a real maneater," said Coleman.

• **Bill Lee (Montreal Expos, 1979):** While jogging in Montreal, Lee jumped into the street to avoid a cat and was hit by a taxi.

• **Pea Ridge Day (St. Louis Cardinals, 1920s):** Famous for his hog calls and his ability to snap leather belts by expanding his chest, Day broke three ribs while demonstrating the latter.

• **Dwight Gooden (New York Mets, 1990):** Suffered a broken toe when teammate Mackey Sasser placed a metal folding chair on his left foot and sat on it without looking. The incident caused Gooden to miss a game; three years later he missed another game when Vince Coleman hit his shoulder with a nine-iron while practicing his golf swing in the locker room.

• **Marty Cordova (Baltimore Orioles, 2002):** Fell asleep in a tanning bed and suffered burns to his face and other body parts.

• **Eric Show (Oakland A's, 1991):** Stabbed himself in the finger with a toothpick; the resulting infection kept him out for 15 days.

• **Jerry May (Pittsburgh Pirates, 1969):** Crashed into the dugout while trying to make a catch. While being rushed to the hospital for that injury, he injured his shoulder when the ambulance he was riding in got into an

---

The Manhattan cocktail was invented by Winston Churchill's mother.

accident. *That* injury cost May his job with the Pirates; his career never recovered.

- **Clarence Blethen (Boston Red Sox, 1923):** Blethen, who'd lost all his teeth by the age of 30, liked to intimidate batters by removing his dentures and grimacing when he pitched. During one game, he forgot to put them back in after batting; they were still in his back pocket when he slid into second base. He is the only player in major league history (as far as we know, anyway) to bite himself in the butt during a game.

- **Greg Minton (San Francisco Giants, 1985):** Drove a nail into his pitching hand while trying to shoe a horse.

- **Wade Boggs (Boston Red Sox, mid-1980s):** Sprained his back after he lost his balance while trying to remove his cowboy boots.

- **Steve Sparks (Milwaukee Brewers, 1994):** Pitcher Sparks dislocated his shoulder while trying to tear a phone book in half, a stunt demonstrated to him earlier in the week by motivational speakers hired by the team.

- **Jose Cardenal (Chicago Cubs, 1972):** Missed a game due to exhaustion when crickets in his hotel room kept him up all night.

- **Randy Veres (Florida Marlins, 1995):** Another hotel-related injury: Veres injured the tendon in his right pinkie while punching his headboard several times when the people in the next room wouldn't quiet down.

- **Bret Barberie (Florida Marlins, 1995):** Missed a game after he was "blinded" by his chili-pepper nachos—he failed to wash his hands thoroughly before putting in his contact lenses.

- **David Wells (San Diego Padres, 2004):** Kicked a 40-lb. iron bar stool, lost his balance, and fell on a beer glass, cutting his left hand and a tendon in his right wrist.

- **Glenallen Hill (Toronto Blue Jays, 1990):** A sleepwalker who's also terrified of spiders, Hill suffered cuts and bruises on his hands, feet, and elbow after he smashed his foot through a glass coffee table and fell down a flight of stairs while "fleeing" the spiders in one of his dreams. The incident landed him on the 15-day disabled list and earned him the nickname "Spiderman."

Ants cannot chew their food.

LATE BLOOMERS

*Sometimes it seems like child prodigies and teenage phenoms
are a dime a dozen. But, as these people prove, it's
never too late to become a spectacular success.*

LATE BLOOMER: Clara Peller

STORY: Peller was a 74-year-old manicurist when a television crew member plucked her out of her salon and asked her to appear as an extra in a commercial—as a manicurist. Eight years later, the commercial's producer remembered Peller when he was casting a series of ads for Wendy's hamburgers. He located her—now 82 and retired from her nail salon—and gave her a role as a grumpy old lady with a catchphrase: "Where's the beef?" Peller's one-line performance was a hit. In the final three years of her life, she worked in commercials and movies, and even made an appearance on *Saturday Night Live*.

LATE BLOOMER: Helen Hooven Santmyer

STORY: Santmyer, born in 1895, always wanted to be a writer. By the age of 33 she'd published two novels, but neither was a commercial success. That wouldn't come for another 55 years when, at the age of 88, she published her landmark novel *...And Ladies of the Club.* The book, which had taken her nearly 10 years to write (and a year and a half to condense down to 1,300 pages), became a runaway success, selling more than a million copies and spending eight months on the *New York Times* bestseller list.

LATE BLOOMER: Jacob Cohen

STORY: At the age of 19, Cohen was determined to become a comedian. But after struggling for nine years, he gave up—he needed a real job to support his family. He worked odd jobs (including selling aluminum siding) until his 40s, when he decided to give show business a second try. Cohen went on to have a very respectable 40-year career in television and films under the name Rodney Dangerfield.

No $%@&! Over a lifetime, the average driver will swear 32,000 times in his or her car.

FREE PORK WITH HOUSE

*Have you ever been stuck in the bathroom with nothing
to read? (Our greatest fear.) Try flipping through
the classifieds to look for ones like these.*

FREE

Beautiful 6-month-old kitten, playful, friendly, very affectionate **OR...** Handsome 32-year-old husband—personable, funny, good job, but hates cats. Says he goes or cat goes. Come see both and decide which you'd like.

Free! 1 can of pork & beans with purchase of 3-Bedroom, 2-bath home

German Shepherd 85 lbs. Neutered. Speaks German.

FOR SALE

1-man, 7-woman hot tub, $850

Amana Washer Owned by clean bachelor who seldom washed.

Cows, Calves never bred... also 1 gay bull for sale.

Tickle Me Elmo, still in box, comes with its own 1988 Mustang, 5l, Auto, Excellent Condition $6800

Georgia Peaches California Grown—89¢ lb.

Fully cooked boneless smoked man—$2.09 lb.

Kellogg's Pot Tarts: $1.99 Box

Exercise equipment: Queen Size Mattress & Box Springs—$175

Used tombstone, perfect for someone named Homer Hendelbergenheinzel. One only.

For Sale: Lee Majors (6 Million Dollar Man)—$50

Turkey for sale: Partially eaten, eight days old, drumsticks still intact. $23 obo

MISCELLANEOUS

Have Viagra. Need woman, any woman between 18 & 80.

Shakespeare's Pizza—Free Chopsticks

Hummels—Largest selection. "If it's in stock, we have it!"

Wanted: Somebody to go back in time with me. This is not a joke. You'll get paid after we get back. Must bring your own weapons. Safety not guaranteed. I have only done this once before.

Hairobért: If we can't make you look good...You ugly!

Tired of cleaning yourself? Let me do it.

It is believed that "canoe" was the first Native American word to be assimilated into English.

MYTH-SPOKEN

*We hate to say it (well actually, we like to say it), but some of
the best-known quotes in history weren't said by the people
they're attributed to...and some weren't even said at all!*

Line: "Go west, young man, go west."
Supposedly Said By: Horace Greeley, publisher of the *New York Tribune*, in 1851
Actually: Even in 1851, big-city media had all the influence. Greeley merely reprinted an article from the Terre Haute, Indiana, *Express*, but ever since, people have identified it with him. The line was really written by a "now forgotten and never very famous" newspaperman named John Soule.

Line: "Taxation without representation is tyranny!"
Supposedly Said By: James Otis, a lawyer arguing in a Boston court against British search warrants, in 1761
Actually: For years, schoolchildren were taught that this was "the rallying cry of the American Revolution." But no one in Otis's time ever mentioned him saying it. It wasn't until 1820, almost 60 years later, that John Adams referred to the phrase for the first time.

Line: "This is a great wall!"
Supposedly Said By: President Richard Nixon
Actually: It's one of the lines used to denigrate Nixon...and he *did* say it to Chinese officials in 1972 when he saw the Great Wall for the first time. But it's a bum rap. As Paul Boller and John George write in *They Never Said It*:

> This was not his complete sentence, and out of context it sounds silly. It is only fair to put it back into its setting: "When one stands here," Nixon declared, "and sees the wall going to the peak of this mountain and realizes it runs for hundreds of miles—as a matter of fact, thousands of miles—over the mountains and through the valleys of this country and that it was built over 2,000 years ago, I think you would have to conclude that this is a great wall and that it had to be built by a great people."

Of the 28,000 people in Japan who are over 100 years old, 85% are women.

Line: "Let them eat cake."

Supposedly Said By: Marie Antoinette, Queen of France, when she was told that conditions were so bad that the peasants had no bread to eat

Actually: She was alleged to have said it just before the French Revolution. But the phrase had already been used by then. It has been cited as an old parable by philosopher Henri Rousseau in 1778—a decade or so before Marie Antoinette supposedly said it. Chances are, it was a rumor spread by her political enemies.

Line: "There are three kinds of lies: lies, damn lies, and statistics."

Supposedly Said By: Mark Twain

Actually: Twain, one of America's most quotable writers, was quoting someone else: Prime Minister Benjamin Disraeli of England.

Line: "Keep the government poor and remain free."

Supposedly Said By: Justice Oliver Wendell Holmes

Actually: Ronald Reagan said it during a speech and attributed the line to Holmes. But Holmes never said it, and it wasn't written by a speechwriter, either. Reagan's "speechwriting office" later told a reporter, "He came up with that one himself.

*   *   *

HOLY BAT FACTS!

• Most species of bats live 12 to 15 years, but some live as long as 30 years. Some species can fly as fast as 60 miles per hour and as high as 10,000 feet.

• Bats are social animals and live in colonies in caves. The colonies can get huge: Bracken Cave in Texas contains an estimated 20 million Mexican free-tailed bats.

• Vampire bats drink blood through a "drinking straw" that the bat makes with its tongue and lower lip. The bats' saliva contains an anticoagulant that keeps blood flowing by impeding the formation of blood clots.

• It's not uncommon for a vampire bat to return to the same animal night after night, weakening and eventually killing it.

How'd they get airmail? From 1939–42, there was an underwater post office in the Bahamas.

PLOP, PLOP, QUIZ, QUIZ

We thought it might be fun to test your ad slogan IQ. How many products and brands can you recognize by their slogans? Answers are on page 284.

1. "Good to the last drop."

2. "You're in good hands."

3. "It takes a tough man to make a tender chicken."

4. "A little dab'll do ya."

5. "When it absolutely, positively has to be there overnight."

6. "The beer that made Milwaukee famous."

7. "We answer to a higher authority."

8. "Plop, plop, fizz, fizz."

9. "When it rains, it pours!"

10. "Don't leave home without it."

11. "Ask the man who owns one."

12. "I liked it so much I bought the company."

13. "Takes a licking and keeps on ticking."

14. "Reach out and touch someone."

15. "Let your fingers do the walking."

16. "It keeps going, and going, and going."

17. "Come to where the flavor is."

18. "It helps the hurt stop hurting."

19. "It does a body good."

20. "It's what's for dinner."

21. "We love to fly and it shows."

22. "And we thank you for your support."

23. "Rich Corinthian leather."

24. "Celebrate the moments of your life."

25. "Manly, yes, but I like it, too."

26. "Generation Next."

27. "We'll leave the light on for you."

28. "Better living through chemistry."

A red blood cell is about 8 microns wide—less than half the width of a human hair.

NOT WHAT THEY SEEM TO BE

Things (and people) aren't always what they seem.
Here are some peeks behind the image.

JOHN JAMES AUDUBON

Image: Considered a pioneer of American wildlife conservation, this 19th-century naturalist spent days at a time searching for birds in the woods so he could paint them. The National Audubon Society was founded in 1905 in his honor.

Actually: Audubon found the birds, then shot them. In addition to painting, he was an avid hunter. According to David Wallechinsky in *Significa*, "He achieved unequaled realism by using freshly killed models held in lifelike poses by wires. Sometimes he shot dozens of birds just to complete a single picture."

WASHINGTON CROSSING THE DELAWARE

Image: One of the most famous paintings of American history depicts General George Washington—in a fierce battle against the redcoats—leading his men across the Delaware River on Christmas Eve 1776.

Actually: It was painted 75 years after the battle by a German artist named Leutze. He used American tourists as models and substituted the Rhine River for the Delaware. He got the style of boat wrong; the clothing was wrong; even the American flag was incorrect. Yet the drama of the daring offensive was vividly captured, making it one of our most recognized paintings.

WEBSTER'S DICTIONARY

Image: The oldest and most trusted dictionary in the United States, created in 1828 by Noah Webster.

Actually: "The truth is," says M. Hirsh Goldberg in *The Book of Lies*, "is that any dictionary maker can put *Webster's* in the name, because book titles can't be copyrighted." And a lot of shoddy publishers do just that. To know if your *Webster's* is authentic, make sure it's published by Merriam-Webster, Inc.

If an animal has a tail, it's *caudate*; if it doesn't have a tail, it's *anurous*.

LEFT-HANDED FACTS

*Here are some tidbits about lefties. Why devote more
than one page to the subject? Because we don't
want the southpaws to feel left out. Alright?*

LEFT-HANDED STATS

• Lefties make up about 5% to 15% of the general population—but 15% to 30% of all patients in mental institutions.

• They're more prone to allergies, insomnia, migraines, schizophrenia and a host of other things than right-handers. They're also three times more likely than righties to become alcoholics. Why? Some scientists speculate the right hemisphere of the brain—the side left-handers use the most— has a lower tolerance for alcohol than the left side. Others think the stress of living in a right-handed world is responsible.

• Lefties are also more likely to be on the extreme ends of the intelligence scale than the general population: a higher proportion of mentally disabled people and people with IQs over 140 are lefties.

LEFT OUT OF SCIENCE

• For centuries science was biased against southpaws. In the 1870s, for example, Italian psychiatrist Cesare Lombroso published *The Delinquent Male*, in which he asserted that left-handed men were psychological "degenerates" and prone to violence. (A few years later he published *The Delinquent Female*, in which he made the same claims about women.)

• This theory existed even as late as the 1940s, when psychiatrist Abram Blau wrote that left-handedness "is nothing more than an expression of infantile negativism and falls into the same category as…general perverseness." He speculated that lefties didn't get enough attention from their mothers.

LEFT-HANDED TRADITIONS

• Why do we throw salt over our left shoulders for good luck? To throw it into the eyes of the Devil, who, of course, lurks behind us to our left.

• In many traditional Muslim cultures, it is extremely impolite to touch

---

Heavy! The Earth's atmosphere weighs about 5,517,000,000,000,000,000 kilograms.

food with your left hand. Reason: Muslims eat from communal bowls using their right hand; their left hand is used to perform "unclean" tasks such as wiping themselves after going the bathroom. Hindus have a similar custom: they use their right hand exclusively when touching themselves above the waist, and use only the left hand to touch themselves below the waist.

• What did traditional Christians believe was going to happen on Judgement Day? According to custom, God blesses the saved with his right hand—and casts sinners out of Heaven with his left.

• Other traditional mis-beliefs:

> ✓ If you have a ringing in your left ear, someone is cursing you. If your right ear rings, someone is praising you.

> ✓ If your left eye twitches, you're going to see an enemy. If the right twitches, you're going to see a friend.

> ✓ If you get out of bed with your left foot first, you're going to have a bad day.

> ✓ If your left palm itches, you're going to owe someone money. If your right palm does, you're going to make some money.

LEFT-HANDED MISCELLANY

• Why are lefties called "southpaws"? In the late 1890s, most baseball parks were laid out with the pitcher facing west and the batter facing east (so the sun wouldn't be in his eyes). That meant left-handed pitchers threw with the arm that faced south. So Chicago sportswriter Charles Seymour began calling them "southpaws."

• Right-handed bias: Some Native American tribes strapped their children's left arms to the mother's cradleboard, which caused most infants to become predominantly right-handed. In South Africa, people achieved similar results by burying the left hands of left-handed children in the burning desert sand.

• The next time you see a coat of arms, check to see if it has a stripe running diagonally across it. Most stripes are called *bends* and run from the top left to the bottom right. A stripe that runs from the bottom left to the top right, is called a "left-handed" bend or a *bend sinister*—and means the bearer was a bastard.

"What if everything is an illusion and nothing exists? In that case...

DRINK UP

The origins of three of America's favorite drinks.

MOUNTAIN DEW. Invented in the 1940s by Ally Hartman of Knoxville, it was intended as a chaser for Tennessee whiskey. The original version looked and tasted like 7-Up, but after Hartman sold the formula in 1954, a succession of new owners tinkered with it. According to one account, credit for the final version goes to William H. Jones, who bought the formula in 1961 and sold it to Pepsi three years later. "He fixed it so it had just a little more tang to it, mainly by adding citrus flavoring and caffeine," a business associate recalls. "He'd take little cups marked A, B, C, and D around to high schools and factories and ask people which mixture tasted best. That's how he developed his formula."

V-8 JUICE. In 1933, W. G. Peacock founded the New England Products Company and began manufacturing spinach juice, lettuce juice, and other vegetable juices. Even though the country was in the midst of a health craze, few people wanted to drink Peacock's concoctions. So he began mixing the drinks together, hoping to find something more marketable. It took about a year, but he finally came up with a drink he called Vege-min— a combination of tomato, celery, carrot, spinach, lettuce, watercress, beet, and parsley juices. The label had a huge V for Vege-min and a large 8 listing the different juices. One day, as he gave a free sample to a grocer in Evanston, Illinois, a clerk suggested he just call the product V-8.

A&W ROOT BEER. Roy Allen made a living buying and selling hotels...until he met an old soda fountain operator who gave him a formula for root beer. "You can make a fortune with a five-cent root beer," the guy told him. It was during Prohibition when beer was illegal, so Allen decided there was a market for a root beer stand that looked like a Wild West "saloon"—including a bar and sawdust on the floor. The first stand, opened in Lodi, California, in 1919, did so well that Allen opened a second one in nearby Stockton and made one of his employees, Frank Wright, a partner. In 1922 they named the company A&W, after their own initials.

FIRSTS

*Q: What does everything in the world have
in common? A: There was a first one.*

First brewery in North America: opened in New Amsterdam (Manhattan) in 1612.

First professional sports organization in the United States: the Maryland Jockey Club, founded in 1743.

First American to fly in a hot air balloon: Edward Warren (1784).

First American cookbook: *American Cookery*, published by Amelia Simmons in 1796.

First refrigerator: invented by Thomas Moore in Baltimore, Maryland, in 1803.

First flea circus performance: took place in New York City in 1835.

First American novel to sell a million copies: *Uncle Tom's Cabin* by Harriet Beecher Stowe (1852).

First drive-in movie theater: opened in Camden, New Jersey, in 1933. (Picture shown: *Wives Beware*, starring Adolphe Menjou.)

First female celebrity to wear pants in public: Actress Sarah Bernhardt was photographed wearing men's trousers in 1876.

First blood transfusion: June 1667, by Jean-Baptiste Denys, a French doctor, to a 15-year-old boy. (He got lamb's blood.)

First electric hand drill: invented by Wilhelm Fein of Norwell, Massachusetts, in 1895.

First tank: built in 1916 and nicknamed "Little Willie," it could only go 2 mph and never saw duty in battle.

First drink of Kool-Aid: taken by chemist Edwin Perkins of Hastings, Nebraska, in 1927.

World's first flight attendant: Ellen Church, hired in 1930. (She wanted to be a pilot.)

First coast-to-coast direct-dial phone call: made from Englewood, New Jersey, to Alameda, California, in 1951.

First *Uncle John's Bathroom Reader*: went to press in 1988.

A polar bear can smell a seal up to 18 miles away under a sheet of ice.

YAH-HAH, EVIL SPIDER WOMAN!

Until recently, law required all movies made in Hong Kong to have English subtitles. But producers spent as little on translations as possible…and it shows. These gems are actual subtitles from action movies.

"Take my advice, or I'll spank you without pants."

"Fatty, you with your thick face have hurt my instep."

"You always use violence. I should've ordered glutinous rice chicken."

"Who gave you the nerve to get killed here?"

"This will be of fine service for you, you bag of the scum. I am sure you will not mind that I remove your toenails and leave them out on the dessert floor for ants to eat."

"A normal person wouldn't steal pituitaries."

"That may disarray my intestines."

"The bullets inside are very hot. Why do I feel so cold?"

"Beware! Your bones are going to be disconnected."

"I am darn unsatisfied to be killed in this way."

"If you don't eat people, they'll eat you."

"She's terrific. I can't stand her."

"Darn, I'll burn you into a BBQ chicken."

"I'll cut your fats out, don't you believe it?"

"Sex fiend, you'll never get reincarnated!"

"How can I make love without TV?"

"I got knife scars more than the number of your leg's hair!"

"Yah-hah, evil spider woman! I have captured you by the short rabbits and can now deliver you violently to your doctor for a thorough extermination."

"What is a soul? It's just a toilet paper."

The first minute of the day officially starts at 12:00 midnight.

CANADIANS ON CANADA

Some quotes from the Great White North.

"Canada is a country whose main exports are hockey players and cold fronts. Our main import is acid rain."
—**Pierre Trudeau**

"I have to spend so much time explaining to Americans that I am not English and to Englishmen that I am not American that I have little time left to be Canadian."
—**Laurence J. Peter**

"Canada is the essence of not being: not English; not American. And a subtle flavour—we're more like…celery."
—**Mike Myers**

"We'll explain the appeal of curling to you if you explain the appeal of the National Rifle Association to us."
—**Andy Barrie, radio host**

"Canadians don't have a very big political lever. We're nice guys."
—**Paul Henderson, athlete**

"Maybe you live somewhere that doesn't have snow in April; if so, I hope you appreciate it."
—**Spider Robinson, author**

"Hockey captures the essence of Canadian experience. In a land so inescapably and inhospitably cold, hockey is the chance of life, and an affirmation that despite the deathly chill of winter we are alive."
—**Stephen Leacock**

"Canadians are the people who learned to live without the bold accents of the natural ego-trippers of other lands."
—**Marshall McLuhan**

"The great themes of Canadian history are as follows: keeping the Americans out, the French in, and trying to get the Natives to somehow disappear."
—**Will Ferguson**

"There's something romantic about being Canadian. We're a relatively unpopulated, somewhat civilized, clean, and resourceful country."
—**k. d. lang**

"I speak English and French, not Klingon. I drink Labatt's, not Romulan Ale…My name is William Shatner and I AM CANADIAN!"
—**William Shatner**

Most of Bill Gates's 50,000-square-foot home is underground.

DIED ON THE JOHN

*From the darker wing of Uncle John's Stall of Fame, here are
some people who took their last breaths in the bathroom.
(Someday we'll probably put Uncle John on the list.)*

In 1016, 27-year-old King Edmund II of England was murdered in the bathroom. An assassin hid behind the primitive toilet and, as Edmund sat, the murderer stepped out and quickly shoved his sword twice "into the king's bowels."

• Another English monarch, King George II, died on the toilet in 1760 at the age of 77. He woke up at six that morning, drank some chocolate, and an hour later went to the bathroom, where he died of a ruptured aorta.

• Evelyn Waugh, one of the greatest English novelists of the 20th century (*Brideshead Revisited, The Loved One*) had just returned home from Easter Mass. In recent years, the 62-year-old had put on a lot of weight. He also drank a lot, smoked cigars, and rarely exercised. He died "straining at stool" in the bathroom, April 10, 1966.

• Perhaps the most famous death-by-toilet is Elvis Presley's. A combination of weight gain and too many prescription drugs gave the 42-year-old singer a heart attack while he was "takin' care of business." (At the time of his death he was reading a book entitled *The Scientific Search for the Face of Jesus.*)

• Movie producer Don Simpson (*Top Gun, Flashdance*) died in 1996. While rumors persisted that he died of a cocaine overdose, the truth was more humble and embarrassing: He died of a heart attack while going to the bathroom.

• It's commonly believed that Catherine the Great of Russia died after being "crushed" by a horse. True? Na-a-a-a-y. On that fateful day in 1796, she suffered a stroke while sitting on the toilet, but died in her bed several hours later.

To be called a "heavy rainfall," it must be raining at least 1/6 of an inch per hour.

FLINTSTONE V. JETSON

Who's the bigger environmental (Hanna) barbarian?

AN ANIMATED DEBATE
One is from the Stone Age, and one is from the distant future, but Fred Flintstone (of *The Flintstones*, 1960–66) and George Jetson (of *The Jetsons*, 1962–63) are a lot alike: Both are middle-class family men just trying to get by. Here's where these two fictional characters from 40-year-old cartoon shows truly and most importantly differ: Who had the larger carbon footprint?

FRED FLINTSTONE: GOOD

• He lives in the Stone Age. All building materials, tools, cars, and consumer products are made out of natural, mostly unadulterated—and extremely eco-friendly—stone. Flintstone lives off of the earth, literally.

• Flintstone doesn't use fossil fuels. He lives alongside plants and animals that will one day putrefy and *become* petroleum. Without a drop of oil, Flintstone powers his car by rapidly pedaling his feet, perhaps the greenest alternative energy source in history. Further, since electricity hasn't been harnessed yet, all of the appliances in his home are powered via the mechanical labor of various birds and animals. Carbon emissions from the Flintstone home: zero.

• One could argue that this is animal cruelty, as the birds and mammoths are forced to work as indentured servants. However, instead of running away, the animals seem perfectly content to insult Fred with their clever wisecracks.

• Finally, Flintstone doesn't wear shoes or pants, so he doesn't contribute much to the pesticide-dependent cotton industry. Conclusion: Fred Flintstone is quite "green."

GEORGE JETSON: BAD

The Jetsons was a product of the early 1960s idea that "the future" would be all about technology and labor-saving devices. What didn't seem to occur to anyone was all the energy it would take to power a world full of robots, flying cars, and self-cleaning kitchens.

• Jetson eats food prepared by a Food-a-Rac-a-Cycle, a microwave-size

---

Who's George Holiday? The man who videotaped the Rodney King beating in 1991.

machine that prepares any meal at the push of a button. Because it's a tiny device that can't store bulky items, it can't produce just *any* food. According to an article by David Freedman in *Discover*, it would only produce "blobs of tasteless but nutritious paste" with flavoring chemicals added. So the Jetsons subsist on highly processed chemicals, decidedly not locally grown or organic.

• The food machine is just one of many sophisticated gizmos that preclude any work for Jetson and his family (his boy Elroy, daughter Judy, and Jane, his wife). The Jetsons enjoy talking watches, machines that control their dreams, holographic 3-D television, video phones, a machine that gets them out of bed and dresses them, and Rosie, the robot maid. Every single one of these gadgets requires a tremendous amount of electricity.

• Jetson drives a flying car. It looks like a cross between a Volkswagen Beetle and a flying saucer, but the closest thing we have to compare it to is a Sikorsky S-76C, a common commercial helicopter that gets terrible gas mileage—less than two miles per gallon. Today's gas-guzzling Hummer H2 gets about 10 mpg, meaning that Jetson's "futuristic" car is only 20% as efficient as a Hummer.

• Even if Jetson wanted to drive an energy-efficient car on the ground, he couldn't. All of the buildings in his hometown of Orbit City are elevated hundreds of feet off the ground—he can't even *walk* anywhere. Flying is the only option. And when Jetson steps out of the car at his destination, the sidewalks move. (It's truly amazing, then, that Fred Flintstone is fatter than George Jetson.)

• And why exactly are all those buildings sky-high? It's not touched upon in the show (creators say they based the buildings on the futuristic Space Needle in Seattle), but maybe Al Gore was right: By the time *The Jetsons* takes place, in the year 2062, all the electricity used to power our labor-saving devices has produced so many carbon emissions that the polar ice caps have melted, covering the surface of the Earth in water, leaving humanity no choice but to build upward. (Sorry, George. Our bad.)

*   *   *

Fred: How can you be so stupid?
Barney: Hey, that's not very nice! Say you're sorry.
Fred: I'm sorry you're stupid.

—*The Flintstones*

No permit required: Beavers in Connecticut have the legal right to build dams.

SOUND SMARTER

Experts say the path to success is built on a good vocabulary. Here are a few words, with examples of their use, that might make you sound smart enough to go into politics. (Hmm…maybe that was a bad example.)

New Word: Endemic (en-DEM-ik)
Meaning: Belonging to a particular region or people
Instead of… "Them Tasmanian Devils are only found in Tazakistan, I'm pretty sure. And zoos."
Sound Smarter: "The Tasmanian Devil is *endemic* only to the Australian island of Tasmania."

New Word: Cavil (KAV-uhl)
Meaning: To quibble or nitpick
Instead of… "Well, I guess that's for the jury to decide."
Sound Smarter: "I hate to *cavil*, darling, but I'm fairly sure that man you just hit was riding a Segway, not a scooter."

New Word: Parlous (PAHR-lous)
Meaning: Dangerous
Instead of… "This won't hurt a bit!"
Sound Smarter: "I assure you there is nothing *parlous* about the intracranial demulsification procedure."

New Word: Imbibe (im-BAHYB)
Meaning: Drink; absorb
Instead of… "Let's go sit on the porch, down a few cold ones and take in the scenery."
Sound Smarter: "Please join me on the veranda to *imbibe* some refreshing beverages and enjoy the spectacular ocean view."

New Word: Soporific (soh-puh-RIF-ik)
Meaning: Sleep-inducing
Instead of… "I could eat a whole 'nuther helping of pie—but I'm just too pooped."
Sound Smarter: "Unfortunately, the *soporific* effects of the turkey, not to

mention all the wine I've imbibed, prevent me from staying awake long enough to partake of dessert."

New Word: Alacrity (uh-LAK-ri-tee)
Meaning: Quick, cheerful enthusiasm
Instead of... "Brian's a go-getter, isn't he? I like him. But he kind of bugs me, too."
Sound Smarter: "Brian's tendency to approach every task with *alacrity* made him not only one of the office's favorite employees, but also one of the most annoying."

New Word: Circumspect (SUR-kuhm-spekt)
Meaning: Cautious
Instead of... "Uh, Fred, you might not want to look down that tube."
Sound Smarter: "Frederick, a more *circumspect* approach to that fireworks cannon you just lit might be advisable."

New Word: Phlegmatic (fleg-MAT-ik)
Meaning: Apathetic; sluggish
Instead of... "Get your lazy butt up off the sofa and answer the phone yourself."
Sound Smarter: "*Guinness World Records* just called to let you know you've been named Most *Phlegmatic* Couch Potato."

New Word: Enmity (EN-mi-tee)
Meaning: Ill will, hostility, or outright hatred
Instead of... "I hate you! I hate, hate, hate you!"
Sound Smarter: "Be assured, my charming friend, that my *enmity* for you is outmatched only by my resistance to having my tonsils extracted through my nasal passages."

New Word: Temerity (teh-MEHR-eh-tee)
Meaning: Foolhardiness; reckless courage
Instead of... "I don't know if that was brave or just stupid, what you just did. Did it really eat your cell phone?"
Sound Smarter: "It takes extreme *temerity* to jump into the grizzly bear enclosure, Jethro. Shall I call an ambulance?"

NOT EXACTLY PRINCE CHARMING

Ever heard of Prince Philip? He's the Duke of Edinburgh and husband of Queen Elizabeth II of England. About the only time he makes headlines is when he, as one newspaper puts it, "uses his royal status to insult and belittle people." His public gaffes are so frequent that they've earned him the title "The Duke of Hazard."

To a driving instructor in Scotland: "How do you keep the natives off the booze long enough to get them through the test?"

To a Nigerian diplomat in traditional Nigerian garb: "You look as if you're ready for bed."

On seeing a fuse box filled with wires, during a visit to an electronics company: "This looks like it was put in by an Indian."

To a chubby 13-year-old boy at a space exploration exhibit, pointing to a space capsule: "You'll have to lose weight if you want to go in that."

To a smoke-detector activist who lost two of her children in a house fire: "My smoke alarm is a damn nuisance. Every time I run my bath, the steam sets it off and I've got firefighters at my door."

To members of the British Deaf Association, while pointing to a loudspeaker playing Caribbean music: "No wonder you are deaf."

To a tourist, during a state visit to Hungary: "You can't have been here long, you've no potbelly."

Speaking to British students studying in China: "If you stay here much longer, you'll all be slitty-eyed."

On the "key problem" facing Brazil: "Brazilians live there."

On his daughter Princess Anne: "If it doesn't fart or eat hay, she isn't interested."

Remark to the Queen on seeing a picture once owned by King Charles I of England in the Louvre in Paris: "Shall we take it back?"

Instant classic: Robert Louis Stevenson wrote *Dr. Jekyll and Mr. Hyde* in six days.

RANDOM ORIGINS

You know what these are…but do you know where they came from?

WOOD-BURNING STOVES

If you wanted to heat your home in the mid-18th century, there was only one way: your fireplace. But because they were usually built into an exterior wall, fireplaces were inefficient—much of the heat was lost to the outside air. In 1742 Benjamin Franklin invented a freestanding metal stove that could be placed in the middle of the room, so *all* the heat radiated into the room. The "Franklin stove," as it came to be known, remains one of Benjamin Franklin's most famous inventions. One problem: it didn't work. Smoke *rises*, which means you have to put the chimney outlet at the top of the stove. Franklin connected his at the base, and because of that the fire would not stay lit. His stove didn't become practical until another inventor, David Rittenhouse, connected the chimney *above* the fire.

MAIL-ORDER CATALOGS

In September 1871, a British major named F. B. McCrea founded the Army & Navy Cooperative in London to supply goods to military personnel at the lowest possible price. Its first catalog was issued in February 1872…six months before an American named Aaron Montgomery Ward put his first catalog in the mail.

ALUMINUM

The Earth's crust contains more aluminum than any other metallic element, yet it was not discovered or extracted until the mid-1820s—when it was so expensive to extract that it was actually considered a precious metal. Then, in 1886, two different inventors—Charles Hall, an American, and Paul Héroult, a Frenchman—discovered a process by which aluminum could be extracted much more cheaply using electricity. The Hall-Héroult process reduced the price of aluminum to less than 1% of its previous cost. But it wasn't until World War I, when German designer Hugo Junkers started building airplanes out of metal instead of the traditional wood and fabric, that aluminum came into its own. Today the world uses more aluminum than any other metal except iron and steel.

Electric eels must surface to breathe every five minutes or they will drown.

THE CHEW-CHEW MAN

Where did the low-calorie diet come from? It started with a guy known as the "Chew-Chew Man" to critics and the "Great Masticator" to fans.

THE BIRTH OF "FLETCHERISM"

In 1895, 44-year-old Horace Fletcher was turned down for life insurance because he weighed 217 pounds (at 5'6" tall), and he drank excessively. "I was an old man at forty, and on the way to a rapid decline," he recalled years later.

In 1898 Fletcher performed an experiment on himself. He began chewing each bite of food 30 to 70 times—even milk and soup, which he swished in his mouth—and never ate when he was upset or wasn't hungry. After five months of "Fletcherizing" each morsel of food, he lost 60 pounds and regained his health. He also found that he could live happily on 1,600 calories a day, far less than the 3,500 to 4,500 calories recommended at the turn of the century.

THE GREAT MASTICATOR

The experience helped Fletcher find a new calling—pitching his chewing habits to the masses. His slogan: "Nature will castigate those who don't masticate." Fletcher's lecture tours and bestselling books attracted tens of thousands of followers, including John D. Rockefeller and Thomas Edison. Adherents formed "Fletcher clubs," where they met to eat slowly and chant ditties like:

I choose to chew, Because I wish to do, The sort of thing that
Nature had in view, Before bad cooks invented sav'ry stew;
When the only way to eat was to chew! chew! chew!

Fletcher died from bronchitis in 1919 at the age of 69, and his chewing theories soon followed him to the grave. But one thing that did survive him was his low-calorie diet: In 1903, a Yale University professor named Russell Chittenden examined Fletcher, found him to be in excellent health, and decided to try the diet himself. Soon after, his rheumatic knee stopped bothering him and his chronic headaches went away, prompting Chittenden to launch a series of studies into diet and health. These and other pivotal studies led to a ratcheting down of the recommended calorie intake from 3,500 a day to the 2,000 recommended today.

The Boston police department purchased America's first cop car in 1903.

FAMOUS FOR 15 MINUTES

Here's proof that Andy Warhol was right when he said that "in the future, everyone will be famous for 15 minutes."

THE STAR: Mark Stutzman, a 34-year-old illustrator living in Mountain Lane Park, Maryland

THE HEADLINE: *Struggling Artist Takes Care of Business*

WHAT HAPPENED: Stutzman was just another artist having trouble making ends meet in 1992 when one of his clients encouraged him to enter a contest to design a stamp commemorating Elvis Presley. He'd never designed a stamp before, but he entered anyway, creating a portrait of the King in his younger days. "It's the first thing I think of when I think of Elvis," he says, "when he was really young and parents didn't want their kids to listen to his music."

Thirty artists submitted designs to the U.S. Postal Service; only Stutzman's (a young Elvis) and another artist's (an old, fat Elvis) were chosen as finalists. The American public would choose between the two designs by voting at their post office or mailing in a special ballot.

What happened? Millions of people cast their votes...and Stutzman's stamp won overwhelmingly.

THE AFTERMATH: The U.S. Postal Service ordered 300 million of the stamps and then, when those sold out in barely a month, ordered 200 million more, making it the most popular commemorative stamp in U.S. history. Estimated profits: $20 million. How much of that went to Stutzman? Zero—he got the standard design fee of $3,000...nothing more.

THE STAR: James Carter, 76, an ex-convict and retired shipping clerk from Mississippi

THE HEADLINE: *Ex-Con Makes It Big with a Song He Can't Remember, in a Movie He's Never Seen*

WHAT HAPPENED: In September 1959, Carter was chopping wood with a Mississippi prison road gang. He frequently led the men in singing

---

Tommy Bolt is the only professional golfer to have been fined for passing gas (1959).

while they worked, and one afternoon he happened to be recorded while singing a song called "Po' Lazarus." Carter served out his sentence and became a shipping clerk when he got out of prison. By 2002 he was retired.

What happened to that recording of "Po' Lazarus" is another story: It was preserved in a music archive, and in 2000 it ended up in the soundtrack of the film *O Brother, Where Art Thou.* The soundtrack was an even bigger hit than the movie: It went on to sell more than seven million copies, generating thousands of dollars in royalties for Carter…if anyone could find him, that is: After more than 40 years, nobody knew whether he was even still alive.

It took the record's producer about a year to track Carter down in Chicago. One day two people showed up at his doorstep, told him about the movie (he'd never seen it) and the soundtrack (he'd never heard it), and handed him a check for $20,000, the first of what would likely be hundreds of thousands of dollars in royalties.

THE AFTERMATH: About a week later, Carter flew to the Grammy Awards in Los Angeles, where he saw the album win five Grammies, including Album of the Year. For all that, Carter has trouble remembering the lyrics to the song that made him an instant celebrity. "I sang that song a long time back," he says.

THE STAR: Patrick Singleton, the only athlete representing Bermuda in the 2002 Winter Olympics in Salt Lake City

THE HEADLINE: *Athlete Comes Up Short(s) in Salt Lake*

WHAT HAPPENED: Did you watch the opening ceremony for the 2002 Winter Olympics? If you did, maybe you saw it: In the sea of athletes who participated in the ceremony, all properly outfitted for the bitter cold, Singleton wore shorts. Bright red shorts. *Bermuda* shorts—the one thing (other than the Bermuda Triangle) that the tiny British colony is known for.

Even before the Olympics were over, Switzerland's Olympic Museum (where the International Olympic Committee is headquartered) contacted Singleton to see if he would be willing to donate his outfit to the museum. "I doubt we will ever see again an athlete walk into the opening ceremony of the Winter Olympics wearing shorts," a museum spokesperson told reporters. "Everyone will remember, because it was so cold!"

To magnetize a sewing needle, rub it about 20 times on a magnet.

NOVEL STARTS

Were you really just resting your eyes in high school lit class? Below are the first lines of classic works by famous authors. Go ahead, test yourself.

1. "Early in the spring of 1750, in the village of Juffure, four days upriver from the coast of Gambia, West Africa, a man-child was born to Omoro and Binta Kinte."

2. "He was an old man who fished alone in a skiff in the Gulf stream and he had gone 84 days now without taking a fish."

3. "When Mary Lennoz was sent to Misselthwaite Manor to live with her uncle, everybody said she was the most disagreeable-looking child ever seen."

4. "Who is John Galt?"

5. "It was a pleasure to burn."

6. "You will rejoice to hear that no disaster has accompanied the commencement of an enterprise which you have regarded with such evil forebodings."

7. "TOM!"

8. "It was a bright cold day in April, and the clocks were striking thirteen."

9. "As Gregor Samsa awoke one morning from uneasy dreams, he found himself transformed into a giant insect."

10. "Call me Ishmael."

11. "Whether I turn out to be the hero of my own life, or whether that station will be held by anybody else, these pages must show."

12. "Buck did not read the newspapers or he would have known that trouble was brewing, not alone for himself, but for every tide-water

dog, strong of muscle and with warm, long hair, from Puget Sound to San Diego."

13. "1801—I have just returned from a visit to my landlord—the solitary neighbor that I shall be troubled with."

14. "Well, Prince, so Genoa and Hucca are now just family estates of the Buonapartes..."

15. "Last night I dreamt I went to Manderly again."

16. "In my younger and more vulnerable years, my father gave me some advice that I've been turning over in my mind ever since."

17. "The cold passed reluctantly from the earth, and the retiring fogs revealed an army stretched out on the hills, resting."

18. "3 May. Bistritz. Left Munich at 8:35 P.M., on 1st May, arriving at Vienna early next morning; should have arrived at 6:46, but train was an hour late."

19. "You better not even tell nobody but God."

20. "It is a truth universally acknowledged, that a single man in possession of a good fortune, must be in want of a wife."

Answers: **1.** *Roots* (Alex Haley); **2.** *The Old Man and the Sea* (Ernest Hemingway); **3.** *The Secret Garden* (Francis Hodgson Burnett); **4.** *Atlas Shrugged* (Ayn Rand); **5.** *Fahrenheit 451* (Ray Bradbury); **6.** *Frankenstein* (Mary Shelley); **7.** *The Adventures of Tom Sawyer* (Mark Twain); **8.** *1984* (George Orwell); **9.** *Metamorphosis* (Franz Kafka); **10.** *Moby Dick* (Herman Melville); **11.** *David Copperfield* (Charles Dickens); **12.** *The Call of the Wild* (Jack London); **13.** *Wuthering Heights* (Emily Brontë); **14.** *War and Peace* (Leo Tolstoy); **15.** *Rebecca* (Daphne du Maurier); **16.** *The Great Gatsby* (F. Scott Fitzgerald); **17.** *The Red Badge of Courage* (Stephen Crane); **18.** *Dracula* (Bram Stoker); **19.** *The Color Purple* (Alice Walker); **20.** *Pride and Prejudice* (Jane Austen)

YOU YELL, WE SHELL!

Every branch of the armed services has its own set of official inspirational mottoes. And behind the scenes, they've got some unofficial ones, too. Here are some examples of both.

MARINE CORPS
Official: *Semper Fidelis* ("Always Faithful"), "Hell in a Helmet," "Whatever It Takes," *Mors De Contactus* ("Death on Contact")
Off the Record: "Uncle Sam's Misguided Children" (USMC), "You Yell, We Shell," "Muscles Are Required, Intelligence Not Essential, SIR!" (MARINES)

ARMY
Official: "It Will Be Done," "This We'll Defend," "Duty, Honor, Country," "Over, Under, and Through," "Hell on Wheels," "Heaven sent. Hell bent."
Off the Record: "Yes My Retarded A** Signed Up" (U.S. ARMY spelled backward)

NAVY
Official: "Can Do," "Honor, Courage, Commitment," "Always ready, always there," "Lead, follow, or get out of the way."
Off the Record: "We've been to Hell…and it snows there too," "You didn't see me, I wasn't there, and I'm not here now," "In God we trust. All others, we monitor." (Naval Intelligence)

AIR FORCE
Official: *Uno Ab Alto* ("One over All"), "Attack to Defend," "Fire from the Clouds," "These things we do that others may live"
Off the Record: "We were going by there anyway," "Nobody goes until we pass them the hose" (Fuel troops), "Without weapons, it's just another airline." (Weapons troops)

COAST GUARD
Official: *Semper Paratus* (Always Ready)
Off the Record: "Support Search and Rescue—Get Lost"

The melting point of cocoa butter is just below 98.6°F. That's why it melts in your mouth.

WHY DON'T *WE* HAVE A WORD FOR THAT?

Americans excel at inventing colorful expressions and slang, but it turns out other countries are pretty good at it, too.

Kummerspeck (Germany): "Grief bacon"—the weight you gain by overeating when you're worried about something.

Attaccabottoni (Italy): A "buttonholer"—someone who corners casual acquaintances or even complete strangers for the purpose of telling them their miserable life stories.

Modré Pondeli (Czech): "Blue Monday"—When you skip coming in to work to give yourself a three-day weekend.

Razbliuto (Russia): The feeling you have for a person you used to love, but don't anymore.

Shitta (Iran): Leftover dinner that's eaten for breakfast.

Tartle (Scotland): To momentarily forget the name of the person you're talking to. The word helps reduce the social embarrassment of such situations: "I'm sorry, I tartled there for a moment."

Pana po'o (Hawaii): To scratch your head in an attempt to remember something you've forgotten.

Ngaobera (Easter Island): A sore throat caused by too much screaming.

Backpfeifengesicht (Germany): A face that's just begging for somebody to put their fist in it.

Papierkrieg (Germany): "Paper war"—bureaucratic paperwork whose only purpose is to block you from getting the refund, insurance payment, or other benefit that you have coming.

Rujuk (Indonesia): To remarry your ex-wife.

Mokita (New Guinea): The truth that everyone knows, but no one will speak about.

Gorrero (Spain, Central America): Someone who never picks up the check.

Fucha (Poland): Using your employer's time and resources for your own purposes. (Uncle John had never heard of such a thing and wanted to ask around the office if anyone else had, but everyone is still out to lunch.)

Which is bigger: Juneau (Alaska) or Los Angeles? Juneau, at 3,108 sq. mi. (LA is 458 sq. mi.)

WRINKLES IN TIME

Time travel has fascinated scientists and writers for centuries. While the mainstream scientific community continues to research it, some already claim to have done it. Are they brilliant visionaries, or just lunatics?

TIME TRAVELER: Father Pellegrino Ernetti

BACKGROUND: In 2002 Francois Brune, a French priest, wrote *The Vatican's New Mystery*, a book about how his friend, Ernetti, an Italian priest, invented a machine he called the *chronovisor* in 1952. Housed in a small cabinet (like a TV set) it displayed events from anytime in history on a screen (like a TV set). The user selected where and to what year they wanted to "travel" with a series of dials (like a TV set). Ernetti said it worked by picking up, decoding, and displaying "radiation" left behind by the passage of time. He claims he was helped on the project by Nobel Prize-winning physicist Enrico Fermi and Nazi rocket scientist Wernher Von Braun. Ernetti said he used the chronovisor to visit ancient Rome to view and later produce an English translation of *Thyestes*, a Latin play thought to be lost. He also heard Napoleon give a speech in Italy in 1804 and saw Christ die on the cross. So what happened to the chronovisor? Brune says the Catholic Church forced Ernetti to disassemble the machine because of its potential for espionage.

WHAT HAPPENED: Scientists have never found any evidence that the passage of time leaves a trail of radiation. And the existence of the chronovisor has never been confirmed.

TIME TRAVELER: John Titor

BACKGROUND: In 2000 Titor posted messages on Internet paranormal discussion boards claiming he was a soldier from the year 2036 sent back in time to retrieve a computer to fix software bugs on machines of the future. He made more posts, offered pictures of his time machine and its instructional manual, and gave incredibly detailed accounts of world events between 2000 and 2036. For instance, Titor claimed an escalating global war ends in 2015 when Russia drops nuclear bombs on the United States, China, and Europe, instantly dismantling all govern-

---

Aw, shoot: It's illegal to use a firearm to open a can of food in Indiana.

ments and killing three billion people. (Millions more die of mad cow disease.) Survivors group into agricultural communes. Despite the bleak post-apocalyptic landscape, technology is well advanced, with wireless Internet providing all phone service, television, and music. Titor achieved a huge following on paranormal websites and talk radio. Many thought he really could be a bona fide time traveler. But a few months later (in March 2001), Titor announced that he had found the computer he needed and he "returned" to the future. He was never heard from again.

WHAT HAPPENED: "Titor" contradicted himself all over the place, claiming that World War III had destroyed all governments, but also that the U.S. government sent him back in time. Other "predictions" just didn't pan out. He said a second American civil war would take place from 2004 to 2008, and that the 2004 Olympics were the last ones ever held. Also, when asked how his time machine (a modified 1967 Chevrolet, which somehow survived nuclear annihilation) worked, Titor claimed ignorance, calling himself a hired hand, not an engineer. So who was Titor? Some speculate it was a hoax concocted by the late author Michael Crichton.

TIME TRAVELER: Darren Daulton

BACKGROUND: Daulton was an all-star catcher for the Philadelphia Phillies and Florida Marlins during the 1980s and '90s. But he's also an amateur metaphysicist. He claims that a little-known dimension causes all objects on Earth to vibrate slightly, and that only a handful of people, Daulton included, can detect it and use this ability to manipulate objects, the weather…and time. Daulton says that instead of dreaming, he leaves his body every night and travels into the future (but not the past). One event he's witnessed: the end of the world, which he says will occur on December 21, 2012. However, Daulton has also been arrested several times for drunk driving, charges he says he's innocent of. "I've been thrown in jail five or six times," he says. "My wife blames everything on drinking. But I'm not a drunk. Nicole just doesn't understand metaphysics."

WHAT HAPPENED: Daulton was a career .245 hitter. If he could manipulate time and objects, one would think he'd be able to give himself a better batting average.

(BAD) DREAM HOUSES

*Everyone thinks their own horror stories about buying a
new home are the worst, but they're not—these are. Note:
Some names have been changed to protect the gullible.*

Dream House: In 1998 John and Mary Jones found theirs in South Carolina.

From Bad... They didn't get a home inspection before closing. Result: Right after they moved in, problems started. The kitchen sink backed up, the washing machine overflowed, and when the plumber came to fix the leaks, the bathroom floor caved in.

...To Nightmare! Then the air conditioner stopped working. The repairman figured the system was missing a filter, so he went into the attic to explore. But instead of a filter, he found bats—thousands of them. Even worse, over the years hundreds of gallons of bat guano had soaked into the insulation and wood of the structure, rendering the home a health hazard and completely uninhabitable. (Mary Jones developed a rare disease due to exposure from bat guano.)

Dream House: Bill Barnes of southern Maryland was trying to sell his house. Ari Ozman, who claimed to be a traveling salesman who was moving his family into the area, didn't want to buy—he wanted to rent. The market was a little slow, so when Ozman offered six months' rent in advance, Barnes jumped at it.

From Bad... Ozman wasn't a traveling salesman—he was a scam artist. He put an ad in the local paper, offering Barnes' house for sale at a bargain price and—no surprise—had more than 100 calls. And when buyers saw the space, they couldn't resist the deal. Ozman's terms: he'd reserve the house—for a $2,000 cash deposit.

...To Nightmare! He repeated the scam 30 times, collected $60,000, and then took off. Barnes was left with nothing except Ozman's security deposit and 30 angry "buyers."

Dream House: Jack Oldman purchased his in Virginia in 2001.

From Bad...A few nights later, Oldman was asleep in bed when a squadron of fighter jets tore across the sky. He practically jumped out of his skin. It

---

...the NHL Stanley Cup to a movie theater and ate popcorn out of it.

turned out that there was a military base nearby and flight training took place 15 nights a month. Still, Oldman decided to tough it out. Until the house started to smell.

...To Nightmare! Oldman couldn't locate the source of the odor, so he called the Department of Environmental Quality, which found the cadaver of a rotting animal in the foundation (the foul smell was filtering in through cracks in the concrete). What else could go wrong? Plenty—the roof structure was caving in; the chimney was disconnected from the house; and the ground under the house was shifting. Oldman's recourse: He had none—the builder had long since filed for bankruptcy and disappeared.

Dream House: Alan and Susan Sykes moved into theirs in West Yorkshire, England, in 2000.

From Bad... One evening a few months after moving in, the couple was watching a TV documentary about Dr. Samson Perera, a dental biologist who murdered his 13-year-old daughter and hid her dismembered body throughout his home and garden. Suddenly they recognized the house on TV: it was *their* house. When they got to the part that said the child's body—which had been cut into more than 100 pieces—was never fully recovered, the Sykeses packed their bags, moved out that same night...and never went back.

...To Nightmare! They sold the house (at a loss) and filed suit against the former owners, James and Alison Taylor-Rose, for withholding the house's history. The judge said that since the Taylor-Roses were unaware of the murder when *they* bought the house in 1998 (they only placed it on the market after a neighbor told them about it), they were not liable, so the Sykeses lost the suit.

Dream House: Cathie Kunkel found hers in Ontario, California.

From Bad... In August 2001, four months after she moved in, Kunkel had a pond dug in her backyard. After removing only a foot of earth, workers discovered something putrid. "We thought it was a dead chicken," said Kunkel. "The smell was horrendous." The contractor filled in the shallow grave, but the odor lingered. Kunkel and her three children had to move out.

...To Nightmare! It wasn't a chicken—it was a dead cow wrapped in plastic. The development was built on 18,000 acres of former dairy land...and they still don't know how many dead cows are buried there.

At one time, a Minnesota tax form required you to list your date of death.

COLD, HARD FACTS

…about the cold, hard continent of Antarctica.

• Antarctica isn't completely covered in ice—98% of the continent is. The ice averages 1.34 miles thick, and is 3 miles at its thickest.

• At 5.5 million square miles, Antarctica is the fifth largest continent (only Europe and Australia are smaller).

• Antarctica is the driest continent. One region has received no precipitation for the last two million years.

• The Bentley Subglacial Trench is 8,383 feet below sea level—the lowest dry location on Earth.

• If Antarctica's ice sheets melted, the world's oceans would rise about 200 feet.

• There are 145 liquid lakes (and counting) beneath the Antarctic ice. One, Lake Vostok, is under 2.5 miles of ice and is about the size of Lake Ontario.

• The lowest temperature ever recorded on Earth was in 1983 at Russia's Vostok Station: –128.6°F.

• Cold, dense air being pulled by gravity down Antarctic mountains create the most extreme *katabatic* (Greek for "go down") winds on the planet. They have been clocked at 200 mph.

• Antarctic ice accounts for 70% of the world's fresh water.

• The largest non-migratory land animal in Antarctica is the *belgica*, a wingless midge (gnat) less than half an inch long. They don't fly (the winds would blow them away); they hop like fleas and live in penguin colonies.

• The Antarctic Treaty, drawn up in 1959, reserves the continent for exploration and scientific research and prohibits its use for military purposes. To date, 47 countries have signed the charter, technically the first arms-reduction treaty of the Cold War.

• Seven countries claim to own parts of the continent: Argentina, Australia, Chile, France, New Zealand, Norway, and the United Kingdom.

Hiking the entire 2,174-mile Appalachian Trail takes an average of **5 to 7 months.**

HOLLYWOOD'S #1 STAR

*For some reason, "answering the call of nature" has worked
its way into nearly every Tom Hanks movie.*

• **The Money Pit (1986):** Beleaguered homeowner Walter Fielding (Hanks) notices a cherub statue in his yard is having trouble "peeing." "Prostate trouble?" he asks. Later, Walter pees on a small tree in his garden and it falls down.

• **Joe Versus the Volcano (1990):** Joe pees off of the luggage raft.

• **A League Of Their Own (1992):** Washed-up baseball star Jimmy Dugan pees for nearly a minute in the girls' locker room. "Boy, that was some good peein'," comments Mae (Madonna).

• **Forrest Gump (1994):** When Forrest meets John F. Kennedy, he informs the president, "I gotta pee."

• **Apollo 13 (1995):** Astronaut Jim Lovell urinates into a collection tube. "It's too bad we can't show this on TV," he says.

• **Saving Private Ryan (1998):** Captain John Miller and Sergeant Horvath (Tom Sizemore) talk about an old war buddy named Vecchio, who would "pee a 'V' on everyone's jacket, for Vecchio, for Victory."

• **The Green Mile (1999):** Warden Paul Edgecomb suffers from a painful urinary tract infection that has him "pissing razor blades."

• **Cast Away (2000):** Marooned Fed-Ex executive Chuck Noland is peeing on the beach at night when he sees the faint light of a passing ship.

• **Road to Perdition (2002):** Mob hit man Michael Sullivan is asked if coffee makes him sweat. His reply: "It also makes me piss."

• **The Terminal (2004):** Stranded immigrant Viktor Navorski must hold his pee for hours while waiting for a pay phone call at New York's JFK Airport.

Ironically, one of the few movies that Tom Hanks *doesn't* pee in, or even mention it, is...1984's *Splash*.

Neither can you! A cat cannot see directly under its nose.

LET'S DANCE!

Even non-dancers will like the story behind this dance craze.

THE POLKA

This fast-paced dance is simple to learn, even for Uncle John. And it has a fun origin story, too…depending on who's telling it. The Bohemian version—the one most often cited—claims that in 1834 a young peasant girl named Anna Slezak was bored one Sunday and decided to make up a new dance. She choreographed a hop-step-close-step pattern while singing a Czech folk song ("Uncle Nimra Brought a White Horse"). A local schoolmaster walked by and asked Anna to show it to him; he wrote down the steps and then introduced the polka (from the Czech word *pulka*, meaning "half-step") in ballrooms in nearby Prague. The Polish version is similar: In the 1830s, a Bohemian man was visiting Poland when he saw a little girl dancing the polka (which may actually date as far back as the 1600s) and took the dance back home to Prague, where it was christened *polka*, meaning "Polish woman."

Either way, thanks to the Bohemian army, the dance spread from dance hall to dance hall all over Europe, making it a huge fad in the mid-19th century. Much like rock 'n' roll would be 100 years later, the polka was embraced by the youth culture and vilified by grown-ups, who had only recently accepted the much slower waltz as their dance of choice.

SQUEEZE BOX

For most of the 19th century, polkas were usually written for violins. But as Polish immigrants moved to America in the 20th century, they brought along their accordions (invented around the same time the polka became popular), a much more versatile instrument that allowed a single musician to play melody, harmony, rhythm, and bass—perfect for polka parties. The polka's second golden age took full swing in the Midwest after World War II, where millions of European refugees settled and brought their culture with them. Polka legends such as Frank Yankovic and Lawrence Welk helped legitimize the lively music for adults—many of whom were appalled by rock 'n' roll.

For more dance crazes, turn to page 162.

YOU WANT A PIECE OF ME?

Organ transplants are a miracle of science and an incredible act of human kinship: A part of one person can help another person live or live better. But it's not just hearts and livers anymore—it seems like doctors can transplant nearly anything these days

BODY PART: Face
RECIPIENT: Isabelle Dinoire
STORY: In May 2005, 38-year-old Dinoire of Valenciennes, France, was depressed and took a large dose of sleeping pills. Her dog tried to wake her up, but couldn't, and became more and more alarmed. In its zeal to rouse Dinoire, the dog inadvertently mauled her, destroying her nose, lips, and chin. Dinoire recovered, but she could barely eat and couldn't speak at all. Two surgeons from Amiens, France, took an interest in the case and proposed a triangular skin graft. The tissues, muscles, arteries, and veins would be taken from the face of a brain-dead donor and transplanted onto Dinoire. The skin had to come from a living donor because live tissue ensured proper blood flow; skin from somewhere else on Dinoire's body would be too different in color and texture. The five-hour procedure took place in November 2005, and it worked. Dinoire's appearance isn't exactly what it used to be—it's more of a hybrid between her old face and the donor's face. (Her nose is narrower and her mouth is fuller.) She still can't move her lips very well, but she's able to speak, eat, and even smoke again. (After all, she's French.)

BODY PART: Head
RECIPIENT: Some monkeys
STORY: On March 4, 1970, a team of scientists at Case Western Reserve University in Ohio, led by Dr. Robert J. White, successfully attached the head of one rhesus monkey to the body of another rhesus monkey. First, White cooled the brain to the point where all neural activity stopped. It would still be chemically "alive" if the volume of blood was kept at a nor-

mal level. This was achieved by carefully cauterizing all the arteries and veins in the head. Then the old head—brain and skull intact—was grafted onto the new body…and it was still alive. After the monkey recovered from the anesthesia, it tried to bite one of the researchers, but it could eat, hear, smell, and follow things with its eyes, meaning all nerves were intact with the brain. It lived for about four hours. Thirty-one years later, White tried the experiment again and this time was able to get the new body breathing on its own, controlled by the transplanted brain, allowing the monkey to live for eight days. Neither the 1970 nor 2001 experiment resulted in the attachment of the spinal cord, so neither monkey could voluntarily control the action of their new bodies. White is now retired, but has a standing offer to perform the procedure on a human being. (So far, no takers.)

BODY PART: Hand

RECIPIENT: Matthew Scott

STORY: In 1985, 24-year-old Scott, a paramedic from New Jersey, severely damaged his left hand from a blast by an M80 firecracker. It had to be amputated and Scott was fitted with a prosthetic hand. In 1998, Scott decided he wanted a real hand. Hand transplants weren't unheard of—the procedure had been attempted before—but it had never been successful in the long term. That's because it's one of the most complicated surgeries conceivable: the hand contains 27 bones, 28 muscles, three nerves, two arteries, tendons, veins, soft tissue, and skin. To get the new hand to perform normally would be more akin to performing several dozen micro-surgeries. The surgery was performed in 1999 at the Jewish Hospital in Louisville, Kentucky, by University of Louisville surgeons Warren Breidenbach and Tsu-Min Tsai. Using a hand from a 58-year-old male cadaver, it took a surgical team of 17 people nearly 15 hours to attach the new hand (heart transplants take about seven). After the surgery, Dr. Breidenbach told the media "it could be at least a year if we know if it's a good functioning hand. We hope for a good grip and some sensation of hot and cold." Amazingly, Scott could move his new fingers just a week later. In April 2000, he threw out the first pitch at a Philadelphia Phillies game. And amazingly, after just one year Scott could sense temperature, pressure, and pain…and could use his new hand to write, turn pages, and tie his shoelaces.

Mars has no plate tectonics, but has a single plate 125 miles thick, twice that of Earth's.

MR. T

If you're a fool, don't read this page, as you will likely end up being pitied.

"'T' stands for 'tender' for the ladies and the kids. For the bad guys and thugs, 'T' stands for 'tough.'"

"As a kid, I got three meals a day. Oatmeal, miss-a-meal, and no meal."

"It takes a smart guy to play dumb."

"When I was growing up, my family was so poor we couldn't afford to pay attention."

"I was born and raised in the ghetto, but the ghetto was not born and raised in me."

"For five years, Mr. T disappeared. Fools went unpitied!"
—on his bout with cancer

"When you see me now, I'm nothing but a big overgrown tough mama's boy. And I speak with that glee because the problem with society is we don't have enough mama's boys."

"Calvin Klein and Gloria Vanderbilt don't wear clothes with your name on it, so why should you wear their name?"

"I believe in the Golden Rule. The man with the gold rules."

"Anger: use it, but don't lose it."

"Pity is between sorry and mercy. See, if you pity him, you won't have to beat him up. So that's why you gotta give fools another chance because they don't know any better."
—on pitying fools

"I thought about my father being called 'boy,' my uncle being called 'boy,' my brother being called 'boy.' What does a black man have to do before he's given respect as a man? So when I was 18 years old, I said I was old enough to be called a man. I self-ordained myself 'Mr. T' so the first word out of everybody's mouth is 'Mister.' That's a sign of respect that my father didn't get."

The term "filibuster" is from the French word for "pirate."

ANIMALS IN
THE OUTFIELD

And the infield, the dugout, the uniforms, the pressbox…

JACOB'S SWATTER

In the 2007 A.L. division baseball series, the Yankees were playing in Cleveland, down by one game but clinging to a 1–0 lead in the eighth inning. Coming in to hold the lead was 22-year-old Yankee reliever Joba Chamberlain, who hadn't blown a save all year. Also entering the game: a giant swarm of tiny gnatlike insects called *midges* (they were attracted to the stadium lights). As they enveloped the mound, Chamberlain tried swatting them with his cap, but that didn't work, so catcher Jorge Posada ran out and sprayed the pitcher with insect repellent. That didn't work, either. So, with tiny midges crawling all over his face and neck, Chamberlain kept pitching. Result: He gave up two walks, threw two wild pitches, and hit a batter, allowing the tying run to score. The Indians, who were used to the bugs, won the game in the 12th inning. Afterward, Chamberlain blamed himself: "Bugs are bugs. It's not the first time I had a bug near me." But Yankee shortstop Derek Jeter disagreed: "I guess that's home-field advantage for them—just let the bugs out."

FANGS FOR THE MEMORIES

During the fourth inning of a 2007 spring training game between the Indians and the Mets in Winter Haven, Florida, play was briefly halted when several reporters started screaming and running out of the press box. The culprit: a three-foot-long black snake that had slithered over their notebooks and computers. While fans (Floridians, who are accustomed to snakes) laughed at the reporters, a member of the grounds crew caught the snake and let it go in some woods near the parking lot.

FLY TO YOUR TOMORROW, SEAGULL

To this day, Dave Winfield swears he didn't do it on purpose. Between innings of a game in Toronto on August 4, 1983, the Yankee outfielder caught one last warm-up toss and then threw it to a ball boy waiting along the foul line. Perched on the field between Winfield and the boy, however, was a small white gull. After taking a short hop, the baseball hit the bird hard…and killed it. As the groundskeepers quickly came in and took it away, Winfield raised his cap. Stunned Toronto fans saw this as disrespectful and threw things at the Yankee slugger for the rest of the game. And after the game, a group of Mounties arrested Winfield (in the visitor clubhouse) for "willfully causing unnecessary cruelty to an animal." Winfield denied it was willful, but cooperated and paid the $500 bail. The charges were later dropped, but Winfield's reputation in Canada was severely damaged. (When the Blue Jays later brought in a falcon to try and curb the ballpark's gull population, they named it "Winfield.")

Redeemed: Ironically, Winfield (the player, not the falcon) was later traded to the Blue Jays and helped win the 1992 World Series with a spectacular game-wining double in Game 6…earning him the nickname "Mr. Jay."

THE CAT'S MEOW

In May 1990, A's manager Tony La Russa was sitting in the dugout during an Oakland home game when a stray cat ran out onto the field. The players tried to catch it, but the frightened cat made a beeline for the dugout, where La Russa—a self-described "cat person"—was able to corral it. The crowd cheered, and the cat spent the rest of the game clinging to La Russa. (He kept the cat and named her Evie.) Inspired, La Russa and his wife Elaine founded ARF, the Animal Rescue Foundation, which auctions off baseball memorabilia and uses the funds to find homes for stray animals (so far, tens of thousands of them). La Russa, who owns three dogs and nine cats, says his animals help him keep things in perspective. "I get home, feeling like hell after we get beat, and then see the faces of my pets telling me that, really, everything's okay."

A TIP O' THE CAP

It's always tough to return to the home park of your former team, but Casey Stengel came prepared when he and his fellow Pirates showed up at Ebbets Field to play the Dodgers (who'd recently traded him) in 1919. The Dodger fans booed mercilessly as Stengel walked up to the plate, when he suddenly paused and turned to face the hecklers. Then, to everyone's astonishment, he tipped his cap and out came…a sparrow. It fluttered a few circles around the plate and then flew off into the sky. The fans roared and—at least temporarily—were in love with Casey again.

Penguins sleep more deeply in the afternoon than in the morning. (Researchers…

KNOW YOUR GEOGRAPHY

There are certain places you hear mentioned on the news or read about in magazines that aren't exactly countries—they're more like regions or "geographic distinctions." But where are they?

IBERIA. The peninsula at the far west of Europe occupied by Spain and Portugal. The name was derived from *Iber*, the Greek name for the river that flows across the peninsula.

THE FERTILE CRESCENT. Coined around 1900 by American archaeologist James Henry Breasted, the term refers to the crescent-shaped area that ranges across Syria, Israel, Jordan, Lebanon, and Iraq. It encompasses ancient Mesopotamia, between the Tigris and Euphrates Rivers, known as "the birthplace of civilization."

THE GREAT STEPPE. A *steppe* is a grassy plain that can be flat or hilly. The Great Steppe in Europe and Asia is a vast expanse bordered by the Black Sea that extends over Russia, eastern Europe, and former Soviet republics Turkmenistan and Kazakhstan. Historically, it was home to nomadic tribes and conquering hordes on horseback.

THE CAUCASUS. This mountain range divides Europe from Asia. It's nestled between the Black and Caspian seas, and bordered by Ukraine and Turkey. The region includes southwest Russia, Azerbaijan, and Armenia. The name comes from the ancient Greek word *kau*, meaning "mountain."

TORA BORA. A cave complex situated at nearly 13,000 feet in the Safed Koh mountain range on the Pakistan-Afghanistan border. *Tora bora* is the local Iranian dialect's term for "black dust." After the 2001 U.S.-led invasion against the Taliban, Tora Bora was the suspected hideout of al-Qaeda leader Osama bin Laden.

BALKANS. Comprising a mostly mountainous region in southeastern Europe, the Balkan Peninsula is bordered by the Adriatic Sea on the west and the Aegean and Black Seas on the east. Countries making up the Balkan states: Albania, Bosnia and Herzegovina, Bulgaria, Croatia,

Greece, Macedonia, Romania, Serbia and Montenegro, Slovenia, and the European tip of Turkey. *Balkan* is the Turkish word for "mountain."

PATAGONIA. A desert in the southernmost parts of Argentina and Chile that extends to the tip of South America. The name comes from *pata*, Spanish for "paw." According to legend, when Magellan explored the area in 1520, he was impressed by the gigantic tracks he found in the snow and thought they must belong to a race of giants. In truth, the marks were probably left by the oversize llama-skin shoes worn by the indigenous Tehuelches people.

THE BALTICS. The three westernmost former Soviet republics Latvia, Lithuania, and Estonia. These eastern European nations are bordered by the Baltic Sea, and other than geographic proximity they have little in common. Latvians and Lithuanians speak related languages, but Estonians use a language similar to Finnish.

ASIA MINOR. A peninsula in western Asia, bounded by the Black Sea on the north and the Mediterranean Sea on the south. The entire land-mass is occupied by Turkey. It gets its name from the fact that it's a small part of Asia that connects the continent to Europe.

THE TROPICS. The Tropics is a band between two imaginary lines that circle the Earth, parallel to the equator. The Tropic of Capricorn is 23° south of the equator, and the Tropic of Cancer is 23° north of it. The distinguishing characteristic of the region is that the Sun is directly overhead at least once a year. This makes for very warm climates in locales like Brazil, Polynesia, and northern Australia. The two Tropics are named after the constellations where the Sun was positioned, in ancient times, during the summer solstice.

SUB-SAHARAN AFRICA. The Sahara Desert stretches across the northern third of Africa through Algeria, Libya, Egypt, Sudan, Niger, Chad, Mauritania, Mali, Morocco, and Tunisia. These nations, some of which have oil-based economies, are largely made up of Muslim Arabic peoples. Nations south of the desert, in sub-Saharan Africa ("below the Sahara"), are inhabited mostly by non-Arabic people. The climate is much hotter and there's little oil.

DUMB CROOKS

*Our favorite crooks are the ones who do something
dumb, and then do something even dumber.*

EMPTY YOUR BRAINS IN THIS TRAY

"Clyde Lamar Pace II made two mistakes. The first, Polk County sheriff's deputies say, was when he emptied his pockets to pass through a courthouse metal detector and apparently forgot about the small bag of marijuana. He threw it in a baggie without realizing it, and the person working the security post said, 'Hey, what's this?' Chief Deputy Bill Vaughn said. 'He gave that old "uh-oh, I've-been-caught" look, and the chase was on.' The second mistake was when he ran away from deputies, directly into a locked revolving door. Pace, 18, was arrested for drug possession and resisting arrest."

—The Des Moines Register

THANKS, MOM

"Trilane A. Ludwig, 24, of Vancouver, was arrested after a traffic stop early New Year's Day. At 5:30 a.m. he called his mother, Angela Beckham, and asked her to bail him out with the money in his wallet. She handed $500 to a clerk, who suspected the money was phony and called police. The police report described the counterfeit bills as bad copies that were the wrong size. Beckham said she wasn't going to shell out any real cash to bail him out. The case has been referred to the Secret Service."

—Kansas City Star

THEY'LL NEVER FIND ME HERE...OR HERE

"In December 1999, Christopher S. Newsome broke into the Delaware County Courthouse in Muncie, Indiana, and stole $25 from the receptionist's desk. He then hid in a closet, where a janitor found him. When the janitor went to call authorities, Newsome sprinted out of the courthouse, through a parking lot, and toward a nearby building. Unfortunately for Newsome, that building was the county jail. Moments later, the 26-year-old was in handcuffs."

—Realpolice.net

Nothing new: The first weight loss pill was marketed in 1893.

HOW'D YOU GUYS FIND ME?

"Police didn't have much trouble finding Joshua W. Kochell, 27, who they say robbed two Lafayette, Indiana, gas stations. They tracked him through the monitoring device he was ordered to wear on a 2001 sentence for theft and habitual offense. Kochell was being held in Tippecanoe County Jail on $60,000 bond."

—Associated Press

GUILTY AND GUILTIER

"A New York woman who was given probation for robbery faces four years in jail after punching a juror outside the court. Octavia Williams came face-to-face with juror Geraldine Goldring just after Goldring and the other jurors found her guilty of stealing $160 from a woman in Times Square. Williams ran off after the assault but was caught and returned to the courtroom, where she was charged with assault and contempt of court for ignoring the judge's instructions to report to probation immediately after the verdict."

—New York Daily News

NOTE TO SELF...

"Police in Hillsborough, North Carolina, responded to a call from a bank about a man who was acting suspiciously. Capt. Dexter Davis confronted the man and asked if he had a weapon. 'He pulled his book bag off his shoulders, opened the bag up and held it open to me to show he didn't have a gun,' Davis said. When Davis looked inside, there was a note in clear view. It read, 'I want $10,000 in $100 bills. Don't push no buttons, or I'll shot [sic] you.' Davis laughed out loud, and then arrested Christopher Fields (who also was carrying a 10-inch knife) and turned him over to the FBI."

—Durham Herald-Sun

CRASH TEST DUMMY

"In Springfield, Illinois, Zachary Holloway, 20, and a pal were arrested and charged with breaking into one car and stealing, among other things, a motorcycle helmet, then attempting to break into another car. To try to get into the second car, Holloway put on the helmet, stood back from the car and charged into it, head-butting a window, unsuccessfully, twice."

—The Oregonian

The light above Big Ben's clock face is only lit when Parliament is in session.

HOW TO AVOID GETTING HIRED

Your resumé is a carefully crafted sales pitch about how indispensable you'll be to prospective employers. That's what it's supposed to be, anyway. This list of real-life resume bloopers appeared in Fortune *magazine.*

"I demand a salary commiserate with my extensive experience."

"I have lurnt Word Perfect 6.0, computor and spreadsheat progroms."

"Received a plague for Salesperson of the Year."

"Reason for leaving last job: maturity leave."

"Wholly responsible for two failed financial institutions."

"Let's meet, so you can 'ooh' and 'aah' over my experience."

"You will want me to be Head Honcho in no time."

"Marital status: single. Unmarried. Unengaged. Uninvolved. No commitments."

"Reason for leaving last job: They insisted that all employees get to work by 8:45 every morning. Could not work under those conditions."

"Note: Please don't misconstrue my 14 jobs as 'job-hopping.' I have never quit a job."

"I am loyal to my employer at all costs....Please feel free to respond to my resume on my office voice mail."

"I procrastinate, especially when the task is unpleasant."

"As indicted, I have over five years of analyzing investments."

"Personal interests: donating blood. Fourteen gallons so far."

"Instrumental in ruining entire operation for a Midwest chain store."

"The company made me a scapegoat, just like my three previous employers."

"Finished eighth in my class of ten."

"It's best for employers that I not work with people."

From 1889 to 1930, over 3,700 people were lynched in the U.S. About 80% were black.

JUST PLANE WEIRD

*These days, no one makes jokes on a plane, least of all
the pilot. Here's the harrowing tale of a practical
joke that almost went horribly wrong.*

CRASH COURSE

In 1947 an American Airlines pilot named Charles Sisto was in command of a propeller-driven DC-4 aircraft carrying 49 passengers from Dallas to Los Angeles. Along with Sisto were his copilot, Melvin Logan, and John Beck, a DC-3 pilot who was learning how to operate the more sophisticated DC-4. While cruising along at 8,000 feet, Captain Sisto invited Beck to take the controls. As Beck was settling into the captain's chair, Sisto thought he'd have a little fun at the rookie's expense—he fastened the gust lock, a device that locks up both the rudder and the elevator and is supposed to be used only on the ground.

Beck was obviously confused when the DC-4 started climbing...and climbing...and kept climbing, no matter what he did. Beck tried everything he could think of, but he couldn't level the plane out. Finally, suppressing his laughter, Captain Sisto decided that the joke had gone on long enough and unlocked the gust lock. Bad idea: while trying to correct the plane's altitude, Beck had left the controls set to an extreme position. Once the gust lock was off, the airplane went straight into a nose dive.

The sudden lurch threw Sisto and Beck, who were not strapped in, out of their seats. They hit the ceiling—which happened to be where the propeller controls were located—and shut off three of the four engines. This actually turned out to be a good thing, because shutting off the propellers slowed the plane's descent and allowed copilot Logan, who *was* strapped in, to level the plane just 350 feet from the ground. They made an emergency landing in El Paso, Texas.

Many of the passengers were injured, but none seriously. At first, the three pilots claimed that the autopilot had failed, but after a lengthy investigation, Sisto finally confessed to his ill-conceived practical joke.

He was fired.

Since Neptune was discovered in 1846, it has made about 3/4 of one orbit of the sun.

UNCLE JOHN'S STALL OF FAME

You'd be amazed at the number of newspaper articles BRI members send in about the creative ways people get involved with bathrooms, toilets, toilet paper, etc. So we created Uncle John's "Stall of Fame."

Honoree: Will Simmons, a freshman at Duke University

Notable Achievement: Turning toilet paper into a political issue

True Story: In his first year at Duke, Simmons discovered that the toilets in his dorm were outfitted with single-ply toilet paper. Outraged, he decided to run for a seat in the student government. His single campaign platform: a promise that students would get two-ply paper in dorm bathrooms.

Simmons won, of course—students know what's important. After the election, university housing officials pledged to cooperate.

Honoree: Donna Summer, pop singer

Notable Achievement: Writing a Top 10 song in the bathroom

True Story: At a posh hotel, Summer was washing her hands in the ladies' room. She mused to herself that the washroom attendant there had to work awfully hard for her money. It suddenly hit Summer that she had a song title. So she rushed into a stall and wrote lyrics for it. "She Works Hard for the Money" was an international hit that went to #3 on the Billboard chart in 1983.

Honoree: Jacob Feinzilberg, a San Jose, California, inventor

Notable Achievement: Inventing the ultimate port-a-potty

True Story: In 1993 Feinzilberg came up with the Inflate-a-Potty, a toilet so portable it can actually fit in a purse. It can be inflated in seconds and is used with an ordinary eight-gallon kitchen bag as a disposable liner. He came up with the idea for it at a picnic when his young daughter suddenly "heard nature's call and found no place to answer it."

The Bible was written in three languages: Hebrew, Aramaic, and Koine Greek.

Honorees: Philip Middleton and Richard Wooton of Chantilly, Virginia

Notable Achievement: Creating a "commode for dogs"

True Story: According to a 1993 news report, it's called the Walk-Me-Not. The dog walks up stairs at the side of the bathroom toilet, steps onto a platform over the toilet bowl, and squats down to use.

Honorees: Chiu Chiu-kuei and Lee Wong-tsong, a Taiwanese couple

Notable Achievement: Creating a public bathroom nice enough for a wedding...and then getting married in it

True Story: In the mid-1990s, Chiu Chiu-kuei designed, and her fiancé Lee Wong-tsong built, a bathroom for a public park in the city of Taichung. According to news reports: "The couple said the lavatory, complete with elaborate decoration, had cost about $1 million to build." Chiu explained: "Since the bathroom is the creation of me and my husband it is very meaningful to us and therefore we decided to have our ceremony in here." Not explained: Why seven other couples joined them, making it the largest group wedding ever performed in a lavatory.

Honoree: Bryan J. Patrie, a Stanford graduate student

Notable Achievement: Inventing the Watercolor Intelligent Nightlight, which informs bleary-eyed midnight bathroom-goers whether the toilet seat up is or down...without turning on a blinding light.

True Story: Patrie introduced the device in the early 1990s. He explained: "When you get within five feet of the dark commode, it will sense your motion. It looks to see if the room is dark. Then it looks upward by sending out an infrared beam. If it gets a reflection, it knows the seat is up. If it is, the red light comes on."

*　　　*　　　*

HIS & HERS BATHROOM PEEVES

According to the *Philadelphia Inquirer*'s Toilet Paper Report, women's #1 bathroom complaint is men leaving the toilet seat up. Men's #1 complaint: waiting for women to get out of the bathroom.

Amphibians' eyes come in a variety of shapes, including square or heart-shaped pupils.

FILTHY WATER PEOPLE

*Did you ever get a lousy nickname that stuck? You're
in good company. Many Native American tribes are
known today by unflattering names given to them
by their neighbors. Here are a few examples.*

CHEYENNE

Meaning: Red-Talkers

Origin: This Great Plains tribe called themselves the
Tsitsistas, which means the "Beautiful People." The neighboring Dakota
people may have agreed, but they couldn't understand what the Tsitsistas
were saying, because they spoke a different language. They called the Tsitsistas the "Red-Talkers," meaning "those who speak unintelligibly," or, in
Dakota, the *Cheyenne*.

APACHE

Meaning: Enemy

Origin: Like many Native American tribes, this one, famous for legendary chief Geronimo, called themselves "the People"—*Dine* (di-nay) in
their native language. But the neighboring tribe—victim of many of their
war parties—the Zuni, called them "the enemy," or *apachu*. Over time,
that evolved into their permanent name, the *Apache*.

ARAPAHO

Meaning: Tattooed People

Origin: These Plains Indians called themselves the *Inuna-ina*, which
translates to "the People." Their neighbors, the Crow, identified them by
their distinctive body markings and called them "Tattooed People," or, in
their language, *Arapahos*.

HURON

Meaning: Boar's Head

Origin: This tribe lived in the area between Lakes Huron and Ontario
and called themselves the *Wyandot*, meaning "Those from the Peninsula."
But the French called them *Hures*, or "Boar's Head," because the men in

Of the world's 100 largest economic entities, 51 are corporations and 49 are countries.

the tribe wore their hair in bristly spikes that resembled boar's hair—and *Hures* eventually became *Huron*.

WINNEBAGO

Meaning: Filthy Water People

Origin: These Great Lakes Indians were named by the *Chippewa* people. Their own name was *Horogióthe*, or "Fish-Eaters." But the Chippewa called them the *Winnebago*—the "Filthy Water People," possibly because the Horogióthe painted themselves with clay when going to war, which made them appear to have bathed in muddy water.

MOHAWK

Meaning: Man-Eaters

Origin: This tribe from upper New York State and eastern Canada called themselves *Kaniengehagaóthe*, or "Flint People." That proved to be a very difficult word to pronounce for Europeans, who called them what their neighbors, the Narragansett, called them: *Mohawk*, or "Man-Eaters." Why? They engaged in ritualistic cannibalism.

GROS VENTRES

Meaning: Big Bellies

Origin: This tribe from what is now Montana and Saskatchewan called themselves the *Ahahninin*, or "White Clay People." When early French fur trappers and traders asked members of neighboring tribes about the name, they responded—in Native American sign language—by sweeping their hand out from their chest and downward, making what appeared to be a "belly" shape. What were they saying? Historians believe they were saying "Waterfall People," referring to the part of the Saskatchewan River where they lived. The French mistook the gesture and called them the name they are still called today, the *Gros Ventres*—"Big Bellies."

*   *   *

"Names are not always what they seem. The common Welsh name Bzjxxllwcp is pronounced Jackson."

—**Mark Twain**

First county to issue postage stamps: Great Britain (1840).

HE'S A CURLY WOLF

Real cowboy slang of the late 19th century was a lot different from the way it's been depicted in movies and on TV. Some examples:

Coffee boiler: A lazy person who sits around the coffee pot instead of helping with the work.

Big bug: Important person; big shot.

Bone orchard: Cemetery.

The boss: The best.

He only gave it a lick and a promise: He did a poor job.

Crow bait: A poor-quality horse.

Shin out: To run away.

Clean someone's plow: To beat them up.

You're all down but nine: You don't understand—refers to missing all the pins in a game of nine-pin bowling.

Coffin varnish: Bad coffee.

Grub-line rider: Someone who travels from ranch to ranch looking for work.

Curly wolf: A very tough, very dangerous person.

Flannel mouth: A smooth talker.

California widow: A wife who lives apart from her husband because he has gone West to seek his fortune.

Gospel sharp: A preacher. (As skilled with the Bible as a card sharp is with cards.)

Indian haircut: A scalping.

Quirley: A cigarette you roll yourself.

Cowboy change: Bullets (sometimes used as quarters or dimes when coins were short).

Fightin' wages: Extra money paid to cowboys for fighting Indians or cattle rustlers.

Take French leave: To desert, or leave without permission.

Dude: An Easterner or well-dressed person (they wear "duds").

Someone to ride the river with: Someone dependable.

Beat the Devil around the stump: To procrastinate.

Honda: The eyelet at the end of a lasso that's used to make the loop.

The towns of Kamas and Samak are Utah neighbors.

BRITS VS. AMERICANS: A WORD QUIZ

People in both countries speak English, but we don't necessarily use the same words. For instance, the British call a raincoat a "mackintosh." See if you can match the British words to their American counterparts.

BRITISH
1) Knackered
2) Crumpet
3) Stone
4) Nick
5) Afters
6) Rubber
7) Lollipop lady
8) Berk
9) Pilchards
10) Chuffed
11) Redundant
12) Yob
13) Brolly
14) Spot on
15) Naff
16) Dodgy
17) Nappy
18) Nutter
19) Butty
20) Plonk
21) Doddle
22) Starkers
23) Tailback
24) Wally
25) Gormless
26) Wonky
27) Ladder
28) Daps
29) Argy-bargy

AMERICAN
a) Dessert
b) Heated argument
c) Moron
d) Umbrella
e) Sandwich
f) Pleased
g) An attractive woman
h) Sneakers
i) Easy task
j) Iffy, suspect
k) Stupid
l) Exhausted
m) Run (in stockings)
n) Crossing guard
o) Worthless, unfashionable
p) Diaper
q) Steal
r) Kook
s) Sardines
t) Cheap wine
u) Unemployed
v) Eraser
w) Perfect
x) Naked
y) Fourteen pounds
z) Traffic jam
aa) Nerd
bb) Unstable
cc) Hooligan

Answers

1) l; 2) g; 3) y; 4) q; 5) a; 6) v; 7) n; 8) c; 9) s; 10) f; 11) u; 12) cc; 13) d; 14) w; 15) o; 16) j; 17) p; 18) r; 19) e; 20) t; 21) i; 22) x; 23) z; 24) aa; 25) k; 26) bb; 27) m; 28) h; 29) b

Kevin Costner, Harrison Ford, and Gene Hackman...

LITTLE THINGS MEAN A LOT

"The devil's in the details," says an old proverb. And in the profits too. The littlest thing can mean big bucks. Here are a few examples.

A MINUS SIGN

In 1962 an Atlas-Agena rocket that was carrying the *Mariner 1* satellite into space was launched from Cape Canaveral. Unfortunately, the rocket went off course and ground controllers had to push the self-destruct button. The whole thing exploded. Investigators found that someone had left a minus sign out of the computer program. Cost to U.S. taxpayers: $18.5 million.

A LETTUCE LEAF

In 1993 Delta Airlines was looking for ways to reduce costs to compete in the cutthroat airline industry. They discovered that by just eliminating the decorative piece of lettuce served under the vegetables on in-flight meals, they could save over $1.4 million annually in labor and food costs.

A SHOE

On September 18, 1977, the Tennessee Valley Authority had to close its Knoxville nuclear power plant. The plant stayed shut for 17 days, at a cost of $2.8 million. Cause of the shutdown: "human error." A shoe had fallen into an atomic reactor.

A DECIMAL POINT

In 1870 the government published a table of nutritional values for different foods. According to the charts, spinach had 10 times as much iron as other vegetables. Actually, a decimal point had been misplaced; spinach has about the same amount as other veggies. But a popular misconception had already taken hold that spinach promotes strength. Long-term benefit: It ultimately gave us Popeye the Sailor, who's "strong to the finish, 'cause I eats my spinach."

...have all appeared in Japanese commercials for Kirin beer.

SWAN SONGS

When someone dies, whether it's sudden or not, the last thing
he or she did often seems poignantly appropriate.
For a musician, that's often a song.

JOHN COLTRANE
Date of Death: July 17, 1967 (age 40)
Last Song: "A Few of My Favorite Things."

Story: The man considered one of the most influential saxophone players in jazz history played his last concert on April 23, 1967, at the Olatunji Center of African Studies in Harlem. That night, Coltrane and his band performed a version of the Rodgers and Hammerstein classic "My Favorite Things," which had long been his signature song. They stretched it out to 34 minutes in a cacophonous, swirling deluge of sound, described as "frightening" and "Picassoesque" by both those who loved it and hated it. Coltrane knew at the time that he was dying of liver cancer; he'd be gone three months later. The performance was released 44 years later, in 2001, on the album called *The Olatunji Concert.*

OTIS REDDING
Date of Death: December 10, 1967 (age 26)
Last Song: "(Sittin' on the) Dock of the Bay"

Story: In his seven years of recording, Redding had never cracked the top 20 on the charts before. But when his song "Dock of the Bay" came out in January 1968, it held the top spot for four weeks. He recorded it on December 6 and 7, 1967—just a few days before he was killed in a plane crash.

MICHAEL HUTCHENCE
Date of Death: November 22, 1997 (Age: 37)
Last Song: "Possibilities"

Story: This song was written by the former lead singer of INXS for his first solo album, simply titled *Michael Hutchence.* He had been working on the album, while recording and touring with INXS, since 1995. He

---

Winnie the Pooh is named for Winnipeg, Manitoba.

recorded "Possibilities" just three days before his death, which some believe was a suicide; others said it was an accident resulting from auto-erotic asphyxiation. *Michael Hutchence* was released in 1999.

BING CROSBY

Date of Death: October 14, 1977 (age 74)

Last Song: "Once in a While"

Story: Crosby ended his final recording session on October 11 at BBC studios in London with the 1937 standard. Three days later, after playing golf with friends in Spain, he uttered a now-famous line as he walked off the course: "That was a great round of golf, fellas." A few seconds later, he died from a massive heart attack. What wasn't widely known until 2001 was that the *very* last song he sang was on that golf course. The summer 2001 issue of *BING* magazine, put out by the still-active "Club Crosby" fan club, carried an interview with Valentin Barrios, who played that round of golf with Crosby that day. "There were some construction workers building a new house just off the ninth hole," Barrios recounted. "The workers recognized Bing and motioned for him to come over to them. Bing was very happy to be recognized and walked over to the men, who asked for a song. The last song Bing Crosby sang, which I remember vividly, was 'Strangers in the Night.'"

GEORGE HARRISON

Date of Death: November 29, 2001 (age 58)

Last Song: "Horse to Water"

Story: Harrison wrote the song with his son Dhani for old friend and pianist Jools Holland (you can hear it on Holland's album *Small World Big Band*). Harrison recorded it in his home on October 1, in the midst of his battle with throat and brain cancer. With his characteristic dark sense of humor, he asked that his songwriting credit be listed as "RIP Limited."

*　　　*　　　*

"We want to be the band to dance to when the bomb drops."

—**Simon Le Bon, of Duran Duran**

Cost of a 3-minute phone call from New York to San Francisco in 1915: $20.70.

A DOTTY IDEA

*Elbert Botts's brainchild may have seemed like just a bump
in the road at the time, but it's saved countless lives.*

MEET DR. BOTTS

You may never have heard of Elbert Dysart Botts, but if you did any driving today, you probably ran over his invention. The invention? Botts Dots, the raised reflective markers seen on roads and freeways throughout the United States.

Botts didn't start out in the public-safety profession. He earned a doctorate in chemistry from the University of Wisconsin in 1924 and taught for 16 years at San Jose State University. When World War II broke out, he went to work for the government as a chemist. Then he landed a job in research and development at CalTrans (the Californian Department of Transportation), where he was assigned the task of creating a reflective paint for freeways that could be seen in heavy rain.

SPIKED

While working for CalTrans, Botts dreamed up the idea of raised markers that would alert drivers when they crossed into a different lane, avoiding unintentional lane changes and, theoretically, serious accidents. He called his innovation reflective pavement markers, or RPMs (later known by the nickname "Botts Dots"). Unfortunately, the ceramic markers cracked apart when cars rolled over them, exposing the spikes that held them to the road surface—which was bad news for tires. But one of Botts' former students came up with a solution: a durable, fast-drying epoxy that replaced the spikes. Glued-on Botts Dots have been the industry standard ever since.

FOLLOWING THE DOTTED LINE

Elbert Botts died in 1962 at age 69, a year before the first working models of his invention were installed in Northern California. Within a few years, Botts Dots were installed on roads all over the country. They've been in use ever since, and his legacy lives on every time we hear a "thump-thump-thump" when we change lanes on the freeway—or almost cross into someone else's.

In bumblebee hives, the entire colony, except for the queen, dies at the end of each summer.

SMITHSONIAN FUN

In his spare time, Scott Williams of Newport, Rhode Island, digs up things from his backyard and submits them to the Smithsonian Institution in Washington, D.C. as authentic "paleological finds." Here is the actual (we think) response from the Smithsonian, proving that some scientists do indeed have a sense of humor.

Smithsonian Institution
207 Pennsylvania Avenue
Washington, D.C. 20078

Dear Mr. Williams,

Thank you for your latest submission to the Institute, labeled "93211-D, layer seven, next to the clothesline post…Hominid skull." We have given this specimen a careful and detailed examination, and regret to inform you that we disagree with your theory that it represents conclusive proof of the presence of Early Man in Charleston County two million years ago. Rather, it appears that what you have found is the head of a Barbie doll, of the variety that one of our staff, who has small children, believes to be "Malibu Barbie." It is evident that you have given a great deal of thought to the analysis of this specimen, and you may be quite certain that those of us who are familiar with your prior findings were loathe to contradict your analysis. However, we do feel that there are a number of physical attributes of the specimen which might have tipped you off to its modern origin:

1. The material is molded plastic. Ancient hominid remains are typically fossilized bone.

2. The cranial capacity of the specimen is approximately 9 cubic centimeters, well below the threshold of even the earliest identified proto-hominids.

3. The dentition pattern evident on the skull is more consistent with the common domesticated dog than it is with the ravenous man-eating Pliocene clams you speculate roamed the wetlands during that time.

This latter finding is certainly one of the most intriguing hypotheses you have submitted in your history with this institution, but the evidence seems to weigh rather heavily against it. Without going into too much detail, let us say that:

A typical Somali pirate "earns" 17 times as much as an average Somali.

A. The specimen looks like the head of a Barbie doll that has been chewed on by a dog.

B. Clams don't have teeth.

It is with feelings tinged with melancholy that we must deny your request to have the specimen carbon-dated. This is partially due to the heavy load our lab must bear in its normal operation, and partly due to carbon-dating's notorious inaccuracy in fossils of recent geologic record. To the best of our knowledge, no Barbie dolls were produced prior to 1956 A.D.

Sadly, we must also deny your request that we approach the National Science Foundation Phylogeny Department with the concept of assigning your specimen the scientific name *Australopithecus spiff-arino*. Speaking personally, I, for one, fought tenaciously for the acceptance of your proposed taxonomy, but was ultimately voted down because the name you selected was hyphenated, and didn't really sound like it might be Latin.

However, we gladly accept your generous donation of this fascinating specimen to the museum. While it is undoubtedly not a Hominid fossil, it is, nonetheless, yet another riveting example of the great body of work you seem to accumulate here so effortlessly. You should know that our Director has reserved a special shelf in his own office for the display of the specimens you have previously submitted to the Institution, and the entire staff speculates daily on what you will happen upon next in your digs at the site you have discovered in your Newport backyard.

We eagerly anticipate your trip to our nation's capital that you proposed in your last letter, and several of us are pressing the Director to pay for it. We are particularly interested in hearing you expand on your theories surrounding the trans-positating fillifitation of ferrous metal in a structural matrix that makes the excellent juvenile Tyrannosaurus rex femur you recently discovered take on the deceptive appearance of a rusty 9-mm Sears Craftsman automotive crescent wrench.

Yours in Science,

Harvey Rowe
Chief Curator–Antiquities

ASK UNCLE JOHN: IN THE BATHROOM

Plumbing the depths of the bathroom's greatest mysteries.

Dear Uncle John:
Is it true that water in sinks and toilets swirls in one direction in the Northern Hemisphere and in the opposite direction in the Southern Hemisphere? And what happens to the water in the toilet bowl if you're on the equator?

The idea that sink or toilet water swirls one way or another depending on what hemisphere you're in is pretty much completely wrong.

The belief in differently draining water is based on the Coriolis force, an actual phenomenon caused by the rotation of the Earth. Because of the Coriolis force, hurricanes, cyclones, and other large weather systems in the Northern Hemisphere rotate in a counterclockwise direction, while those in the Southern Hemisphere rotate clockwise. (So what happens to a hurricane when it moves from one hemisphere to another? Nothing, because hurricanes don't leave their hemispheres of origin—in fact, they don't even form within five degrees of the equator, because the Coriolis forces at the equator are too weak to allow it to happen.)

But the effect of the planet's rotation on the average bathroom fixture is miniscule; the Coriolis force does almost nothing to your sink or toilet water. The things that *do* affect how the water goes down the drain are much more mundane, like air currents, the shape of the sink, or the fact that your dog just lapped out of the john. Water drains in all sorts of directions, no matter where on Earth you are.

Dear Uncle John:

I get into the shower, and after a few minutes, my shower curtain starts attacking me. What's up with that? Is it possessed?

This is one of those things that people have wondered about for years, but the explanation for weird, clingy shower curtains didn't come about until

---

If you're average, you'll produce about 10,000 gallons of saliva in your lifetime.

2001—and it required some fairly advanced computer modeling to figure it out. Who spends his time modeling the physics of a clingy shower curtain? David Schmidt, a professor of mechanical engineering at the University of Massachusetts.

First, Schmidt created a computer model of his mother-in-law's bathtub. Then he filled the virtual bathtub with thousands of computerized "cells" that measured pressure and velocity. Then he turned on a virtual showerhead to see what would happen.

What Schmidt discovered was that a typical shower creates a miniature, spinning weather system, caused in part by the aerodynamic drag that water droplets encounter when they spritz out of the showerhead. In the center of this tiny weather system is a low-pressure area that sucks on the shower curtain. The top of the shower curtain is held in place by the curtain rod, but the bottom of the curtain is free to wander into the vortex. And so it does. It's not earth-shattering science, but it is one less thing for us to wonder about.

Dear Uncle John:

I was told that if you put soap on your bathroom mirror and then wipe it off after it dries, the next time you shower, your mirror won't fog up. Is this true, and if so, how does it work?

It usually does work. Why? Because, in addition to getting your hands and body clean and germ-free, soap has another quality: It acts as a *surfactant*. Surfactants lower the surface tension of water, making it "wetter" and less able to form droplets. Surface tension is an important element in fogging up your mirror because it lets water droplets form and grow on the mirror's surface. Coating your mirror with soap and then wiping it off leaves a bit of soap residue on the mirror's surface so that later, when you shower, water that collects is unable to generate enough surface tension to allow it to bead. Instead, it just slides down the mirror. Result: no misting.

But after you've soaped up your mirror, don't forget the important "wiping off" step. If you don't, it mirror won't steam up, but you still won't be able to see yourself in it because you'll have a layer of dried soap all over it.

ODD SUPERHEROES

But are they really any odder than a guy who wears his red underwear
over his blue tights or a guy who shoots goo out of his wrists?

BOUNCING BOY. First appearing in a 1961 Action comic, Chuck Taine drank what he thought was a bottle of soda, but it was really a "super-plastic fluid" that gives him the ability to turn into a gigantic bouncing ball. He even gets to join the Legion of Superheroes (sidekicks of Superboy) along with other uniquely powered characters, such as Matter-Eater Lad (his superpower: He can eat anything).

ZSAZSA ZATURNNAH. By day, Ada is the meek owner of a beauty salon in a small town in the Philippines (where the comic originates). At night, he eats a piece of magic rock and transforms himself into Zsazsa, a muscular, curvaceous, crime-fighting woman.

SUPER PRESIDENT. On this 1967 cartoon show, American President James Norcross gets caught in a "cosmic storm" and gains the ability to turn himself into steel, water, stone, or electricity.

SUPERDUPONT. Satirizing French stereotypes, this 1972 French-made superhero is a snooty, mustachioed Frenchman who wears a beret, carries a baguette, drinks red wine, and smokes Gauloise cigarettes. He flies around foiling the schemes of an enemy organization called "Anti-France."

LEECH. His parents abandoned him at birth because he had green skin and hollow eyes. Even his superhero friends (Leech is a minor character in *X-Men* comics) avoid him because his power is to negate the powers of those around him.

AQUANUS. An Indonesian version of Aquaman, he can breathe underwater and communicate with fish. But he can do something Aquaman can't—he can shoot rainbows from his belt.

GENERATION TESLA. In this 1995 Serbian comic, inventor Nikola Tesla transports himself to another dimension and reanimates a bunch of dead people and gives them all superpowers.

...the ocean, yet there are over 1,000,000 swimming pools in the state.

SPEAKING "TOURIST"

Here at the BRI, we have nothing but respect for park rangers. Not only do they brave bears, avalanches, and forest fires, they cope with a little-understood phenomenon called "tourists." Here are some of the silliest comments and questions park rangers have received from tourists at U.S. and Canadian national parks.

"How far is Banff from Canada?"

"At what elevation does an elk become a moose?"

"Do you have a glacier at this visitor center?"

"Is this a map I'm looking at?"

"We had no trouble finding the park entrances, but where are the exits?"

"The coyotes made too much noise last night and kept me awake. Please eradicate those annoying animals."

"Where does Bigfoot live?"

"When do they turn off the waterfalls?"

"There are too many rocks in the mountains."

"Don't all Canadians wear raccoon hats? Where can I buy one?"

"How come all of the war battles were fought in national parks?"

"How many miles of undiscovered caves are there?"

"Are the national parks natural or man-made?"

"Is there anything to see around here besides the scenery?"

"Are you allowed to stay overnight in the campgrounds?"

"Is this island completely surrounded by water?"

At Glacier National Park

Tourist: How did these rocks get here?

Ranger: They were brought down by a glacier.

Tourist: But I don't see any glacier.

Ranger: Really? I guess it's gone back for more rocks.

Sesame Street has been brought to you by the letter B more often than any other letter (200+ times).

NAME YOUR POISON

What's the difference between Scotch and bourbon?
Vodka and gin? Port and sherry? We've always
wondered, so we looked them up

WHERE ALCOHOL COMES FROM

Ethyl alcohol (the kind you can drink) is created by a process known as *fermentation*. Yeast is added to fruit juice or a "mash" (a cooked mixture of grain and water), and the yeast consumes the sugars, creating two by-products: carbon dioxide and alcohol. But there's a natural limit to this process. When the alcohol content of the mixture reaches about 15 percent, the yeast loses its ability to convert any more sugars into alcohol. If you want alcohol with a stronger kick than that, you have to continue on to a second process: *distillation*.

Distilled spirits are made in a device called a *still*, which consists of a boiler, a condenser, and a collector. The fermented liquid is heated in the boiler to at least 173°F, the boiling point for alcohol. All the alcohol (and some of the water) boils off in the form of vapor. The vapor flows into the condenser, where it cools back to liquid form and is collected in the collector. The process can be repeated to increase the alcohol content even further.

All distilled liquor is colorless when it is first made, but it can darken during the aging process, especially when aged in wooden barrels or casks. Some manufacturers use caramel or artificial coloring to darken their spirits.

BAR CODES

• **Whiskey.** The word comes from the Gaelic *uisce beatha*, meaning "water of life." It's alcohol distilled from fermented grains such as barley, rye, corn, wheat, or a combination. In Ireland and the United States, whiskey is spelled with an "e." In Scotland, Canada, and Japan, it's spelled *whisky*.

• **Scotch.** Whiskey made in Scotland. According to international law, only whiskey made in Scotland may be called Scotch.

• **Bourbon.** American whiskey of the type originally made in Bourbon

---

According to studies, grapefruit scent can make women appear as much as 6 years younger to men.

County, Kentucky, typically made from 70 percent corn and 30 percent wheat, rye, or other grains. Tennessee whiskey is similar to bourbon, except that it's produced in—you guessed it—Tennessee. It's filtered through a ten-foot layer of maple charcoal, which gives it a milder, distinctive flavor.

• **Brandy.** Alcohol distilled from fermented fruit juices. Brandy is short for brandywine, which comes from the Dutch *brandewijn*, which means "burnt wine." It can be made from grapes, blackberries, apples, plums, or other fruits. Cognac is a type of brandy produced in the Cognac region of France.

• **Gin.** Distilled grain alcohol flavored with juniper berries. Sloe gin is gin flavored with sloe berries from the blackthorn bush instead of juniper berries.

• **Rum.** Alcohol distilled from molasses and sugarcane juice, both of which are by-products of the process used to turn sugarcane into refined sugar.

• **Vodka.** Distilled alcohol originally made from potatoes, but today mostly made from grain. "Vodka" is the diminutive form of *voda*, the Russian word for water, and means "little water." All vodka produced in the United States is required by law to be colorless, odorless, and nearly tasteless, which accounts for its popularity in mixed drinks.

• **Sherry.** White wine that has been fortified by the addition of distilled spirits. It gets its name from *Shareesh,* the Arabic name for the town of Jerez in southwestern Spain, where it originated.

• **Port.** Fortified red or white wine. It gets its name from the city of Porto in northern Portugal, where it originated.

• **Vermouth.** Fortified white wine flavored with aromatic herbs and spices. It's no longer true, but the flavorings were originally used to mask the flavor of inferior wines. Vermouth gets its name from *wermut,* German for wormwood, one of the traditional flavors.

• **Cordials.** Distilled spirits combined with sweetened fruit pulp or fruit juices. Liqueurs are similar to cordials, except that the flavoring is provided by flowers, herbs, seeds, roots, or the bark of plants. Many traditional cordial and liqueur recipes are centuries old and started out as medicinal products.

Number of glaciers in Glacier National Park in 1910: 150. Today: 27.

"BUNGA BUNGA!"

Sophomoric clown or a brilliant satirist of British imperialism? Either way,
Horace de Vere Cole was responsible for one of the best pranks in history.

HIS MAJESTY REQUESTS...
In the years before World War I, Britain had the most powerful navy in the world. And the HMS *Dreadnought*, armed with 10 large guns and powered by a steam engine, was the pride of the fleet. Considered the superweapon of its day, the huge battleship lay anchored under the tightest security in Weymouth. Few outside the Navy's top officers had ever stepped on board, much less toured its "top-secret" state-of-the-art weaponry.

On February 10, 1910, Sir William May, the ship's captain, received a telegram from the Foreign Office, signed by Under-Secretary Sir Charles Hardinge, announcing the impending arrival of the emperor of Abyssinia and his court in England. The emperor was to receive the royal treatment, including a tour of the HMS *Dreadnought*. The captain immediately ordered his officers and crew to prepare to greet the emperor with all due pomp and circumstance. Guns were polished, decks swabbed, and uniforms washed and pressed in anticipation of the royal tour.

V.I.P. TREATMENT

But the telegram was a fake—it was sent by a practical joker named Horace de Vere Cole. A few days later, he and five co-conspirators (including author Virginia Woolf and her brother) blackened their faces and hands with burnt cork, glued false beards to their chins, donned long red robes topped with makeshift turbans (all rented), and took a cab to London's Paddington Station. Brazenly declaring that he was a state official named "Herbert Cholmondley," Cole talked the stationmaster into giving them a VIP train to Weymouth, where the delegation was met with a full honor guard and a brass band.

An Abyssinian flag couldn't be found (no one knew what one looked like), so one from Zanzibar was used instead. And the band played the Zanzibar national anthem, since that was the only African anthem they knew. (The pranksters didn't know the difference.) The Navy had no translator either: fortunately, the delegation supplied their own, and his

---

According to German folklore, Great Danes were once used to guard against evil spirits.

translations were so eloquent that none of the navy officers noticed that the language spoken by the "Abyssinians" bore a striking resemblance to fractured Latin. And as they were shown all of the ship's accoutrements, they shouted "Bunga Bunga!" in approval at everything they saw.

There were a few anxious moments. One was when the pranksters realized one of the Navy officers knew Woolf. But the officer never caught on. Another came when their "interpreter" sneezed and almost blew off his whiskers. Again, no one noticed. Weather almost sank the prank, too: Rain began to fall as the delegation arrived at the *Dreadnought*; Cole managed to talk their way onto a lower deck just as their makeup started to run.

Finally, Cole decided it was time to get out. They refused lunch (they weren't sure what dietary restrictions might go along with their made-up religion) and left quickly on the excuse that there were no prayer mats for their daily devotionals.

The delegation was given a military escort back to their train. Still in disguise and under Naval supervision, the "Abyssinians" requested that waiters serving them dinner wear white gloves. (The train stopped and was held up in Reading to purchase the gloves.)

SHIP OF FOOLS

Five days later a photograph appeared in the *Daily Mirror*, showing the "Abyssinian" delegation with their Naval hosts. In the accompanying article, Cole exposed the hoax and ridiculed the Navy for being so gullible. All over London, sailors were harassed with cries of "Bunga Bunga!" The Admiralty was furious, but its attempt to charge Cole and his party with treason (the delegation had seen top-secret areas of the ship) was hooted down in Parliament and the press. After all, as people pointed out, the only "treasonous" thing they'd done was make the Admiralty and its officers look like fools. Besides, the only actual crime committed was sending a telegram under a fake name.

The Navy decided to not press charges, but still felt that somebody had to be punished. As the pranksters were all upper class, they could get away with a symbolic act to settle the dispute as gentlemen. Naval officers visited Cole and gave him six symbolic taps on the buttocks with a cane. Cole insisted he be allowed to do the same to the officers. Amazingly, the officers agreed.

During the Christmas season, Americans use their Visa cards about 5,340 times per minute.

IRONIC DEATHS

You can't help laughing at some of life's—and death's—
ironies…as long as they happen to someone else.
These stories speak for themselves.

BOB TALLEY, *centenarian*
Final Irony: Talley passed away in London during his 100th birthday party, moments after receiving a telegram of congratulations from the Queen and telling friends, "Yes, I made it to 100."

RALPH BREGOS, *heart patient*
Final Irony: Bregos, 40, spent more than two years wondering if a suitable donor heart would ever become available. Finally in 1997, doctors told him that one had been found. Bregos became so excited at the news that he suffered a massive heart attack and died.

STANLEY GOLDMAN, *candidate for mayor of Hollywood*
Final Irony: At a campaign stop, Goldman chided his opponent for being "too old for the job." Moments later, he dropped dead from a heart attack.

ROBERT SHOVESTALL, *gun enthusiast in Glendale, California*
Final Irony: Shovestall, 37, died from an accidental gunshot wound. According to news reports, he placed a .45-caliber pistol he thought was unloaded under his chin and pulled the trigger. The incident took place "after his wife's complaints about his 70 guns prompted him to demonstrate they were safe."

ANONYMOUS MAN, *from West Plains, Missouri*
Final Irony: According to news reports, the suicidal man set himself on fire, only to change his mind moments later and jump into a pond to extinguish the flames. Cause of death: drowning.

ELIZABETH FLEISCHMAN ASCHEIM, *pioneering X-ray technician at the turn of the 20th century*
Final Irony: Ascheim often X-rayed herself to show patients that the treatment was safe. Cause of death: "severe skin cancer."

MY OTHER VEHICLE IS IN ORBIT

We keep thinking that we've seen every clever bumper sticker that exists, but every year readers send us new ones. Have you seen the one that says…

I'm Still Hot. It Just Comes in Flashes.

Remember: It's pillage *first,* then burn.

I'll rise, but I won't shine

It's my cat's world. I'm just here to open cans.

Whenever I feel blue, I start breathing again.

The closer you get, the slower I go

Coffee makes it possible to get out of bed; chocolate makes it worth it.

My dog is smarter than your honor student.

If all else fails, stop using all else.

Don't Drink and Derive. Alcohol and Calculus Don't Mix.

What would Scooby do?

EVERYTHING I NEED TO KNOW I LEARNED IN PRISON

BOTTOMLESS PIT OF WANTS AND NEEDS

I'm so old that "getting lucky" means finding my car in the parking lot.

Welcome to Middle Earth. Now go home.

PHYSICALLY *PFFFFFT!*

The only difference between a rut and a grave is the depth.

Dangerously under-medicated.

A barrel full of monkeys would not be fun— it would be horrifying

When life gives you lemons, shut up and eat your lemons

Worldwide, more than 250 lakes are reported to be home to a lake "monster."

YOU STOLE WHAT, NOW?

Thieves…you just never know what they're gonna steal next.

STICKY FINGERS

Someone stole the head off a life-size wax statue of Wolfgang Amadeus Mozart from a museum in Salzburg, Austria, in 2005. "It must have happened between 8 p.m. Friday, when we closed, and today before 9 a.m.," employee Elisabeth Stoeckl told reporters. "When we opened up again, Mozart's head was gone," she said, adding that the stolen head was worth about $18,000.

HE'S A LITTLE SLOW

In 1999 a man in Los Angeles was arrested after leading police on a slow-speed chase…on a stolen steamroller. An officer stopped the runaway steamroller by climbing aboard and shutting it off. The man's excuse: "I was tired of walking."

TIKI TACKY

Security cameras in a Wellington, New Zealand, library captured shots of three masked vandals as they walked up to a tiki—a wooden figurine made by the country's indigenous people, the Maori—chopped off its wooden penis with chisels, and then ran away. The artist who had carved the tiki, Kerry Strongman, called the theft an insult to the *mana*, or "pride," of the city, and immediately began work on a replacement penis for the statue.

IS THIS HOT?

In September 2006, *USA Today* reported that at least seven men had been electrocuted and killed since July trying to steal copper wire from live power lines. Three of the deaths were in Detroit, the latest being when the body of a 24-year-old man was found near a utility box. A pair of wire cutters was found next to his body. Authorities said the would-be thieves were motivated by record-high copper prices—the price of scrap copper has doubled in the last year, according to the report, to about $3 per pound.

You could make over two million different sandwich combinations from the Subway menu.

NASCAR 101

Stock car racing has a rich history...and a complicated set of rules and guidelines. Here's a quick guide for the uninitiated.

How did stock car racing begin? During Prohibition (1920–33), bootleggers in the southern United States relied on fast cars to stay ahead of the law. To maintain a low profile, they souped up their engines and shock absorbers but kept the *stock*, or factory-made, bodies. After a night on the run, the bootleggers would sometimes meet to boast about their cars and race them against each other on oval dirt tracks. This soon became a Sunday tradition, complete with picnic baskets.

How did NASCAR begin? In 1938 Bill France Sr., a mechanic and amateur race-car driver, began running operations at a track in Daytona Beach, Florida, near a stretch of beach where several early land-speed records had been set. The young sport of racing was in trouble, though: Shady promoters often wouldn't pay the drivers, and the lack of consistent car guidelines led to frequent disagreements. France worked to legitimize the sport. After a series of meetings that culminated in Daytona Beach on February 21, 1948, he convinced the drivers and promoters to form a single entity—the National Association for Stock Car Auto Racing. France ran NASCAR until 1972, when his son, Bill France Jr., took over. The younger France ran the organization until 2000.

What's the difference between stock cars and other race cars? Race cars such as Formula One are built specifically for auto racing, while stock cars are made by auto manufacturers for use on regular roads. In NASCAR's early days, the cars were *strictly* stock. But starting in the 1950s, certain modifications were allowed to the engines and chassis to make the cars faster and safer.

How fast do stock cars go? It depends on the track. On *short tracks*, which are less than a mile long, the average speed is about 82 mph. On *intermediate tracks*, between one and two miles long, the fastest speeds top out at about 150 mph. Tracks over two miles in length are called *super-*

A 1792 law made coin defacement, counterfeiting, and embezzlement...

speedways, and there are only two: Talladega, in Alabama, and Daytona, Florida, where the season begins each year. These two tracks boast an average speed of 188 mph. It used to be higher…until a horrific wreck at Talladega in 1987 when Bobby Allison's car nearly flew into the stands. NASCAR now uses *restrictor plates* at these two tracks—a device placed over the intake valve to reduce the car's power.

Why are the cars covered with ads? In 1972, two years after losing the right to advertise tobacco products on television, the R. J. Reynolds Company tried a new marketing tactic by sponsoring the first Winston Cup series (now called the Sprint Cup). In the mid-'70s, partial races were telecast on ABC's *Wide World of Sports*, giving NASCAR a wider audience. But it its biggest boost came with the 1979 Daytona 500, the first NASCAR race broadcast live on national television. On a day when the northeastern U.S. was paralyzed by a snowstorm, millions of TV viewers watched the race—which ended in a dramatic wreck on the final lap, followed by a fistfight between Cale Yarborough and Donnie Allison. After that, more companies jumped on the sponsorship bandwagon, creating a marriage of convenience: Stock cars make perfect blank slates for ads, and stock car racing is so expensive that teams can't do it week after week without the millions they receive from sponsors.

How does the point system work? In each race, a driver receives points for every lap in which he or she leads (there have been 17 female NASCAR drivers). The winner of the race gets an additional 185 points, second place gets 170, third 165, and so on. Because this system rewards consistency over winning, fans complained that the racing was getting too conservative. After Matt Kenseth won the 2003 NASCAR Championship with only one victory (but 25 top-10 finishes), NASCAR implemented a playoff system. Now after the first 26 races are completed, the top 12 drivers' point totals are reset to 5,000, plus an additional 10 points for each race they've won. This means that for the final 10 races, now called "The Chase for the NASCAR Sprint Cup," the top 12 are far ahead of the pack and battle each other for the championship. Adding to the drama: *All* of the drivers still participate in the final 10 races, so drivers farther down in the rankings can often act as "spoilers."

DIALOGUES WITH WORLD LEADERS

Here are some unofficial exchanges involving heads of state at official state functions.

Queen Elizabeth II: How do you do, Mr. King?

Alan King: How do you do, Mrs. Queen?

President Nixon: You dress pretty wild, don't you?

Elvis Presley: Mr. President, you got your show to run and I got mine.

At an old folks home, President Bush approaches an old lady.

George H. W. Bush: Do you know who I am?

Old Lady: No, but if you ask in reception I'm sure they will be able to tell you.

William Gladstone: I predict, Sir, that you will die either by hanging or of some vile disease.

Benjamin Disraeli: That all depends, Sir, upon whether I embrace your principles or your mistress.

At French President Charles de Gaulle's retirement luncheon:

English guest: Madame de Gaulle, what are you looking forward to in the years ahead?

Madame de Gaulle: A penis....

...embarrassed silence...

Charles de Gaulle: My dear, I don't think the English pronounce the word like that. It is 'appiness.'

George H.W. Bush: Tell me, General, how dead is the Dead Sea?

General Zayid bin Shakr: Very dead, sir.

Woman at dinner party: You must talk to me, Mr. Coolidge. I made a bet with someone that I could get more than two words out of you.

Calvin Coolidge: You lose.

"A body of men holding themselves accountable to nobody ought not to be trusted by anybody."
—Thomas Paine

Motto of Springfield, the town in *The Simpsons*: "A noble spirit embiggens the smallest man."

LOCAL HEROES

*Here are the stories of ordinary people who were
faced with an extraordinary situation…
and did something about it.*

SPILT MILK

Local Hero: Steve Leech, a milkman in Cornwall, England

Heroic Deed: Putting out a dangerous fire

The Story: Leech was making his regular deliveries one morning when he noticed smoke pouring out of a gift shop along his route. He called 999 (the English equivalent of 911) but then decided not to wait for the fire fighters to arrive. "I saw the row of apartments up above the shop," he explains, "and I thought, bloody hell, I'd better do something!"

What did Leech do? He kicked open the door of the shop and started pouring milk on the fire. By the time the firefighters arrived 15 minutes later, the fire was under control—and Leech is credited with saving the row of eight shops, as well as the lives of the people living in the apartments above them. "It was hard work opening all those bottles, since they have tamper-proof lids," he says, "but it was even harder trying to explain to my boss where all the milk (320 pints) had gone."

Update: Leech needn't have worried about his boss—he not only kept his job, in January 2002 England's National Dairymen's Association named him the "Hero Milkman of the Millennium."

FIRST-RATE THIRD GRADER

Local Hero: Austin Rosedale, a third-grader at Sunny Hills Elementary School in Issaquah, Washington

Heroic Deed: Saving his teacher from choking

The Story: Austin was in the computer lab one day in November 2001 when his teacher, Mrs. Precht, started choking on a cough drop. She was just about to pass out when he sprang into action.

Luckily for Precht, Austin's parents had given him a Day Planner organizer that happened to have an instructional diagram of the Heimlich maneuver printed on the cover. Austin had read it so many times that

---

Surgeons who play video games have 37% fewer operating room errors than those who don't.

helping Mrs. Precht was a snap. With two thrusts to her abdomen, he dislodged the cough drop. "I just visualized the pictures," he says, "and remembered what I'd read."

BLUE'S BROTHER

Local Hero: Art Aylesworth, a Montana insurance agent

Heroic Deed: Helping to save the mountain bluebird and the western bluebird from extinction

The Story: A longtime conservationist, Aylesworth had worked on a few wildlife habitat restoration projects. But in the mid-1970s he became alarmed when he learned that extensive logging in the state was pushing the bluebirds—which nest in the cavities of old trees—toward extinction. So he got some scrap lumber and built some nest boxes for the birds; then he founded an organization called the Mountain Bluebird Trails Group and recruited hundreds of volunteers to do the same thing.

The organization gave the boxes to anyone willing to put them up and keep an eye on them; it estimates that over the next 25 years, it gave away more than 35,000 boxes. Did it work? Yes—when Aylesworth started handing out the boxes in 1974, only a handful of the bluebirds were thought to still exist; by 1998 the count had grown to more than 17,000.

GUN CONTROL

Local Hero: Dale Rooks, a crossing guard at Suter Elementary School in Pensacola, Florida

Heroic Deed: Finding a unique way to get speeding motorists to slow down in front of the elementary school

The Story: For years Rooks had tried everything he could think of to get drivers to slow down in front of the school—including waving his hands and yelling—but nothing worked. Then inspiration struck him—he got an old hair dryer and covered it with gray duct tape so that it looked like a radar gun, and started pointing it at speeders. That did the trick. "People are slowing down, raising their hands at me apologetically," he says. "It's amazing how well it works."

Update: Inspired by his example, fifth-graders at the school set up a lemonade stand and raised $93 to buy Rooks a *real* radar gun. "I don't mean it to be funny," he says, "but it looks just like a hair dryer."

A *klaxon* is an electric horn. The name comes from a German word meaning "shriek."

THE ICEMAN COMETH

*Not all mummies are wrapped in bandages. Here's one
who was buried in ice, fully clothed, for 5,000 years.*

SURPRISE ENCOUNTER

On September 19, 1991, some people hiking in the Alps along the
Austrian/Italian border spotted a body sticking out of a glacier. The
corpse was brown and dried out and looked like it had been there for a
long time. But neither the hikers nor the Austrian officials who recovered
it four days later had any idea *how* long.

When scientists carbon-dated the remains, the "Iceman" (as he was
dubbed in the press) turned out to be more than 5,300 years old. It was
the world's oldest fully preserved human body, and the first prehistoric
human ever found with "everyday clothing and equipment"—including
an axe, dagger, and bow and arrows. Other bodies that have been found
were either buried following funerals or sacrificed in religious cere-
monies…which means they had ceremonial objects and clothing that
didn't shed much light on what everyday life was like.

CLOSE CALL

Because no one realized how old or valuable the Iceman was until five
days after he was discovered, no one took any precautions to ensure he
wasn't damaged during removal and shipment to the morgue. In fact, it
seems they did just about everything they could to *damage* him. An Austrian police officer tried to free the Iceman from the ice by using a jackhammer—shredding his garments and gashing his left hip to the bone. He
probably would have done more damage, except that he ran out of com-
pressed air for the jackhammer and had to quit.

Next, as word of the unusual discovery spread, locals and gawkers
traveled to the site to view the remains. Many pocketed the Iceman's
tools and shreds of garment as souvenirs. And when forensics experts
finally removed the body from the ice, they did so using clumsy pickaxes,
destroying the archaeological value of the site in the process.

Longest distance ever traveled in a hang glider: 437 miles, by Manfred Ruhmer (2001).

By now the Iceman, clothed from the waist down when initially discovered, was buck naked save for pieces of a boot on his right foot and shards of clothing strewn around the body. Even worse, his private parts were missing, perhaps stolen by one of the visitors to the site. They were never recovered.

MODERN PROBLEMS

When scientists did get around to studying him, they found a dark-skinned male between the ages of 25 and 40 who stood 5'2" tall. The Iceman surprised archaeologists with his shaved face, recently cut hair, and tattoos; experts thought that humans did not "invent" shaves, haircuts, and tattoos until thousands of years later.

He also suffered from some surprisingly modern ailments. A body-scan revealed smoke-blackened lungs—probably from sitting around open fires, but definitely not from smoking—as well as hardening of the arteries and blood vessels. He also had arthritis in the neck, lower back, and hip. But he didn't die from any of them.

CAUSE OF DEATH

The fact that the Iceman's body survived so long may provide a clue about how he died. Most bodies recovered from glaciers have literally been torn to pieces by slow-moving ice. But the Iceman's wasn't. He was found in a small protective basin, 10 to 15 feet deep, that sheltered him as glaciers passed overhead. This leads archaeologists to speculate that he sought shelter in the basin when a surprise winter storm hit. "He was in a state of exhaustion perhaps as a consequence of adverse weather conditions," a team of experts theorized in *Science* magazine in 1992. "He therefore may have lain down, fallen asleep, and frozen to death." Snow covered the body, the glacier eventually flowed over it…and the body remained completely preserved and undisturbed for the next 53 centuries.

FINAL RESTING PLACE

The Iceman now resides in a freezer in Austria's Innsbruck University, kept at 98% humidity and 21°F, the same conditions that preserved him for more than 5,000 years. Scientists only examine the body for 20 minutes every two weeks—anything more than that would cause the mummy to deteriorate.

House dust can vary in composition from room to room.

FAMOUS TIGHTWADS

For some bizarre reason, really rich people are often the most uptight about spending money. Here are a few examples of people who've gone over the deep end about loose change.

MARGE SCHOTT, former owner of the Cincinnati Reds. Told her staff in 1995 that she couldn't afford Christmas bonuses and gave out candies instead. They turned out to be free samples from a baseball-card company…and they came with coupons inviting consumers to "win a trip to the 1991 Grammys."

CARY GRANT. Nicknamed "El Squeako" by Hollywood friends, he counted the number of firewood logs in his mansion's garage and used a red pen to mark the level of milk in the milk bottles in his refrigerator, both to make sure his servants weren't taking them.

FRANKLIN D. ROOSEVELT. Mooched dollar bills off of his presidential valet to drop in the collection plate at church.

GROUCHO MARX. Wore a beret, which became one of his trademarks, "so he wouldn't have to pay to check his hat."

CORNELIUS VANDERBILT, American financier. When his doctor told him on his deathbed that a glass of champagne a day would moderate his suffering, Vanderbilt —then the wealthiest man in America—replied, "Dammit, I tell you Doc, I can't afford it. Won't sodywater do?"

J. PAUL GETTY, oil baron. Installed a pay phone in his mansion to keep visitors from running up his long-distance bill, and put locks on all the other phones. "When you get some fellow talking for ten or fifteen minutes," the billionaire explained, "well, it all adds up."

LEE IACOCCA, former head of Chrysler Corp. Threw himself lavish holiday parties and charged the gifts to underlings. Popular saying at Chrysler: "If you have lunch with someone who looks like Iacocca and sounds like Iacocca, rest assured—if he offers to pick up the check, it's not Iacocca."

The red maple leaf on Canada's flag has 11 points. (The number has no national significance.)

UNDERWORLD LINGO

Every profession has its own jargon—even the criminal world. These terms were compiled by someone else. We stole them fair and square... and we're not giving them back, and no copper's gonna make us!

Walk the plank. Appear in a police lineup.

Barber a joint. Rob a bedroom while the occupant is asleep.

Chop a hoosier. Stop someone from betting because they've been continuously winning.

Dingoes. Vagrants who refuse to work even though they claim to be looking for a job.

California blankets. Newspapers used to sleep on or under.

Wise money. Money to be wagered on a sure thing.

Ride the lightning. Be electrocuted.

Rolling orphan. Stolen vehicle with no license plates.

Put [someone] in the garden. Swindle someone out of their fair share of money or property.

Swallow the sours. Hide counterfeit money from the police.

Frozen blood. Rubies.

Square the beef. Get off with a lighter sentence than expected.

Toadskin. Paper money—either good or counterfeit.

Vinegar boy. Someone who passes worthless checks.

Trojan. A professional gambler.

White soup. Stolen silver melted down so it won't be discovered.

Grease one's duke. Put money into someone's hand.

Irish favorites. Emeralds.

Fairy grapes. Pearls.

High pillow. The top man in an organization.

Nest with a hen on. Promising prospect for a robbery.

Trigging the jigger. Placing a piece of paper (the trig) in the keyhole of a door to a house that is suspected to be uninhabited. If the trig is still there the next day, a gang can rob the house later that night.

NFL statistic: Americans consume 8 million pounds of guacamole on Super Bowl Sunday.

HOW TO READ
A DOLLAR BILL

Looking for emergency bathroom reading the next time you're without this book? Try a dollar bill. It's packed with info, from the obvious to the symbolic.

FIRST, THE BACK OF THE BILL...

• The pyramid stands for permanence and strength. It's unfinished to represent the country's future growth.

• The eye over the pyramid represents the overseeing eye of God.

• The Latin phrase *Annuit Coeptis* above the pyramid means "He Has Favored Our Undertakings."

• The Roman numeral MDCCLXXVI on the bottom of the pyramid is the number 1776 (the year the U.S. was founded).

One in five Americans cannot say which president is on the $1 bill without looking.

• *E Pluribus Unum* is a Latin phrase meaning "Out of Many, One" (50 states united into one nation).

• The eagle's head turns toward peace (symbolized by an olive branch); it turns away from war (represented by arrows). Check out how many olive leaves and arrows there are.

AND NOW, GEORGE'S SIDE OF THE BILL...

• First, a historical note: Ever wonder why George Washington's not smiling in his portraits? Historians suspect it's because of his unattractive and ill-fitting false teeth.

• To the left of Washington is a letter in the center of a seal. That shows which Federal Reserve Bank issued the bill: Boston (A), New York (B), Philadelphia (C), Cleveland (D), Richmond (E), Atlanta (F), Chicago (G), St. Louis (H), Minneapolis (I), Kansas City (J), Dallas (K), or San Francisco (L).

• Below the seal is a series of numbers. This is the bill's serial number. Every bill has a different number.

• Also to the left of Washington is the signature of the Treasurer of the United States at the time the bill was printed.

Pop science quiz: Why does peanut butter stick to the roof of your mouth?...

JELLIED MOOSE NOSE

In 1967 the Canadian government published a collection of backwoods recipes from native and non-native peoples in the nation's far north. It's now out of print, but here are a few highlights. And if ever you find a copy of The Northern Cookbook, *grab it—it's a classic.*

MUSKRAT TAILS

"Cut off the tails and dip them into very hot water. Pull off the fur. Either cook them on top of the stove, turning them after a few minutes, or boil them. (This is the same method as for beaver tails. Both are very sticky to eat.)"

STUFFED MUSKRAT

"Clean the rats well and put them in a roaster with bread stuffing on top. Roast until the muskrats are soft."

BOILED PORCUPINE

"Make a fire outside and put the porcupine in it to burn off the quills. Wash and clean well. Cut up and boil until done."

GRIZZLY BEAR STEAKS

"Cut up meat as for frying and fry in deep grease in frying pan."

BEAR FAT PASTRY

"1½ cups flour, ½ tsp. salt, ⅓ cup bear fat (from a little black bear that was eating berries). Makes rich white pastry."

MUKTUK (meat inside skin and fat of a whale)

"After taken from whale leave 2 days hanging up to dry. Cut into 6" x 6" pieces. Cook until tender. After cooked, keep in a cool place in a 45-gallon drum of oil, in order to have muktuk all year."

OVEN-ROASTED LYNX

"Wash and clean the hind legs of the lynx and roast it with lard and a little water."

BOILED LYNX

"Cut up the lynx and boil it until it is soft and well cooked. Good to eat with muktuk."

STEAMED MUSKRAT LEGS

"Cut off the muskrat's legs, dip in a bowl of flour with salt, pepper, and other strong seasoning. Put grease into a large frying pan. Put in the muskrat legs. Cover and cook for a long time as they take long to become tender. The strong seasoning takes away the actual taste of the muskrat."

...A: Its high protein content sucks away moisture.

BOILED REINDEER HEAD

"Skin and wash the head well. Then chop it in quarters, splitting it between the eyes with an axe. Cover with cold water and boil until soft. One can also roast in an open pan in an oven very slowly."

BOILED REINDEER OR CARIBOU HOOFS

"Put hoofs (skin still on them) in a large pot. Cover and boil for a couple of hours. The skin will peel off easily. The muscles are soft and very good to eat. The toe nails also have some soft sweet meat inside them."

BOILED SMOKED BEAVER

"Smoke the beaver for a day or so. Cut up the meat and boil it with salted water until done."

FROZEN FISH EGGS

"Take fish eggs out and freeze them. They are good to eat like this."

BOILED BONE GREASE

"Boil whatever bones are left after all the meat has been cut off. Boil them all in a big pot for two hours. Then let the grease get cold in the pot. It is easy to pick the grease off. Keep the grease to eat with dry meat or add to pounded meat."

BOILED REINDEER TONGUES

"Boil tongues until thoroughly cooked. Potatoes and vegetables are good with this."

DRY FISH PUDDING

"Pound up 5 to 6 dry fish. Throw away skin. Add sugar, a little grease, and cranberries."

JELLIED MOOSE NOSE

"Cut the upper jaw bone of the moose just below the eyes. Boil in a large kettle for 45 minutes. Remove and chill. Pull out all the hairs (like plucking a duck) and wash until none remain. Place nose in a kettle and cover with fresh water. Add onion, garlic, spices, and vinegar. Bring to a boil, then reduce heat and simmer until meat is tender. Let cool overnight. When cool, discard the bones and cartilage. You will have white meat from the bulb of the nose and dark meat from the bones and jowls. Slice thinly and alternate layers of white and dark meat in a loaf pan. Let cool until jelly has set. Slice and serve cold."

BAKED SKUNK

"Clean, skin, wash. Bake in oven with salt and pepper. Tastes like rabbit (no smell)."

WHERE'S YOUR MECCA?

You've probably heard of the pilgrimage to the city of Mecca in Saudi Arabia that is a requirement of the Islamic faith. But have you heard about the Kumbh Mela? *How about the…*

HOLY SITE: Sites around Mecca, Saudi Arabia
THE JOURNEY: The *Hajj* pilgrimage is the duty of all Muslims, if they are physically and financially able to make the journey. It always takes place in the 12th (and holy) month of the Islamic year, *Ramadan*. Some requirements of the Hajj: Pilgrims are not allowed to hunt, wear perfume, have marital relations, or argue; they must walk around the *Ka'aba*—the ancient mosque said to be built by Islam's patriarch, Abraham, and his son Ishmael—seven times. (The *Ka'aba* is the direction that all Muslims face during prayer.) They must also stone the three pillars of *Jamraat*, which represent Satan, symbolizing Abraham's rejection of temptation. More than 2 million people make the Hajj to Mecca every year.

HOLY SITES: Four cities in India
THE JOURNEY: The *Kumbh Mela* is the world's largest religious pilgrimage. It centers around a Hindu myth: Long ago the gods and demons fought a battle over the *Kumbh*, a pitcher containing the nectar of immortality. During the battle, four drops of nectar spilled onto the Earth. Those drops fell in the Indian cities of Allahabad, Nasik, Ujjain, and Haridwar. Every three years a *mela* (fair) is held in one of the cities, rotating so that each is visited every 12 years. *The Guinness Book of World Records* called Allahabad's 1989 gathering "the largest number of human beings to ever assemble with a common purpose in the entire history of mankind." An estimated 25 million people—nearly the population of Canada—attended.

HOLY SITE: Ise Jingu (The Grand Shrine of Ise), Mie, Japan
THE JOURNEY: The Ise Jingu is the Shinto shrine dedicated to Amaterasu Omikami, the Great Sun Goddess and mythological ancestor of the Japanese royal family. In the 600s A.D., Emperor Temmu declared it the most important shrine in Shintoism. At first, only Japanese royalty were

allowed in, but it in the 1600s it was opened to the public. Ise Jingu also has the distinction of being one of the oldest—and newest—pilgrimage sites in the world. Every 20 years it undergoes *shikinen sengu*—all the shrine's buildings are destroyed and rebuilt, using the same construction techniques that were used 13 centuries ago. (The next *shikinen sengu* is in 2013.) Today more than 6 million make the trip every year, with more than a million showing up around New Years Day alone.

HOLY SITE: Chek Chek shrine near Yazd, Iran

THE JOURNEY: Zoroastrianism was founded in the 6th century B.C. and was the official religion of the ancient Persian Empire. Legend says that in 640 A.D. Muslim armies chased the daughter of Persian Emperor Yazdgird III to the mountains near Yazd. There she prayed to the Zoroastrian creator, Ahura Mazda, for her freedom, and the mountain opened up and saved her. A holy spring still runs at the site (Chek Chek means "drip drop"). Every June, thousands of pilgrims make their way up the mountain to a sacred cave, where they pray and drink the water from the spring.

HOLY SITE: Hill Cumorah, near Palmyra, New York

THE JOURNEY: Hill Cumorah is where Joseph Smith had visions in the 1820s, upon which the Mormon faith is based. There, Mormons believe, Smith was visited by the Angel Moroni, who gave him the Book of Mormon—the history of the New World on gold tablets. A huge statue of Moroni stands on the hill, and every July, nearly 100,000 Mormons come for "The Cumorah Pageant: America's Witness for Christ," during which dramatic reenactments of the Book of Mormon are performed.

HOLY SITE: The Saut d'Eau waterfall near Ville Bonheur, Haiti

THE JOURNEY: Many Haitians follow a combination of Voodooism and Christianity. In 1847, believers say, an image of the Virgin Mary was seen in a tree near the falls. In the Voodoo faith, the Virgin Mary is often associated with Erzuli, the Voodoo goddess of love. Every July, pilgrims journey to Ville Bonheur (the Village of Bliss) and the Saut d'Eau falls. There they stand in the falls and sing, chant, and pray to Mary and/or Erzuli and other Voodoo spirits. Anywhere from hundreds to tens of thousands of Haitians (depending on political conditions in the country) make the trip each year.

STAR TREK WISDOM

Is there intelligent life in TV's outer space? You decide

"Is there anyone on this ship who, even remotely, looks like Satan?"
—**Kirk**

Tuvok: "The phaser beam would ricochet along an unpredictable path, possibly impacting our ship in the process."
Janeway: "All right, we won't try that."

"Mr. Spock, the women on your planet are logical. That's the only planet in the galaxy that can make that claim."
—**Kirk**

"I'm a doctor, not an escalator."
—**McCoy**

"I must say, there's nothing like the vacuum of space for preserving a handsome corpse."
—**Doctor**

"It's difficult to work in a group when you're omnipotent."
—**Q**

"The best diplomat I know is a fully-loaded phaser bank."
—**Scotty**

"Mr. Neelix, do you think you could possibly behave a little less like yourself?"
—**Tuvok**

"What am I, a doctor or a moon shuttle conductor?"
—**McCoy**

"Time travel. From my first day on the job I promised myself I'd never let myself get caught up in one of these God-forsaken paradoxes. The future is the past; the past is the future. It all gives me a headache."
—**Janeway**

"I'm attempting to construct a mnemonic memory circuit, using stone knives and bearskins."
—**Spock**

Data: "Tell me, are you using a polymer-based neuro-relay to transmit organic nerve impulses to the central processor of my positronic net?"
Borg Queen: "Do you always talk this much?"

"I'm a doctor, not a bricklayer."
—**McCoy**

The word "grandmother" appears in the Bible only once: 2 Timothy 1:5.

JUZT NUTZ

Each year, The Onion's A.V. Club receives thousands of records from up-and-coming bands, some with really, really strange names. Here are a few that we can print (but we can't vouch for their music).

- Dear and the Headlights
- The Dead Kenny Gs
- Human Being Lawnmower
- Happy Butterfly Foot
- Orb of Confusion
- Best Fwends
- The Color Fred
- Tigers Can Bite You
- To Live and Shave in L.A.
- Butt Stomach
- Shapes Have Fangs
- Harmonica Lewinsky
- Earth Dies Screaming
- Shoot for the Stars… and Kill Them
- Secret Lives of Freemasons
- Unicorn Dream Attack
- Chevy Metal
- The Pleasures of Merely Circulating
- Garrison Killer
- Penguins with Shotguns

- DD/MM/YYYY
- Mel Gibson & the Pants
- Doofgoblin
- Ringo DeathStarr
- General Patton & His Privates
- Let's French
- The Shark That Ate My Friend
- I Would Set Myself on Fire for You
- Dyslexic Speedreaders
- Clown Vomit
- Les Breastfeeders
- Happy Mothers Day, I Can't Read
- Neil Diamond Phillips
- Broke Up This Year, Alas
- Juzt Nutz
- If Your Hands Were Metal That Would Mean Something
- We All Have Hooks For Hands
- The House That Gloria Vanderbilt

In Flowery Branch, Georgia, it is illegal to yell "Snake!" within city limits.

NUDES & PRUDES

Nudity can be shocking…and so can prudery.
Which side of the fence do you fall on?

NUDE
In April 2000, a state trooper stopped a car in the Houston suburb of Sugarland and discovered that all four passengers—three women and a three-year-old girl—were naked. God, the women claimed, had told them to burn their clothes and drive to Wal-Mart to get some new clothes. "It's always something," the state trooper says. "No two days are the same in this job."

PRUDE
Police in Brazil arrested a minor league soccer player named William Pereira Farias after he stripped off his uniform and threw it into the crowd to celebrate the scoring of a goal. "He broke the laws of respectful behavior," police officer Alfredo Faria told reporters. "He offended the townspeople and will likely be suspended from the team."

NUDE
Norway's Radio Tango has become the first radio station to offer live nude weather reports. The reports, billed as "more weather, less clothes," air on the station's morning show; listeners can view the naked weather forecasters on the Internet. "This is a world exclusive," says morning host Michael Reines Oredam. "It has never been done before. It brings a certain atmosphere to the studio which we hope our listeners are able to pick up on."

PRUDE
Police in Seremban, a town south of Kuala Lumpur, Malaysia, have raided several cellular phone stores and seized "obscene" plastic cellular phone covers that feature naked images of well-known celebrities. "The phones are modified to light up the private parts of actors or actresses when a user receives or makes a call," says police superintendent Abdul Razak Ghani.

NUDE
Portland businessman Mark Dean hopes to expand his topless nightclub

---

business by running it as a topless doughnut shop during breakfast hours, with his strippers doubling as waitresses. What are the odds that his new venture will succeed? Not as good as you might think—a topless doughnut shop in Fort Lauderdale, Florida, went under after less than a year; a topless car wash operated by the same businessman lasted only a few months.

PRUDE

The executor of the estate of the late basketball legend Wilt Chamberlain reports that he is having trouble selling the Big Dipper's Bel Air estate, even after reducing the price from $10 million to $4.3 million and tearing out the "playroom," which featured a waterbed floor covered with black rabbit fur and a wraparound pink velvet couch. (The retractable mirrored roof over the master bed has been preserved; so has the traffic light in the bedroom that signals either a green light to "Love," or a red light for "Don't Love.") Executor Sy Goldberg admits that Chamberlain's boasting that he slept with more than 20,000 women in his lifetime may be part of the problem, but he says that holding that against the house is "ridiculous."

NUDE

A Dutch telemarketing company has found a novel way around the tight labor market in the Netherlands: They've created a special division of the company that allows employees to work in the nude. "We had about 75 applicants in the first four hours," a spokesman for the company—which did not release its name "for fear of offending existing clients"—told reporters. "With a normal call center, you'd be lucky to get one or two applicants an hour."

PRUDE

Officials at Los Angeles International Airport covered images of "bounding nude men" with brown paper in 2001 pending a decision on whether to remove them permanently. The naked men, who were supposed to represent the earliest human attempts at flight, were sandblasted into the granite floor of a newly renovated terminal at the airport. American Airlines paid Los Angeles artist Susan Narduli $850,000 to create the work, which was approved by both the airline and the city's cultural affairs commission. The figures' private parts were "completely obscured," but no matter: "If the city decides it wants the artwork changed," said an American Airlines spokesperson, "we'll change it." Several weeks later, city officials said the artwork could remain…and the brown paper was removed.

Barely known fact: "Naked" means to be unprotected; "nude" means unclothed.

HE SLUD INTO THIRD

Verbal gems actually uttered on the air by sports announcers.

"If only faces could talk."
>—**Pat Summerall,**
NFL announcer

"Hector Torres, how can you communicate with Enzo Hernandez when he speaks Spanish and you speak Mexican?"
>—**Jerry Coleman,**
San Diego Padres announcer

"A lot of good ballgames on tomorrow, but we're going to be right here with the Cubs and the Mets."
>—**Thom Brennaman,**
Chicago Cubs announcer

"Lance Armstrong is about to join a list which includes only himself."
>—**Mark Brown,**
ESPN sports analyst

"I don't think anywhere is there a symbiotic relationship between caddie and player like there is in golf."
>—**Johnny Miller, golf analyst**

"Referee Richie Powers called the loose bowel foul on Johnson."
>—**Frank Herzog, Washington**
Bullets basketball announcer

"It's a great advantage to be able to hurdle with both legs."
>—**David Coleman,**
British sports announcer

"The Minutemen are not tall in terms of height."
>—**Dan Bonner,**
college basketball analyst

"Jose Canseco leads off the 3rd inning with a grand slam."
>—**John Gordon,**
Minnesota Twins announcer

"The offensive linemen are the biggest guys on the field, they're bigger than everybody else, and that's what makes them the biggest guys on the field."
>—**John Madden,**
NFL announcer

"Watch the expression on his mask."
>—**Harry Neale, hockey analyst**

"The game's in the refrigerator, folks. The door's closed, the light's out, the eggs are cooling, the butter's gettin' hard, and the Jell-O's a-jigglin'."
>—**Chick Hearn,**
L.A. Lakers announcer

It's impossible to create a beverage of more than 18% alcohol by fermentation alone.

WORD ORIGINS

Ever wonder where words come from?
Here are some interesting stories.

JACKPOT
Meaning: A huge prize
Origin: "The term goes back to draw poker, where stakes are allowed to accumulate until a player is able to 'open the *pot*' by demonstrating that among the cards he has drawn he has a pair of *jacks* or better." (From *Dictionary of Word and Phrase Origins, Vol. II*, by William and Mary Morris)

GRENADE
Meaning: A small, hand-thrown missile containing an explosive
Origin: "The word comes from the French *pomegrenade*, for pomegranate, because the military missile, which dates from the sixteenth century, both is shaped like the fruit and explodes much as the seeds burst out from it." (From *Fighting Words*, by Christine Ammer)

SNACK
Meaning: A small amount of food eaten between meals
Origin: "A snack is something grabbed in a hurry, from the Dutch *snacken*, meaning to snap at something, although that word was only used for dogs." (From *Word Origins*, by Wilfred Funk)

AMMONIA
Meaning: A potent, odorous cleaning fluid
Origin: "*Ammonia* is so called because it was first made from the dung of the worshippers' camels at the temple of Jupiter Ammon in Egypt." (From *Remarkable Words with Astonishing Origins*, by John Train)

HEATHEN
Meaning: An ungodly person
Origin: "Christianity began as primarily an urban religion; people in rural districts continued to worship older gods. The Latin word for countryman

was *paganus*—whence, of course, pagan; the Germanic tongues had a similar word, something like *khaithanaz*, 'dwelling in the heath' (wilderness)—whence heathen." (From *Loose Cannons and Red Herrings*, by Robert Claiborne)

CALCULATE

Meaning: Add, subtract, divide, and/or multiply numbers or money

Origin: "In Rome 2,000 years ago the merchant figured his profit and loss using what he called *calculi*, or 'little stones' as counters. So the Latin term *calculus*, 'pebble,' not only gave us 'calculate' but our word 'calculus,' one of the most complicated forms of modern mathematics." (From *Word Origins*, by Wilfred Funk, Litt. D.)

MUSEUM

Meaning: Building or collection of art, music, scientific tools, or any specific set of objects

Origin: A shrine to the Greek Muses. "Such a shrine was known as a *mouseion*. When the Museum at Alexandria was destroyed in the fourth century, the word nearly dropped out of use. Three hundred years ago, a scholar rediscovered the word." (From *Thereby Hangs a Tale*, by Charles Earle Funk)

DOPE

Meaning: Drugs

Origin: "This word was originally a Dutch word, *doop*, meaning a sauce or liquid. Its first association with narcotics came when it was used to describe the viscous glop that results from heating opium. Then, by rapid extension, it came to mean any narcotic." (From *Dictionary of Word and Phrase Origins, Vol. III*, by William and Mary Morris)

RIVAL

Meaning: Competitor

Origin: "A rival is etymologically 'someone who uses the same stream as another.' The word comes from Latin *rivalis*, meaning 'of a stream.' People who use or live by the same stream are neighbors and, human nature being as it is, are usually in competition with each other." (From *Dictionary of Word Origins*, by John Ayto)

...from sitting in their cars with the engine running.

LITTLE WILLIE

*These morbid "Willie" poems were popular in the 1950s, although most were
written in the 1890s. Either way, they're still funny (in a sick sort of way).*

Little Willie hung his sister,
She was dead before
we missed her.
Willie's always up to tricks!
Ain't he cute? He's only six!

Willie poisoned Father's tea.
Father died in agony.
Mother was extremely vexed.
"Really, Will," she
said, "What next?"

Into the family drinking well
Willie pushed his sister Nell.
She's there yet
because it kilt her.
Now we have to buy a filter.

Little Willie, on the track,
Didn't hear the engine squeal.
Now the engine's
coming back,
Scraping Willie off the wheel.

The ice upon our
pond's so thin
That Little Willie's fallen in!
We cannot reach
him from the shore
Until the surface freezes more.
Ah me, my heart
grows weary waiting—
Besides, I want
to do some skating.

Willie saw some dynamite,
Couldn't understand it quite;
Curiosity never pays:
It rained Willie seven days.

Willie with a thirst for gore
Nailed his sister to the door.
Mother said with
humor quaint,
"Willie dear, don't
scratch the paint."

Little Willie fell down a drain;
Couldn't scramble out again.
Now he's floating in the sewer
The world is left
one Willie fewer.

Willie, in one of
his nice new sashes,
Fell in the fire and
was burnt to ashes.
Now, although the
room grows chilly,
We haven't the heart
to poke poor Willie.

Willie coming
home from school,
Spied a dollar near a mule.
Stooped to get it,
quiet as a mouse.
Funeral tomorrow
at Willie's house.

How big is the principality of Monaco? 370 acres.

THE BUGS AND THE BEES

*We sometimes wonder about insects creeping and crawling
in the garage or out in the garden. What do they do all
day? It turns out that even with six or eight legs,
they still have a one-track mind.*

CHEAPSKATE FLIES

The mating ritual of a type of fly called *Hilara*, commonly known as the "dance fly," involves gift-giving. The male catches a small insect, wraps it in silk, and then presents it—along with a wing-waving mating dance—to his potential mate. When she accepts it, he mounts her while she's busy eating the gift. But some dance flies are too lazy to even catch the bug. In one species, the male offers the female what *looks* like a gift-wrapped insect. While she unwraps it, he mates with her, trying to complete the act before she discovers there's no bug in the bag.

TRICKY ORCHIDS

The female tiphiid wasp can't fly. So she climbs to the top of a tall plant and releases her pheromones into the air. The male flies by, grabs her, and flies away. Mating takes place in midair.

One type of orchid has made an interesting adaptation: its flower looks just like a female tiphiid. Not only that, its scent is almost identical to her pheromones. The unsuspecting male wasp grabs the flower and tries to take off with it; in the struggle, he brushes against the pollen before becoming frustrated and flying away. He goes on to the next orchid and goes through the same routine, thus pollinating the orchids.

HUNGRY SPIDERS

The female black widow spider is genetically programmed to control the black widow population in her neighborhood, based on available food supply. Here's how she does it: A male approaches her web, sits on the edge, and bobs his abdomen, causing the web to vibrate. If she's not in the mood, she won't respond. If she is willing to mate, she'll send out an answering pattern of vibrations calling him toward her. But if she's hungry, she'll send the male the *exact same* mating response. And when he gets close enough… she eats him.

Early recipes for beer included mushrooms, bay leaves, butter, and bread crumbs.

WHAT DREAMS MEAN

Psychologists say dreams reflect our waking lives. Although translations will vary with each individual, researchers say everybody's dreams share some common themes. Here are some examples.

• **If you're naked,** you're dreading an upcoming event because you feel unprepared, ashamed, or vulnerable.

• **If you're falling,** it's a subconscious response to real-life stress. However, some experts say the "stress" could be something as simple as a mid-sleep leg or arm spasm.

• **If you die,** it doesn't portend death (yours or anybody else's)—it suggests insecurity or anxiety.

• **If you dream about a dead relative,** you've come to terms with the loss. Dream psychologists say we only dream about deceased loved ones when the grief process is complete.

• **If you see a car wreck,** a big undertaking in your life may feel bound for failure.

• **If you're being chased,** you're probably running away from something in real life. Being unable to run in a dream indicates feeling overwhelmed by daily pressures.

• **If your teeth fall out or crumble,** you're unhappy with your physical appearance. It may also mean you're excessively concerned about how others perceive you.

• **If you're giving birth,** great change is unfolding. Dreaming about babies indicates a desire to behave more maturely.

• **If you can fly,** you've just conquered a stressful situation. If you dream that you're able to control where you fly, it's a sign of confidence. Flying aimlessly suggests you're cautiously optimistic about your success.

• **If you dream about water,** it represents a general sense of your emotional state. Clear water means satisfaction with work and home. Muddy water is a sign of skepticism and discontent.

• **If you're urinating,** you may be expressing desire for relief from a difficult situation. Or you may really have to pee. Or you may be doing so already.

The American bison was pictured on a 1901 U.S. dollar. It was nicknamed "the buffalo bill."

UNINTENDED CONSEQUENCES

Sometimes when a plan is put into action, the result can be something that no one could have predicted. But, hey—that's what makes life interesting.

WHAT HAPPENED: The approval of the drug Viagra by the FDA in 1998

INTENDED: Improved sexual performance in men and, thus, better physical relationships between couples

UNINTENDED: A sharp rise in the divorce rate among the elderly. Reports released between 2001 and 2003 dubbed the problem the "Viagra divorce." *USA Today* reported that "husbands previously unable to perform now confront 'Viagra wives' not excited to be asked once again for sex." This, according to the reports, often led the men to have affairs, which often resulted in divorce.

WHAT HAPPENED: The Roman army's victories in Asia Minor between 161 and 166 A.D.

INTENDED: Armenia, Syria, and Mesopotamia were annexed to the Roman Empire

UNINTENDED: The plague. Returning soldiers brought it back with them, and as much as half the entire population of Rome was decimated by the disease.

WHAT HAPPENED: The use of salicylic acid as early as the fifth century B.C. and its modern form, acetylsalicylic acid—better known as aspirin

INTENDED: Pain relief

UNINTENDED: The prevention of countless heart attacks and strokes. British scientist John Vane showed in 1971 that aspirin suppresses not only inflammation, fever, and the transmission of pain signals to the brain, it also affects the blood's ability to clot. Blood clots are a major factor in heart attacks and strokes—the leading cause of death in the Western world. Vane's research, which showed that small regular doses of aspirin could prevent their occurrence, won him a Nobel Prize.

Over a lifetime, the average driver releases 900 pints of gas inside their car.

WHAT HAPPENED: A ban on smoking in bars in Winnipeg, Manitoba
INTENDED: A decrease in the health risks of cigarette smoke to bar-goers and workers in the city
UNINTENDED: The discovery of a mummified body in the wall of a bar. In December 2003, police found the body of Eduardo Sanchez, 21, behind a wall in the Village Cabaret. The club's owners said they had been aware of an offensive smell for a year but thought it was just normal bar odors: stale beer and cigarettes. When the smoking ban went into effect, the odor stood out and neighbors called police. Sanchez was a DJ at the club; police had been unable to solve the mystery of his disappearance in October 2002. They said it now appeared that Sanchez had crawled into a gap between two walls in the basement—for an unknown reason—and gotten stuck.

WHAT HAPPENED: The U.S. government's $1.3 billion "War on Cocaine" in Colombia
INTENDED: A decrease in cocaine use in the United States
UNINTENDED: An increase in heroin use in the U.S. In 2001 the *Chicago Sun-Times* reported that under the U.S. plan, Colombian planes and helicopters were being used to go after coca plantations—the same aircraft that had previously been used to search for poppy plantations. Poppy growers took advantage and started making record amounts of heroin…and shipping it to the U.S.

WHAT HAPPENED: The creation of the DMZ (Demilitarized Zone) between North and South Korea at the end of the Korean War in 1953
INTENDED: The barbed wire–enclosed 2.5-by-150-mile strip of land would help preserve peace between two nations that are still officially "at war."
UNINTENDED: The DMZ is an environmental paradise. It's been virtually human-free for more than 50 years. Result: According to scientists, nearly 3,000 species of plants and animals thrive in the zone today—many that no longer exist in either country. That includes several severely endangered animals, such as Asiatic black bears, Siberian tigers, and two of the most endangered birds in the world: the white-naped crane and the red-crowned crane. In 1999 environmental leaders created a group called the DMZ Forum, which is still working to convince the two countries to turn the strip into a permanent nature reserve.

Ouch! The term "alimony" is from the Latin for "eating money."

LUCKY FINDS

Ever found something really valuable? It's one of the best feelings in the world. Here's an installment of a regular Bathroom Reader *feature.*

A SHAKY PROSPECT

The Find: A dirty, moldy, wobbly old card table

Where It Was Found: At a lawn sale, for $25

The Story: In the late 1960s, a woman named Claire (no last name—she prefers to remain anonymous) moved to a new house and needed a small table for one of the rooms. She found one at a yard sale but it was dirty and it wobbled; a friend advised against buying it, telling her that "it would never hold a lamp." She bought it anyway—after bargaining the price down from $30 to $25, because that was all the money she had in her purse. When she cleaned the table up, she noticed a label on the underside of it that read "John Seymour & Son Cabinet Makers Creek Square Boston." Claire did some research on it, but didn't learn a lot.

Nearly 30 years passed. Then in September 1997, Claire took her table to a taping of the PBS series *Antiques Roadshow*. There she learned that Seymour furniture is among the rarest and most sought-after in the United States; until Claire's table showed up, only five other pieces in original condition with the Seymour label were known to exist. Claire thought the table might be worth $20,000; the *Antiques Roadshow* appraiser put it at $300,000. Not even close—the table sold at auction at Sotheby's for $490,000.

I YAM WHAT I YAM

The Find: A diamond

Where It Was Found: In Sierra Leone...under a yam

The Story: In 1997 three hungry boys were scrounging for food near the village of Hinnah Malen in the African country of Sierra Leone. The boys, orphaned since 1995 when their parents had been killed in a rebel attack, had gone two days without food. They spent three unsuccessful hours searching for yams that morning and were on their way home when their luck changed. They found a yam under a palm tree and dug it up. Right under the yam they found a flawless 100-carat diamond. Estimated value: $500,000. "It was easy to see," according to the oldest boy, 14-year-old Morie Jah. "It was shining and sparkling."

NOT BAA-AA-AD

The Find: A lost Hindu shrine

Where It Was Found: In a cave in the Himalayas, in India

The Story: In September 2001, a shepherd named Ghulam Qadir lost some of his sheep and set out to look for them. He crawled into a small cave, thinking they might be there…but instead of his sheep, he found a 12-inch idol of the Hindu god Shiva. The cave turned out to be a 1,500-year-old shrine, one that had been forgotten and undisturbed for centuries. Government officials were so excited by the discovery that they promised to pay Qadir 10% of the cash offerings left at the shrine from 2002 to 2007, followed by a large final payment when the five years were up. (He never did find his sheep.)

FOWL PLAY

The Find: A piece of paper stuffed into a leather-bound datebook from 1964

Where It Was Found: In a box of old books in Shelbyville, Kentucky

The Story: Homeowners Tommy and Cherry Settle found the datebook while looking through boxes in their basement. Inside the datebook they found a recipe for fried chicken, one that called for 11 herbs and spices—a number that immediately clicked with the Settles, because their home was once owned by Kentucky Fried Chicken founder Colonel Harland Sanders. The Settles believe the recipe may be a copy of Colonel Sanders's "Original Recipe," a carefully guarded trade secret and the foundation upon which the $20 billion fast-food chain is built. Only a handful of KFC employees know the recipe, and each of them is sworn to secrecy. When the company subcontracts out the recipe to other manufacturers, they always use at least two companies, so that no one else knows the complete recipe.

So is the Settles' find the genuine article? The Settles think so, because when they asked KFC about it, the chain filed a lawsuit to force them to hand the recipe over. "They didn't say anything," Cherry Settle says, "They just sent this court document." Estimated "value," priceless. If the recipe ever gets out, KFC is powerless to stop anyone else from using it.

MADISON AVENUE
MUTTS

From beer to burritos, these dogs mean business.

NIPPER, THE RCA DOG

Nipper, a fox terrier, was born in England in 1884 and got his name because he liked to bite visitors on their legs. His original owner was Mark Barroud, brother of English painter Francis Barroud. When Mark died, Francis inherited the dog. According to legend, when a recording of Mark's voice was played at his funeral, Nipper recognized it and stood on Mark's coffin, looking into the horn of the phonograph. Francis Barroud later painted the scene in a work titled *His Master's Voice*.

Around 1900, the Victor Talking Machine Company started using the painting as its logo. Then, in 1928, Nipper (minus the coffin) became the symbol of the Radio Corporation of America when Victor's American rights were sold to RCA.

SPUDS MCKENZIE

"Some guy in our Chicago agency drew a rough sketch of a dog called the Party Animal, for a Bud Light poster," Anheuser-Busch's marketing director told *Sports Illustrated*. "So we had to find a real dog that looked like this drawing." The company picked Honey Tree Evil Eye, a female English bull terrier from Illinois. The poster was supposed to be distributed only to college students, but the beer company's spokesdog was such a hit that the ads started showing up everywhere.

After Spuds made her TV debut during the 1987 Super Bowl, Bud Light sales shot up 20 percent. Spuds retired amid controversy sometime later when the group Mothers Against Drunk Driving accused Anheuser-Busch of using the dog to encourage underage drinking. Honey Tree returned home to Illinois, where she lived until her death in 1993. She was 10 years old.

THE TACO BELL CHIHUAHUA

The most famous fast-food character of the 1990s was invented by chance when two advertising executives, Chuck Bennett and Clay Williams, were eating lunch at the Tortilla Grill in Venice, California. "We saw a little Chihuahua run by that appeared to be on a mission," Bennett says. "We both looked at each other and said, 'That would be funny.'"

The men went on to make Gidget—the model Chihuahua used in the ads—an international superstar. The dog spawned toys, bobbleheads, and a renewed interest in the Chihuahua breed. A respected canine thespian in her own right, Gidget also starred in other projects, most notably as Bruiser's mother in the 2003 film *Legally Blonde 2: Red, White, and Blonde*. She died in 2009 at the age of 15.

MCGRUFF THE CRIME DOG

In the late 1970s, the Ad Council—the organization responsible for producing most public-service announcements—made a deal with the U.S. Justice Department to create an ad campaign to discourage crime. Their first task: invent a spokes-character to deliver the message in commercials. Adman Jack Keil began riding with the New York police to get ideas. He remembers:

> We weren't getting anywhere. Then came a day I was flying home from the West Coast. I was trying to think of a slogan—*crunch crime, stomp on crime.* And I was thinking of animal symbols—*growling at crime, roaring at crime.* But which animal? The designated critter had to be trustworthy, honorable, and brave. Then I thought, you can't crunch crime or defeat it altogether, but you can snap at it, nibble at it—*take a bite out of crime.* And the animal that takes a bite is a dog.

A bloodhound was the natural choice for a crime fighter, and the campaign (dog included) debuted in 1980. But Keil still needed a name for his watchdog, so the Ad Council sponsored a nationwide contest to name the dog. Entries included Shure-lock Bones, Sarg-dog, J. Edgar Dog, and Keystone Kop Dog. The winner was submitted by a police officer from New Orleans—McGruff. In the ads, Keil supplies the dog's voice. When he retires, Steve Parker, a sheriff's deputy from Indiana, will take over.

*　　*　　*

"Scratch a dog, and you'll find a permanent job."

—Franklin P. Jones

In scientific measurement, a unit of beauty is called a *millihelen*.

PLEASED TO MEAT YOU

*Uncle John once saw a sign on an electrician's truck that
said "Let us fix your shorts." He's been collecting
wacky business mottos like these ever since.*

Concrete company: "We dry harder."

Taxidermist: "We really know our stuff."

Podiatrist: "Time wounds all heels."

Butcher: "Let me meat your needs."

Pastry shop: "Get your buns in here."

Septic services: "We're number 1 in the number 2 business."

Dry cleaner: "Drop your pants here."

Towing company: "We don't want an arm and a leg…just your tows!"

Window cleaner: "Your pane is our pleasure."

Restaurant: "Don't stand there and be hungry, come in and get fed up."

Diaper service: "Let us lighten your load."

Funeral home: "Drive carefully, we'll wait."

Chimney sweep: "We kick ash."

Trash service: "Satisfaction guaranteed or double your trash back."

Garden shop: "Our business is growing."

Auto body shop: "May we have the next dents?"

Muffler shop: "No appointment necessary. We'll hear you coming."

Car wash: "We take a bite out of grime."

Massage studio: "It's great to be kneaded."

Sod installation: "We just keep rolling a lawn."

Auto repair: "We meet by accident."

Bakery: "While you sleep, we loaf."

Plumber: "A good flush beats a full house."

Butcher: "Pleased to meat you."

Vacuum cleaners: "Business sucks."

TO TELL THE TRUTH

Can we ever really know for sure if someone is telling a lie? Most experts agree that the answer is no—but that hasn't stopped society from cooking up ways to sort out the liars from the honest people.

ANCIENT LIE DETECTORS

• The Bedouins of the Arabian peninsula forced suspected liars to lick red-hot pokers with their tongues, on the assumption that liars would burn their tongues and truth tellers wouldn't. The method was cruel but it may have also been accurate, since the procedure measured the moisture content of the suspect's mouth—and dry mouths are often associated with nervousness caused by lying.

• The ancient Chinese forced suspected liars to chew a mouthful of rice powder and spit it out; if the rice was still dry, the suspect was deemed guilty.

• The ancient British used a similar trick: They fed suspects a large 'trial slice' of bread and cheese, and watched to see if he could swallow it. If a suspect's mouth was too dry to swallow, he was declared a liar and punished.

• The preferred method in India was to send the suspects into a dark room and have them pull on the tail of a sacred donkey, which was supposed to bray if the person was dishonest...at least that's what the suspects thought. The way the system really worked was that the investigators dusted the donkey's tail with black powder (which was impossible to see in the unlit room). Innocent people, the investigators reasoned, would pull the tail without hesitation...but the guilty person, figuring that no one could see them in the darkness, would only pretend to pull the tail but would not touch it at all.

MODERN METHOD

The first modern lie detector was invented by Cesare Lombroso, an Italian criminologist, in 1895. His device measured changes in pulse and blood pressure. Then, in 1914, another researcher named Vittorio Benussi invented a machine that measured changes in breathing rate. But it wasn't until 1921 that John A. Larson, a medical student at the University of

---

A piano's notes cover the full range of all orchestral instruments...

California, invented a machine that measured pulse, blood pressure, and breathing rate simultaneously. His machine became known as a *polygraph*, because it measured three types of physiological changes. Today's polygraphs use these methods, as well as more sophisticated measurements.

THE QUESTIONS

The most common questioning method is called the Control Question Test (CQT), in which the polygraph operator asks three types of questions: neutral questions, key questions, and control questions.

• Neutral questions like "What kind of car do you drive?" are designed to measure the suspect's general level of nervousness, because nearly anyone who takes a polygraph test is going to be nervous.

• Key, or "guilty," questions quiz the suspect on information that only the guilty person would know. (For example: If the person taking the test were suspected of murdering someone, and the murder weapon was a knife, questions about knives would be considered key questions.)

• Control, or "innocent," questions would be indistinguishable from key questions by someone who did not have knowledge of the crime—but the guilty person would know. Questions about weapons not used in a murder would be considered control questions. An innocent person with no knowledge of the murder weapon would show the same level of nervousness during all the weapon questions—but the guilty person would be more nervous during questions about knives—and would be easy to identify using a polygraph...at least in theory.

Lie detectors really work. True or false?
To find out, turn to page 223.

*   *   *

"Police in Radnor, Pennsylvania, interrogated a suspect by placing a metal colander on his head and connecting it with a metal wire to a photocopy machine. The message, "He's lying," was placed in the copier and police pressed the copy button each time they believed the suspect wasn't telling the truth. Believing the 'lie detector' was working, the suspect confessed."

—News of the Weird

...from below the lowest note of the double bassoon to above the top note of the piccolo.

ALWAYS...

Uncle John's credo: Always follow the advice of experts.

"Always forgive your enemies.... Nothing annoys them so much."
—**Oscar Wilde**

"Always do sober what you said you'd do drunk. That will teach you to keep your mouth shut."
—**Ernest Hemingway**

"Always remember before going on stage, wipe your nose and check your fly."
—**Alec Guinness**

"Always remember that you are absolutely unique. Just like everyone else."
—**Margaret Mead**

"Always hold your head up, but be careful to keep your nose at a friendly level."
—**Max L. Forman**

"Always read stuff that will make you look good if you die in the middle of it."
—**P. J. O'Rourke**

"Always take hold of things by the smooth handle."
—**Thomas Jefferson**

"Always dream and shoot higher than you know you can do. Don't bother just to be better than your contemporaries or predecessors. Try to be better than yourself."
—**William Faulkner**

"Always give a word or a sign of salute when meeting or passing a friend, even a stranger."
—**Tecumseh, Shawnee**

"Always listen to experts. They'll tell you what can't be done and why. Then do it."
—**Robert Heinlein**

"Always be nice to people on the way up; because you'll meet the same people on the way down."
—**Wilson Mizner**

"Always do what you are afraid to do."
—**Ralph Waldo Emerson**

"Always do right. This will gratify some people and astonish the rest."
—**Mark Twain**

"Always and never are two words you should...

NEVER...

Uncle John's credo: Never follow the advice of experts.

"Never hire a cleaning lady named Dusty."
—**David Corrado**

"Never trust the advice of a man in difficulties."
—**Aesop**

"Never assume the obvious is true."
—**William Safire**

"Never play peekaboo with a child on a long plane trip. There's no end to the game. Finally, I grabbed him by the bib and said, 'Look, it's always gonna be me!'"
—**Rita Rudner**

"Never pet a porcupine."
—**Kid on** *Sesame Street*

"Never send a man to do a horse's job."
—**Mr. Ed**

"Never trust a wolf's tameness, a horse's health, or an enemy's smile."
—**Israel Boone,** *Daniel Boone*

"Never trouble trouble till trouble troubles you."
—**John Adams**

"Never give in, never give in, never, never, never, never—in nothing, great or small, large or petty—never give in except to convictions of honor and good sense."
—**Winston Churchill**

"Never spend your money before you have it."
—**Thomas Jefferson**

"Never miss a good chance to shut up."
—**Will Rogers**

"Never get married in the morning, 'cause you may never know who you'll meet that night."
—**Paul Hornung**

"Never explain—your friends do not need it and your enemies will not believe you anyway."
—**Elbert Hubbard**

"Never believe in mirrors or newspapers."
—**Tom Stoppard**

"Never eat more than you can lift."
—**Miss Piggy**

...always remember never to use." —**Wendell Johnson**

FOOD SUPERSTITIONS

What can you do with food, besides eat it? Use it to drive evil spirits away, of course. People once believed in these bizarre rituals.

"Sprinkle pepper on a chair to ensure that guests do not overstay their welcome."

"If cooking bacon curls up in the pan, a new lover is about to arrive."

"Eating five almonds will cure drunkenness."

"If the bubbles on the surface of a cup of coffee float toward the drinker, prosperous times lie ahead; if they retreat, hard times are promised."

"Cut a slice from the stalk end of a banana while making a wish. If a Y-shaped mark is revealed, the wish will come true."

"Feed red pistachio nuts to a zombie—it will break his trance and allow him to die."

"When a slice of buttered bread falls butter-side-up, it means a visitor is coming."

"Put a red tomato on the window sill—it scares away evil spirits."

"If bread dough cracks during baking, a funeral is imminent."

"It's lucky to see two pies, but unlucky to see only one."

"A wish will come true if you make it while burning onions."

"Feeding ground eggshells to children cures bedwetting."

"Stirring a pot of tea stirs up trouble."

"It's bad luck to let milk boil over."

"Bank up used tea leaves at the back of the fire to ward off poverty."

"If you find a pod with nine peas in it, throw it over your shoulder and make a wish. It will come true."

"Finding a chicken egg with no yolk is unlucky."

"If meat shrinks in the pot, your downfall is assured. If it swells, you'll experience prosperity."

"Beans scattered in the corners of a home will drive out evil spirits."

"It is unlucky to say the word 'salt' at sea."

LEBOWSKI 7:16

Lots of movies have inspired their own fan conventions. Let's see, there's Star Trek *and* Star Wars *and…*The Big Lebowski?

BIG FLOPSKI

When *The Big Lebowski* hit theaters in 1998, it didn't make much of a splash. Though it met with critical acclaim and was well received by loyal fans of Joel and Ethan Coen, the film's director, producer, and co-writers, it barely broke even at the box office. Following on the heels of *Fargo*, the Coens' most successful film to that point, *Lebowski*'s modest earnings came as a disappointment. But then in 1999 it was released on video and became a cult classic.

As *Lebowski* fans will tell you, this is a movie that gets better with repeat viewings. There are so many threads woven into the complicated plot, and so much dry humor and memorable dialogue, that the film simply can't be taken in at a single glance. *The Big Lebowski* is one of those movies where you catch something new every time you watch it.

Here's the basic plot: In a case of mistaken identity, Jeff "The Dude" Lebowski—a lazy, unemployed, hippie bowler—is assaulted by thugs who are actually looking for a paraplegic millionaire named Jeffrey Lebowski, whose trophy wife "owes money all over town." During the course of the assault, the assailants pee on The Dude's living room carpet. Deciding to seek restitution from the real Lebowski (because "the carpet really tied the room together, man"), The Dude and his two bowling buddies, Walter and Donny, are drawn into a web of intrigue involving kidnapping, pornographers, and nihilists; Lebowski's avant-garde daughter, Maude; a high-school student whose father used to write for the TV western, *Branded*; and intricately choreographed bowling-dream sequences. There's a lot more, but you'll have to watch the movie a few times to figure it all out…which is exactly what thousands of devoted fans have been doing for nearly a decade.

WHY NOT?

Three years after the movie's release on video, two *Lebowski* fans, Will Russell and Scott Shuffitt, were killing time while manning a T-shirt booth at a tattoo convention in Louisville, Kentucky. Business was so

---

The largest ant colony in the world is in Southern Europe—it stretches for over 3,700 miles.

slow that the two friends began entertaining themselves by quoting lines from *Lebowski*. The people at the next booth turned out to be fans as well, and soon joined in. Eventually, Russell and Shuffitt's booth became the most popular spot in the convention hall, with bored vendors congregating to repeat their favorite bits of dialogue from the film. At some point, according to Russell, "Scott and I were like, man, if they can have this goofy tattoo convention, we should have a *Big Lebowski* convention."

BOWLING AND WHAT-HAVE-YOU

Because bowling is a central theme in the movie, they decided the event should be held in a bowling alley. Unfortunately, the only alley in Louisville that they could afford was a Baptist-run establishment that prohibited both drinking and bad language—a problem because it's hard to quote lines from the film without cursing, and because The Dude is rarely seen without a White Russian in hand (at one point he can't find any half-and-half, so he mixes his White Russian using powdered nondairy creamer). Nevertheless, the alley was rented and, with a $42 advertising budget, the "First Annual *Big Lebowski* What-Have-You Fest" was scheduled for October 2002. They expected a handful of their friends to show up and were surprised when 150 people—dressed up as their favorite characters from the movie—arrived for a night of bowling and a screening of the film.

Russell and Shuffitt immediately began making plans for the second festival. Word got around on the Internet, and it proved to be almost too successful: 1,300 devotees showed up to a venue that could only hold 800. The following year 4,000 fans came…and the event's organizers have never looked back—they've added festivals in Las Vegas, New York, Los Angeles, Austin, Seattle, San Francisco, Chicago, Portland, Boston, and London.

THE DUDE ABIDES

The event has taken on a life of its own. A few years ago, strange signs began appearing in the crowds at concerts and sporting events. Back in 2003 they read, "Lebowski 7:19." The next year: "Lebowski 6:19." These are not references to some book of cinematic scripture, they are the dates of the next annual Lebowskifest in Louisville. Keep your eyes peeled—in 2010 they read "Lebowski 7:16."

That spot on your back that you can't scratch is called the *acnestis*.

RANDOM ORIGINS

Once again, the BRI asks—and answers—the question: Where does all this stuff come from?

WATERBEDS

The waterbed has actually been developed—unsuccessfully—numerous times. The first was more than 3,000 years ago, when Persians filled goat skins with water, sealed them with tar, and left them out in the sun to warm the water. The next time was in 1832, when Scottish doctor Neil Arnott filled a rubber-coated, mattress-sized piece of canvas with water, hoping to prevent bedsores. It wasn't a big seller (even in hospitals), nor was it when English doctor James Paget copied the design in 1873. The main reasons: The beds leaked, and they were cold. But in 1926, scientists at B.F. Goodrich came up with a synthetic material that could make waterbeds both leakproof and warm: vinyl. Sold via mail order, they were, once again, a commercial disappointment. Then in 1968, a San Francisco State University student named Charles Hall was trying to create an ultra-soft piece of furniture. After rejecting a gigantic vinyl bag filled with Jell-O, he tried filling it with water. Hall called his creation the Pleasure Pit and patented it. Waterbeds finally caught on, at least with Bay Area hippies. They became a national fad in the early 1980s.

THE KAZOO

Similar instruments, called *mirlitons*, had been used in Africa for hundreds of years, either to imitate the sounds of animals when hunting or in religious rituals. The sound comes from the user humming (not blowing air) across a membrane, which causes it to vibrate. An African-American named Alabama Vest based the modern kazoo on these instruments. He invented his in Macon, Georgia, in the 1840s. They were mass-produced to Vest's specifications by German clockmaker Thaddeus von Clegg and were first demonstrated at the 1852 Georgia State Fair.

HEIMLICH MANEUVER

Throat surgeon Dr. Henry Heimlich had long noticed the high number of deaths that resulted from simple choking incidents. In the early 1970s, the common method used to relieve choking was a slap on the back.

Though it sometimes worked, it often forced food farther into the windpipe, making the choker's situation worse. Heimlich had a theory: a sudden burst of air pressure up through the esophagus would expel an obstruction. He tested it on dogs and found that it worked. Heimlich's "maneuver" forced any food caught in the throat *up*, rather than down, the way a back slap sometimes did. The technique: the person applying the maneuver stands behind the victim with interlocked fingers held below the rib cage and above the navel, and pulls upward. Heimlich published his findings in 1974. Within a week, the Heimlich maneuver was used to save a person from choking. It has saved tens of thousands since.

TARTAR SAUCE

Before there was tartar sauce, there was *steak tartare*, a French dish that consists of chopped and seasoned raw beef topped with onions and capers. Whoever invented it (that person is lost to history) named it after the Tatars, a nomadic Turkic group who lived in Russia in the medieval era and, according to legend, were known for eating raw meat. *Sauce de tartare* was created in France the 18th century to accompany the entree. It consisted of mayonnaise, pickles, capers, onions, and tarragon. The thick, goopy sauce made its way to England in the late 19th century, where *tartare* was anglicized to *tartar* and was served alongside a distinctively English dish: fried fish.

MAD LIBS

In November 1953, TV writer Leonard Stern was stuck trying to describe the appearance of a new character he'd created for *The Honeymooners*. His friend, game-show host Roger Price, was in the next room and Stern called out, "Give me an adjective." But before Stern could finish his sentence—he'd needed a word to describe "nose"—Price responded, "Clumsy." The two found the idea of "a clumsy nose" absurdly funny and spent the rest of the day writing short stories, then removing certain words and replacing them with blank spaces, prompting the reader for a certain part of speech: a noun, adjective, verb, etc. When the stories were read back with all the blanks filled, the results were hilarious. For the next five years, Price and Stern tried, in vain, to get *Mad Libs* published. Finally, in 1958, they printed up 14,000 copies themselves. By then, Stern was writing for *The Steve Allen Show* and convinced his boss to use Mad Libs as a comedy bit. All 14,000 copies sold out in a week.

In Tokyo, the "911" emergency number is 119.

HOW DO YOU SAY…"MULLET"?

Remember the mullet? That quintessential '80s haircut (think MacGyver, or Billy Ray Cyrus) was short on the top, long in the back…and ridiculed by people all over the world, as you'll see here.

• **France:** *Coupe à la Waddle* (named after a famous 1980s footballer who sported the 'do)

• **French Canadian:** *coupe Longueuil*

• **Sweden:** *hockeyfrilla*

• **Norway:** *hockeysveis*

• **Czech Republic:** *colek* ("newt")

• **Poland:** *Czeski pi karz* ("Czech football player hair")

• **Romania:** *chica*

• **Australia:** *Freddie Firedrill* (as if the haircut was interrupted by a fire alarm)

• **Chile:** *chocopanda* (referring to the typical haircuts of ice cream sellers)

• **Colombia:** *greña paisa*

• **Turkey:** *aslan yelesi* ("lion's mane")

• **Brazil:** *Chitãozinho e Xororó*

• **Denmark:** *bundesliga-hår*

• **Croatia:** *fudbalerka* (referring to the soccer-player haircuts of the 1980s)

• **Finland:** *takatukka* ("rear hair")

• **Germany:** *vokuhila* (short for *vorne kurz, hinten lang* "short in the front, long in the back")

• **Greece:** *laspotiras* ("mudflap")

• **Hebrew:** *vilon* ("curtain")

• **Argentina:** *Cubano*

• **Japan:** *urufu hea* ("wolf hair")

• **Puerto Rico:** *playero* ("beach-comber")

• **Serbia:** *Tarzanka* ("Tarzan")

• **Italy:** *capelli alla tedesca* ("German-style hair"), or *alla MacGyver* (hair that resembles Richard Dean Anderson's from the TV show)

• **American terms:** B&T (bridge and tunnel), ape drape, Tennessee top hat, Kentucky waterfall, Missouri compromise

Your remote control works by shooting an invisible beam of infrared light at the TV.

WHAT THE #!&%?

Here are the origins of several symbols we use in everyday life.

? QUESTION MARK

Origin: When early scholars wrote in Latin, they would place the word *questio*—meaning "question"—at the end of a sentence to indicate a query. To conserve valuable space, writing it was soon shortened to *qo*, which caused another problem—readers might mistake it for the ending of a word. So, they squashed the letters into a symbol: a lowercase *q* on top of an *o*. Over time the *o* shrank to a dot and the *q* to a squiggle, giving us our current question mark.

! EXCLAMATION POINT

Origin: Like the question mark, the exclamation point was invented by stacking letters. The mark comes from the Latin word *io*, meaning "exclamation of joy." Written vertically, with the *i* above the *o*, it forms the exclamation point we use today.

= EQUAL SIGN

Origin: Invented by English mathematician Robert Recorde in 1557, with this rationale: "I will sette as I doe often in woorke use, a paire of paralleles, or Gemowe [i.e., twin] lines of one length, thus: =====, bicause noe 2 thynges, can be more equalle." His equal signs were about five times as long as the current ones, and it took more than a century for his sign to be accepted over its rival: a strange curly symbol invented by Descartes.

& AMPERSAND

Origin: This symbol is a stylized *et*, Latin for "and." Although it was invented by the Roman scribe Marcus Tullius Tiro in the first century B.C., it didn't get its strange name until centuries later. In the early 1800s, schoolchildren learned this symbol as the 27th letter of the alphabet: X, Y, Z, &. But the symbol had no name. So, they ended their ABCs with "and, per se, and", meaning "&, which means 'and.'" This phrase was slurred into one garbled word that eventually caught on with everyone: *ampersand*.

According to DC Comics, the ancestors of Superman's adoptive family, the Kents...

OCTOTHORP

Origin: The odd name for this ancient sign for numbering derives from *thorpe*, the Old Norse word for a village or farm that is often seen in British placenames. According to typographers, the symbol was originally used in mapmaking, representing a village surrounded by eight fields, so it was named the *octothorp*.

$ DOLLAR SIGN

Origin: One theory on the origin of this symbol says that when the U.S. government began issuing its own money in 1794, it used the common world currency: the *peso*—also called the Spanish dollar. The first American silver dollars were identical to Spanish pesos in weight and value, so they took the same written abbreviation: Ps. That evolved into a P with an s written right on top of it, and when people began to omit the circular part of the p, the sign simply became an S with a vertical line through it.

OLYMPIC RINGS

Origin: Designed in 1913 by Baron Pierre de Coubertin, the five rings represent the five regions of the world that participated in the Olympics: Africa, the Americas, Asia, Europe, and Oceania. While the individual rings do not symbolize any single continent, the five colors—red, blue, green, yellow, and black—were chosen because at least one of them is found on the flag of every nation. The plain white background is symbolic of peace.

"THE SYMBOL"

Origin: Okay, so we're running out of symbols, but this is a great pop culture story: In 1993, Prince's dissatisfaction with his record label, Warner Bros., finally reached its peak. Despite his superstar status and his $100 million contract, the Purple One didn't feel he had enough creative control over his music. So "in protest," Prince announced that Prince would never perform for Warner Bros. again—this unpronounceable symbol would instead. The symbol for the Artist Formerly Known as Prince combined three ancient symbols: the male symbol, the female symbol, and the alchemy symbol for soapstone, which was supposed to reflect his artistic genius. Prince retired the symbol when his contract with Warner Bros. ran out in 2000. Today, he is again Prince.

...were noted abolitionists in the 19th century.

GROUNDS FOR DIVORCE

Think you're in a bad relationship? Take a look at these folks.

In Loving, New Mexico, a woman divorced her husband because he made her salute him and address him as "Major" whenever he walked by.

One Tarittville, Connecticut, man filed for divorce after his wife left him a note on the refrigerator. It read, "I won't be home when you return from work. Have gone to the bridge club. There'll be a recipe for your dinner at 7 o'clock on Channel 2."

In Lynch Heights, Delaware, a woman filed for divorce because her husband "regularly put itching powder in her underwear when she wasn't looking."

In Honolulu, Hawaii, a man filed for divorce from his wife, because she "served pea soup for breakfast and dinner...and packed his lunch with pea sandwiches."

In Hazard, Kentucky, a man divorced his wife because she "beat him whenever he removed onions from his hamburger without first asking for permission."

In Frackville, Pennsylvania, a woman filed for divorce because her husband insisted on "shooting tin cans off of her head with a slingshot."

One Winthrop, Maine, man divorced his wife because she "wore earplugs whenever his mother came to visit."

A Smelterville, Idaho, man won divorce from his wife on similar grounds. "His wife dressed up as a ghost and tried to scare his elderly mother out of the house."

In Canon City, Colorado, a woman divorced her husband because he made her "duck under the dashboard whenever they drove past his girlfriend's house."

No escape: In Bennettsville, South Carolina, a deaf man filed for divorce from his wife because "she was always nagging him in sign language."

The Last Straw: In Hardwick, Georgia, a woman divorced her husband because he "stayed home too much and was much too affectionate."

America's first DJ: Dr. Elman Myers, in 1911.

THE LEAGUE OF COMIC BOOK CREATORS

By day, they were mild-mannered writers and artists. But at night…well, they stayed mild-mannered writers and artists, but they also thought up some of the most popular comic book characters the world has ever known. Come meet the men behind the Man of Steel, the Dark Knight, and the mutants.

SUPERMAN: Joe Schuster & Jerry Siegel

Schuster & Siegel created *Superman* in 1936, when the Cleveland duo (Siegel born there, and Schuster having moved there at age nine from Toronto) tried selling the Man of Steel as a comic strip to the newspapers. No one bought it until 1938, when DC Comics gave *Superman* a tryout in its Action Comics book. The rest is history, and Schuster & Siegel would go on to fame and fortune, right? Not exactly. By contract, DC Comics retained all rights in the Superman character, and so while the publishing company was making millions from *Superman*, Schuster & Siegel were not. They weren't doing poorly—in 1940 *The Saturday Evening Post* noted that the two of them were making $75,000 a year between them—but they knew they could be doing much better.

They sued DC Comics in 1946, and in 1948 received a relatively small settlement (a reported $120,000). But the flip side of the settlement was that the duo's byline, previously on every *Superman* story, was removed from all future products. Schuster soon left the comic book field, and Siegel's work slowed to a trickle. In the 1970s, while Hollywood geared up for the *Superman* movie starring Christopher Reeve, Schuster & Siegel again got the word out about how badly they had been treated by DC and sued the company once more. Although the courts decided the writers didn't have a case, DC was pressured by the comic book community into providing both men with a $35,000-per-year stipend for as long as they lived. Schuster died in 1992; Siegel passed away in 1996.

BATMAN: Bob Kane

Like Schuster & Siegel, Kane handed over his comic book creation, *Batman*, to DC Comics, where the Caped Crusader made his first appearance in

---

Look next time you yawn: 55% of people yawn within 5 minutes of seeing someone else yawn.

1939. However, unlike Superman's creators, Kane maintained a small percentage of the take every time the cash register rang up a Batman sale. How did he do it? He had a lawyer in the family, who advised him to retain his copyright interests.

Keeping a stake in the Dark Knight did good things for Kane's income and his leisure time. Although his name was kept on all the Batman stories, he handed off most of the work to underlings in what was one of the biggest open secrets in comics. Kane himself headed to Hollywood to create animated TV shows (such as *Courageous Cat*) and to advise in the development of the campy 1960s *Batman* TV series. He even had a cameo in 1997's *Batman and Robin*, as did his wife. Kane died in 1998.

THE X-MEN & THE INCREDIBLE HULK: Jack Kirby

Kirby, who started working in comics in 1938, was arguably the most prolific comic book character creator around. Characters he created or co-created include the X-Men, the Incredible Hulk, and the Fantastic Four, as well as Captain America, Iron Man, the Silver Surfer, and Thor (the last one with a little help from Norse mythology). Some comic fans also give him a shared credit (along with DC's Stan Lee) for Spider-Man. Most of Kirby's greatest creations are associated with Marvel Comics, but he worked off and on for a number of comic book publishers, including DC; he bounced between the two majors for much of his career.

Kirby was also not above doing grunt work. In the mid-1950s, when worries about the morality of comic books caused the industry to collapse and the superhero genre was gutted (350 comic book titles stopped publication), Kirby stayed in business by drawing romance comics. His artistic output throughout his career was staggering—more than 24,000 pages of comic book art. In 1994, at the age of 76, Kirby died at his home in California.

*　　　*　　　*

"The right answer to a fool is silence."
—Afghani proverb

ANATOMY OF A HICCUP

Have the…hic…hiccups? Reading this page won't cure them…hic…but at least…hic…you'll have a better idea of what you're…hic…dealing with.

WHAT YOU MIGHT NOT KNOW

• A hiccup occurs when a stimulus causes an involuntary contraction of the diaphragm, the muscle separating the lungs from the abdomen. The contraction makes the sufferer take a quick breath, causing the glottis (located in the voice box) to close, which makes the "hic" sound.

• Technical term for hiccups: a diaphragmatic spasm, or *singultus*.

• Unlike other body reflexes (coughs, sneezes, vomiting), hiccups serve no useful purpose.

• Most common causes: too much alcohol, spicy food, cold water, carbonated drinks, indigestion, or asthma. They can also be caused by liver or kidney problems, abdominal surgery, or a brain tumor.

• The word "hiccup" may come from the French *hocquet*, which was used to describe the sound of a hiccup. The earliest known version in English is *hicket*, dating from the 1500s.

• Hiccup lore: In ancient Greece, a bad case of the hiccups meant an enemy was talking about you. To get rid of them one had to guess the enemy's name. The Scots thought holding your left thumb (or your chin) with your right hand while listening to someone singing a hymn would stop the hiccups.

• Some forms of *encephalitis* (swelling of the brain) can cause hiccuping. During the encephalitis pandemics of the 1920s, several cities reported cases of mass hiccuping.

• Fetuses hiccup in the womb.

• Charles Osborne of Anthon, Iowa, holds the title of "World's Longest Hiccuper." It started in 1922, hiccuping as often as 40 times per minute. Sometimes he hiccuped so hard his false teeth fell out. In 1987—nearly 70 years later—the hiccups stopped.

• Folk cures: eat peanut butter, eat Wasabi, drink vinegar, eat Lingonberry jam, drink a glass of water while urinating.

After WWI, the German government trained the first guide dogs to assist blind war veterans.

WHY ASK WHY?

Sometimes the answer is irrelevant—it's the question that counts.

If money doesn't grow on trees, why do banks have branches?

What disease did cured ham have?

Why do we say we "slept like a baby" when babies wake up every hour and a half?

Why do alarm clocks "go off" when they start making noise?

Instead of "All things in moderation," shouldn't it be "Some things in moderation"?

Why do we yell "Heads up!" when we should be yelling "Heads down!"?

Why is it so hard to remember how to spell "mnemonic"?

Why is it called quicksand when it sucks you down very, very slowly?

If everyone lost five pounds at the same time, would it throw the Earth out of its orbit?

Why is it called the Department of the Interior when they are in charge of everything outdoors?

Why are they called marbles if they're made out of glass?

When French people swear, do they say, "Pardon my English"?

What color hair do bald men put on their driver's license?

How do you know when it's time to tune your bagpipes?

If practice makes perfect, and nobody's perfect, then why practice?

How do you throw away a garbage can?

Why do we put our suits in a garment bag and our garments in a suitcase?

When two airplanes almost collide, why is it a "near miss"? Shouldn't it be a "near hit"?

How can something be both "new" and "improved"?

Why do we shut up, but quiet down?

How did the "Keep Off the Grass" sign get there in the first place?

Storm rule of thumb: If it has wind speeds greater than 74 mph, it's a hurricane.

DIVA OF THE DESERT

This unique performer craved the spotlight…but didn't
much care about the size of the audience.

IF YOU BUILD IT…

In the scorched wasteland of Death Valley, California, lies one of the most unusual theaters in America: the Amargosa Opera House. The quirk is that for years, no opera was ever performed there—only ballet. And there was only one performer: a prima ballerina named Marta Becket, who, well into her 70s, performed her solo show in the desert as she had for nearly 40 years.

In 1967 Becket, a dancer and artist from New York, was on a camping trip in the desert with her husband. When they had a flat tire on their trailer, a local park ranger told them they could get it fixed in Death Valley Junction. The town had been built in the 1920s by the Pacific Coast Borax Company to house its mine workers. While her husband stayed at the gas station with the trailer, Marta poked around the small compound of adobe buildings. Aside from the old company offices, there was a 23-room hotel with a lavishly painted lobby, still open for business, and something that really caught her eye: a rundown community center known as Corkhill Hall.

Peeking through a hole in Corkhill's door, she saw a small stage with tattered cotton curtains. Trash was strewn between the wooden benches that faced the stage. Marta said later, "Peering through the tiny hole, I had the distinct feeling that I was looking at the other half of myself. The building seemed to be saying, 'take me…do something with me…I offer you life.'"

…THEY WILL COME

Marta tracked down the town manager and talked him into renting her the hall for $45 a month. Six months later, on February 10, 1968, she gave her first daily performance. There were 12 people in the audience, all of them locals curious to see what the peculiar lady from New York was up to. Occasionally, curious tourists would wander in. Sometimes no one was there at all. Marta always performed no matter what. One night she had just begun her performance to an empty house when four people came in. They sat quietly, applauded politely at the curtain call, and left. Becket thought nothing of it until a few months later, when an article

---

17% of sales reps who golf with clients say they let the clients win.

about her appeared in *National Geographic* magazine. After that, audiences grew. Locals kept coming back; at first they came to gawk and laugh, but left strangely moved by the sight of this intense woman following her muse wherever it led her. Word spread, and soon tour buses were making the newly named Amargosa Opera House a stop on their itineraries. Celebrities would pop over from nearby Las Vegas (comedian Red Skelton was so charmed that he visited four times).

PAINT THE WALLS

Part of the ongoing attraction of the Amargosa is the whimsical, brilliantly colored murals Becket has painted on its walls. Starting in July 1968, driven partly by her loneliness at playing to such small audiences, Marta spent four years covering the walls with a permanent audience. A king and queen hold court in the royal box. Bullfighters sit next to 17th-century Spanish nobility. Monks and nuns stare disapprovingly at the garish prostitutes leering from the opposite wall. The central dome has 16 women playing musical instruments beneath a flight of doves, and there are jugglers, dancing cherubs, dowdy matrons, and little children—whatever took Marta's fancy. The result is an arts institution unlike any other. The town of Death Valley Junction (now owned by the Amargosa Opera House) was added to the National Register of Historic Places in 1980.

CURTAIN CALL

Becket's husband wasn't as dedicated to the venture—he left in 1983. But Becket soldiered on, assisted by Tom Willett, who started out as her stage manager and became her emcee and partner. Willett died in 2005, and though Becket still runs the Amargosa, most of the shows now feature a younger performer, Sandy Scheller.

"I am grateful," Becket says, "to have found the place where I can fulfill my dreams and share them with the passing scene...for as long as I can."

*   *   *

FOUR THINGS MICK JAGGER
(BORN IN 1943) IS OLDER THAN

The transistor (1947)	Velcro (1948)
Israel (1948)	Cake mix (1949)

It takes 3,000 cows to supply the NFL with enough leather for a year's supply of footballs.

GAMES PEOPLE PLAY

When you think about it, baseball is kind of an absurd game: hit a ball with a stick, and then run around a square as fast as you can. But that's nothing compared to these actual games and sports played around the world.

Contest: Vinkenzetting
Played in: Flanders, a region of Belgium
How it's played: In *vinkenzetting*, or "finch-sitting," competitors put a male finch in a box cage. Whoever's bird makes the highest number of complete calls in an hour wins. Winning birds usually make several hundred calls per hour. In one competition, a bird called 1,278 times, inviting doping allegations.

Contest: The Tough Guy
Played in: England
How it's played: This grueling competition begins with a 10-mile cross-country run. It's followed by an obstacle course with an electrified fence, underground tunnels, under*water* tunnels, barbed wire, and waist-deep patches of mud. And it's held in the winter, so the temperature is well below freezing. Around 4,000 people compete every year; their entry fees are donated to charity.

Contest: World Screaming Championships
Played in: Poland
How it's played: The rules are simple: One by one, participants step forward and scream really, really loudly. Loudest scream wins. The record scream was produced in 2000 by Dagmara Stanek, who registered a scream of 126.1 decibels, as loud as a jackhammer.

Contest: Kabaddi
Played in: South Asia
How it's played: Two seven-player teams each occupy half of a court about the size of a soccer field. The teams take turns sending a "raider" into the opposition's territory; the raider tries to tag as many players as possible—without getting blocked or tackled—and then return to his

The tradition of a man proposing with a gold ring dates as far back as 860 A.D.

home side…all in one breath. To prove he's not inhaling, the player has to chant "KABADDI" throughout the raid.

Contest: Rootball
Played in: North Carolina
How it's played: Invented by Max Chain, owner of an Asheville bar called the Root, it's a combination of horseshoes and lawn bowling, played outdoors on a court made of sand. Two metal stakes are placed 32 feet apart. The player stands at one stake and tosses a plastic ring at the opposite stake, and then tosses a spiky plastic ball. The closer to the stake, the more points awarded, with bonuses for landing the ball inside the plastic ring, throwing the ball through the ring, leaning the ring against the stake, etc. (It's patented, by the way.)

Contest: Unicycle Hockey
Played in: England and Germany
How it's played: It's actually been played since 1925, when European unicycle manufacturers first suggested it as a new use for the one-wheeled contraptions. No skates are used, and it's played on flat pavement, not ice. Ice hockey may be hard, but balancing on a unicycle while reaching out with a stick to hit a plastic ball is even harder. It's actually more like polo than hockey…if polo were played on wobbly horses.

Contest: Noodling
Played in: The American South and Southwest
How it's played: It's not exactly a sport. A 200-year-old tradition along the Mississippi River, it's catfish fishing without a pole, without a net, without even bait. Noodlers stick their arms (called "noodles") into stagnant river water where catfish are usually found, often behind or inside of large logs. When they find a catfish, they splash in the water to get the fish's attention, then plunge their arms directly into the throat of the fish, which may weigh as much as 50 pounds. The fish—who are often guarding eggs—respond to the attack by clamping down on the angler's arm. It's so dangerous—hazards can include drowning or being bitten by snapping turtles and water snakes—that it's illegal in 11 states. It's popular (and legal) in Louisiana, Mississippi, Oklahoma, Tennessee, Kansas, and Missouri.

LOVE AT FIRST SIGHT?

*Uncle John actually fell in love at first sight. So smooth
and shiny. Those perfect proportions. That beautiful
white…porcelain. You thought we were talking
about Mrs. Uncle John? Oh, yeah. Her too.*

HERE'S LOOKING AT YOU

You're looking around a crowded room, and your eyes meet the eyes of another. Pow! A shock runs through your whole body! Are you in love? Maybe. Read on to find out. That jolt isn't imaginary. Scientists say that part of your brain actually perks up when you exchange looks with a person you consider attractive.

And just how did they discover that? British researchers used a special helmet to scan the brains of 16 volunteers (8 men and 8 women). Wearing an fMRI (functional magnetic resonance imaging) helmet, each volunteer looked at 160 photos of 40 complete strangers.

In some photos, the strangers were looking directly at the camera—which made them appear to be looking directly at the volunteer. In others, the stranger's eyes were turned away.

As the photos went flashing by—one every 3.5 seconds—the helmets recorded which part of the volunteer's brain was active. After the brain scan was finished, the volunteers went back to the pictures and rated each one for attractiveness. The results of the experiment were published in 2001 in *Nature* magazine.

REAL SPARKS

Every time a volunteer saw an attractive person looking right at them, the volunteer's ventral striatum lit up—that part of the brain is linked to the anticipation of a reward. But when the stranger in the photo was looking away, the magic didn't happen; there was much less brain activity, no matter how attractive the person in the photo. The researchers attributed that to disappointment—the volunteer had failed to make eye contact with an attractive face.

The brain response happened fast—in just nanoseconds. Researchers think this means that it's automatic, that we're all wired for that kind of reaction.

The first recorded ruler of Japan was a woman…the Empress Himiko (3rd century A.D.).

EYES OF THE BEHOLDER

Does this mean that everybody responds to certain kinds of looks? The leading researcher, Dr. Knut Kampe of the Institute of Cognitive Neuroscience in London, commented that we all might naturally respond to people who look strong and healthy. That could be connected with survival. But Kampe said that each of the volunteers defined attractiveness in different ways, and conventional beauty wasn't the only important thing. Some looked for cheerfulness, others for a face that seemed to show empathy. Some even looked for motherliness.

IS IT LOVE?

So does it mean that love at first sight is real? Can we expect to instantly recognize our perfect mate? Probably not. Consider the following:

• Seeing a certain someone can get your brain buzzing—but so can seeing food when you're hungry. The ventral striatum that responded to the photos is the same area that lights up in hungry lab animals who think they're about to get fed. Gamblers and drug addicts have the same kind of reaction to the objects of their desire. That part of your brain gets excited when it expects *any* kind of reward.

• The brain's quick response helps explain why we make snap judgments about people we meet. But first impressions can be wrong.

• The same brain area lit up for any attractive face—no matter whether it was the opposite sex or the same sex as the volunteer. Researchers think that's because attractiveness often gets associated with social status. So maybe your brain assumes that hanging out with attractive people could improve your position. (In the case of monkeys, bonding with an animal higher up in the pecking order brings increased social status.)

So if you're expecting a future with someone based on the jolt you got when your eyes met—slow down. You'll have to engage some other part of your brain to find out whether the two of you actually get along.

*　　*　　*

A SHOWER OF STATS

According to surveys, 57% of Americans shower daily, 17% sing in the shower, 4% shower with the lights off, and 3% clean their pets by showering with them.

MYTH AMERICA

*A few things you probably didn't know about the
founding fathers who wrote the U.S. Constitution.*

THE MYTH

The men who attended the Constitutional Convention in 1787 were a sober, well-behaved group. They showed up on time, stuck it out 'til the end, and were all business when it came to the important task at hand.

THE TRUTH

Not quite. According to historical documents found by researchers at the National Constitution Center in 1992:

• Nineteen of the 74 people chosen to attend the convention never even showed up. (At least one of them had a good excuse, though—William Blount of New York refused to make the horseback ride to Philadelphia because of hemorrhoids.)

• Of the 55 who *did* show up, only 39 signed the document. Twelve people left early, and 4 others refused to sign. "A lot of them ran out of money and had to leave because they were doing a lot of price gouging here," observes researcher Terry Brent. Besides, he adds, the hot weather and high humidity must have been murder on the delegates, who wore wool breeches and coats. "They must have felt like dying. Independence Hall must have smelled like a cattle barn."

• And how did the Founding Fathers unwind during this pivotal moment in our nation's history? By getting drunk as skunks. One document that survived is the booze bill for a celebration party thrown two days before the Constitution was signed on September 17, 1787. According to the bill, the 55 people at the party drank 54 bottles of Madeira, 60 bottles of claret, 8 bottles of whiskey, 22 bottles of port, 8 bottles of cider, 12 bottles of beer, and 7 large bowls of alcoholic punch. "These were really huge punch bowls that ducks could swim in," Brent reports. "The partiers were also serenaded by 16 musicians. They had to be royally drunk—they signed the Constitution on the 17th. On the 16th, they were probably lying somewhere in the streets of Philadelphia."

...A: The *Dartmouth,* the *Eleanor,* and the *Beaver.*

WERE YOU RAISED IN A BARN?

*Tell the truth—how are your manners? Maybe you need
some help from these old etiquette books. You may
not believe it, but these are all real.*

"Although asparagus may be taken in the fingers, don't take a long drooping stalk, hold it up in the air, and catch the end of it in your mouth like a fish."

—*Etiquette* (1922)

"Do not move back and forth on your chair. Whoever does that gives the impression of constantly farting or trying to fart."

—*On Civility in Children* (1530)

"If a dish is distasteful to you, decline it, but make no remarks about it. It is sickening and disgusting to explain at a table how one article makes you sick, or why some other dish has become distasteful to you. I have seen a well-dressed tempting dish go from a table untouched, because one of the company told a most disgusting anecdote about finding vermin served in a similar dish."

—*Martine's Handbook of Etiquette* (1866)

"It is not the correct thing to put the spoon or fork so far into the mouth that the bystanders are doubtful of its return to the light."

—*The Correct Thing in Good Society* (1902)

"No decent person laughs at a funeral."

—*The Bazar Book of Decorum* (1870)

"When you have blown your nose, you should not open your handkerchief and inspect it, as though pearls or rubies had dropped out of your skull. Such behavior is nauseating and is more likely to lose us the affection of those who love us than to win us the favor of others."

—*The Book of Manners* (1958)

"Never put your cold, clammy hands on a person, saying, 'Did you ever know anyone to have such cold hands as mine?'"

—*Manners for Millions* (1932)

The word "arena" is from the Latin word for "sand."

"It is unmannerly to fall asleep, as many people do, whilst the company is engaged in conversation. Their conduct shows that they have little respect for their friends and care nothing either for them or their talk. Besides, they are generally obliged to doze in an uncomfortable position, and this nearly always causes them to make unpleasant noises and gestures in their sleep. Often enough they begin to sweat and dribble at the mouth."

—*The Book of Manners* (1958)

"Peevish temper, cross and frowning faces, and uncomely looks have sometimes been cured in France by sending the child into an octagonal boudoir lined with looking glasses, where, whichever way it turned, it would see the reflection of its own unpleasant features, and be constrained, out of self-respect, to assume a more amiable disposition."

—*Good Behavior* (1876)

"If you ask the waiter for anything, you will be careful to speak to him gently in the tone of request, and not of command. To speak to a waiter in a driving manner will create, among well-bred people, the suspicion that you were sometime a servant yourself, and are putting on airs at the thought of your promotion."

—*The Perfect Gentleman* (1860)

"It is bad manners, when you see something to nauseate you by the roadside, as sometimes happens, to turn to your companions and point it out to them. Still less should you offer any evil smelling object for others to sniff, as some people do, insisting upon holding it up to their noses and asking them to smell how horrible it is."

—*The Book of Manners* (1958)

"When not practicable for individuals to occupy separate beds, the persons should be of about the same age, and in good health. Numerous cases have occurred where healthy, robust children have 'dwindled away' and died within a few months, from sleeping with old people."

—*The People's Common Sense Medical Adviser* (1876)

"Applause is out of order at any religious service."

—*Your Best Foot Forward* (1955)

Song played by the *Titanic* band while the ship sank: "Nearer My God to Thee."

WHO WANTS TO MARRY A MILLIONAIRE?

Trying to cash in on the success of Who Wants to Be a Millionaire?, *the "we'll-try-anything" Fox Network came up with this concept for a reality show, easily one of TV's darkest hours. (Two hours, actually.)*

THE CONCEPT

Quite possibly the most degrading and humiliating moment in network television history—for contestants and viewers—*Who Wants to Marry a Multi-Millionaire* was exactly what the show's title suggested: a chance to marry a millionaire live on TV. Fifty eligible females vied to win the hand of a mystery millionaire, who had supposedly been chosen from a pool of more than 100 millionaire bachelors—all of whom presumably would have been willing to marry a "nobody," only moments after meeting them for the first time, on national TV.

WHO WANTS TO MARRY A STRANGER?

The mysterious future husband would remain hidden behind a screen, quizzing his potential mates-for-life as they strutted across the stage in swimsuits, wedding gowns, and other attire. Then, after nearly two hours of edge-of-your-seat suspense, he would step out, reveal his true identity, and marry his chosen bride on the spot. The show was kind of like a high-stakes "till-death-us-do-part" *Dating Game*...only with better prizes: The bride got a $35,000 engagement ring, a Caribbean cruise honeymoon, and an Isuzu Trooper. Estimated value: $100,000. The husband didn't get quite as much, but it didn't matter—after all, he was a multi-millionaire.

Religious leaders condemned the show for undermining the institution of marriage, but Fox went ahead with it anyway...and on February 15, 2000, more than 23 million people tuned in to watch real estate developer Rick Rockwell, 42, step out from behind the screen to choose Darva Conger, 34, a Gulf War veteran and emergency room nurse, as his bride.

THE MORNING AFTER

The Rockwell-Conger union wasn't exactly love at first sight; many viewers found their first kiss almost too creepy to bear, and things got worse after that. They slept in separate rooms during their "honeymoon" cruise, and within a week of returning to port, Conger was in Las Vegas seeking a quickie annulment.

By then, Rockwell's Prince Charming image was taking quite a beating. The Smoking Gun website revealed that in 1991 a judge had issued a restraining order against Rockwell after his ex-fiancée accused him of hitting and threatening to kill her. (Rockwell denied hitting her.)

That was just the beginning—it turned out that Rockwell wasn't a millionaire real estate developer after all; he was a stand-up comedian and occasional motivational speaker with a lot less than the $2 million in assets he was supposed to have to qualify for the show. The *Vancouver Province* newspaper quoted real estate agents who described him as a "flake" and a "loser whose only investment property is a low-end condo that leaks."

As for Conger, it turns out that she wasn't what she claimed to be, either. She wasn't a Gulf War veteran—she spent the entire war stationed at Scott Air Force Base in Illinois. "You can't call yourself a Gulf War veteran if you've never been to the Gulf," retired army colonel Daniel Smith explained to reporters.

CASHING IN... AND CASHING OUT

A judge annulled the marriage on April 5, 2000; by that time, Conger and Rockwell both were well on their way to making the most—financially, at least—of their brush with fame. Conger, who donated her $35,000 engagement ring to charity, signed a deal to pose in *Playboy* for an estimated $500,000. She later launched her own website, *www.darvashouse.com*. As for Rick Rockwell, his once-sleepy comedy show suddenly sold out all over the country.

About the only people involved who didn't cash in were the folks at Fox—as soon as the network learned of Rockwell's restraining order, it cancelled its scheduled rebroadcast of the show and later announced it was abandoning its entire lineup of upcoming "exploitative reality specials," including *Plastic Surgery Nightmares*, *Busted on the Job 5*, and *The World's Biggest Bitches*.

"They're gone," a spokesperson told reporters. "They're over."

I APOLOGIZE

*With our sincerest regrets, we're very sorry to bring you this collection
of some of the funniest and strangest apologies ever uttered.*

"We apologize for the error in last week's paper in which we stated that Mr. Arnold Dogbody was a defective in the police force. We meant, of course, that Mr. Dogbody is a *detective* in the police farce."

—Ely Standard (U.K.)

"My family and I are deeply sorry for all that Vice President Cheney and his family have had to go through this past week."

—Harry Whittington, Washington lawyer, after Dick Cheney shot *him* in the face

"In previous issues of this newspaper, we may have given the impression that the people of France were snail swallowing, garlic munching surrender-monkeys whose women never bother to shave their armpits. We now realise that the French football team can stop the Portuguese from getting to the World Cup Final. We apologise profusely to France. *Vive la France!*"

—Daily Star (U.K.), after France beat the U.K.'s rival, Portugal, in the 2006 World Cup semifinals

"I am so terribly sorry for urinating outside of a public place in your city. It was not a very intelligent thing to do."

—a man charged with public urination in Fond du Lac, Wisconsin, where all offenders now have to write letters of public apology

"I'm sorry I bet on baseball."

—Pete Rose, written on 300 baseballs that he then sold at $1,000 each

"Oh, goodness, I regret it, it was a mistake! I'm solely responsible for it, and I'm very, very sorry. It was a mistake, I was wrong, it's my fault, and I'm very, very sorry to hurt anyone."

—Sen. George Allen (R–VA), after referring to an Indian-American constituent as a "macaca"

"We ate everything but his boots."

—part of an apology from the Navatusila tribe of Fiji, who killed and ate a British missionary in 1867, to the missionary's descendants

---

First people to use sails on their ships: the ancient Phoenicians (around 2000 B.C.).

WRONG WAY CORRIGAN

While rummaging through our "Dustbin of History" file recently, we discovered the story of this colorful character. He snookered his way into the hearts of people on both sides of the Atlantic by heading in the wrong direction and ending up in the right place.

THAT'S MY STORY...

On the foggy morning of July 17, 1938, a 31-year-old pilot named Douglas Corrigan took off from Brooklyn's Floyd Bennett Field on a solo, nonstop trip to California. Twenty-eight hours later, he landed in Ireland…with a lot of explaining to do. He had no passport or papers of any kind, nor had he received permission from U.S. officials to make the transatlantic flight.

Safely on the ground, Corrigan offered this explanation to Irish customs: Heavy fog in New York had forced him to navigate using only his compass. The fog continued all that day and into the night; there was never good visibility. When the sun rose the next morning—26 hours into his flight—he was surprised to find himself over an ocean. Taking a closer look at his compass, Corrigan realized he'd been following the wrong end of the needle—heading due east instead of west! But by now he was almost out of fuel; he couldn't turn around. His only hope was to continue east and hope to reach land before he ran out of gas. Two hours later he saw fishing boats off a rocky coast and knew he was safe. From there, he made his way to Baldonnel Airport in Dublin. His first words upon exiting the plane: "Just got in from New York. Where am I?"

...AND I'M STICKING TO IT!

He repeated the story to the American ambassador and then to Ireland's prime minister. By this third telling—to the Irish cabinet—the European and American press had got wind of the story and ran with it. When he got to the part about misreading his compass, the cabinet ministers all laughed and Corrigan knew that things would work out. Ireland graciously sent him home without penalty.

When he got back to New York, Corrigan was amazed to find out

---

The first Allied bomb dropped on Berlin in WWII killed the only elephant in the Berlin Zoo.

he'd become a folk hero. In the bleak days of the Great Depression, Corrigan's achievement and amusing explanation lifted people's spirits. Over a million well-wishers turned out for a ticker-tape parade in his honor (more than had turned out to honor Charles Lindbergh after his transatlantic flight). The *New York Post* even ran a backward headline that read "!NAGIRROC YAW GNORW OT LIAH!" ("Hail To Wrong Way Corrigan!").

THE TRUTH
So what really happened? It's no secret that Corrigan's dream was to fly solo across the Atlantic. He got his start in the airplane business in 1927 working for the company that built Lindbergh's *Spirit of St. Louis*. Corrigan helped assemble the wing and install the instrument panel on the famous plane. His greatest honor was meeting Lindbergh. ("Even more than if I had met Abraham Lincoln himself!") After Lindbergh made the first solo transatlantic flight in 1927, Corrigan vowed to follow in his footsteps.

He spent the early 1930s barnstorming the country, landing near small towns and charging for airplane rides to pay for gas. In 1933 he bought a secondhand Curtiss Robin J-6 monoplane for $310, which he named *Sunshine*, and began overhauling it for a trip across the ocean. In 1936 and again in 1937, Federal Aviation officials denied Corrigan's requests to attempt the Atlantic flight.

So it's unlikely that when Corrigan took off from New York in 1938, he didn't know where he was going. Not only was he an accomplished pilot and navigator who had a history of flying without the proper paperwork, but he'd been working 10 straight years toward his dream of flying nonstop to Europe. Wrong Way Corrigan knew one end of a compass from the other.

COME ON, JUST ADMIT IT
For the rest of his life (he died in 1995), people tried to get Corrigan to come clean—but he never did, not even in his autobiography. In 1988 Corrigan took *Sunshine* on a national tour to celebrate the 50th anniversary of his famous flight. He was continually asked the same question: "Were you *really* trying to fly to California?" "Sure," he answered. "Well, at least I've told that story so many times that now I believe it myself."

FAMILY REUNIONS

*You know how strange it seems when you find out you have an
unexpected connection to someone. But what if the person
were closely related to you? These stories are almost
too weird for words, but they're all true.*

WHO: James Austin and Yvette Richardson, brother and
sister

SEPARATION: When James was seven months old and
Yvette was three, their father and mother separated. The father took
James; the mother took Yvette. That was the last time the siblings saw
or heard of each other.

TOGETHER AGAIN: James went to school in Philadelphia and got a
job at the main post office. He worked the 4 p.m. shift, along with 4,100
other people. One day in 1995, he was talking to his shop steward, Barrie
Bowens, about his life. As the *Boston Globe* reported:

> Austin told her that his father died young and that he never knew
> his mother. Bowens asked his mother's name and realized it was the
> same name as another employee's mother. For two years, James and
> Yvette had worked side by side, shooting the breeze but never prying
> into each other's personal life.…Now they discovered they were
> brother and sister.

They were stunned. "Working in the same department for two years,"
the 34-year-old Richardson said, shaking her head. "The same place, the
same time, every day. What are the odds of that?"

WHO: John Garcia and Nueng Garcia, father and son

SEPARATION: During the late 1960s, John Garcia was stationed in
Thailand with the U.S. Air Force. He lived with a woman named
Pratom Semon, and in 1969, they had a son, whom they named Nueng.
Three months later, Garcia was shipped back to the United States; he
wanted to take Semon, but she refused to go. For two years, Garcia regularly wrote and sent checks to support his son. Then Semon started
seeing another man and told Garcia to end his correspondence. Garcia
lost touch with his son. Although he tried to find him, even sending

---

The guillotine was used as a method of execution in France until 1977.

letters to the Thai government requesting an address, he was unsuccessful. He reluctantly gave up.

TOGETHER AGAIN: In 1996 Garcia, now living in Colorado, was driving through Colorado Springs when he decided to stop at a gas station. He filled up and bought two lottery tickets, then handed the clerk a check for $18. According to news reports, when the clerk saw the name on the check, the conversation went like this: "Are you John Garcia?" "Yes." "Were you ever in the Air Force?" "Yes." "Were you ever in Thailand?" "Yes." "Did you ever have a son?"

"With that question," writes the *San Francisco Chronicle*, "the two stared at each other and realized at the same moment that they were the father and son who had been separated 27 years ago and half a world away." Nueng's mother, it turned out, had married an American and moved to Colorado in 1971.

Incredibly, Garcia had never been to that gas station before and wasn't even particularly low on fuel. "I don't even know why I stopped for gas," he admitted on *Good Morning America*. "I started thinking—this couldn't be. I was totally shocked."

WHO: Tim Henderson and Mark Knight, half-brothers

SEPARATION: When Mark Knight was a year old, his parents divorced. His father remarried and had a son named Tim. His mother remarried, too, and Mark took his stepfather's last name. The brothers met once, when Mark was five and Tim three, but the families fought and never saw each other again.

TOGETHER AGAIN: In February 1996, 29-year-old Henderson needed to travel from Newcastle, England, to London. He couldn't afford the train fare, so he called the Freewheelers Lift Share Agency, which matches hitchhikers and drivers. Out of the 16,000 names on file, the name they gave him was Mark Knight.

According to a report in the *Guardian*: "As they drove, they started talking about friends and relatives. 'There was a moment of complete silence as we both stared at each other in disbelief,' said Mr. Henderson. 'Then one of us said, "You must be my brother." It was pretty mind-blowing. I always knew I had a half-brother but never thought we would meet.'"

According to scientists, octopuses do not have eight legs. They have six arms and two legs.

TOM SWIFTIES

This classic style of pun was originally invented in the 1920s. They're atrocious and corny, so of course we had to include them.

"I've had my left and right ventricles removed," Tom said half-heartedly.

"We've taken over the government," Tom cooed.

"Dawn came too soon," Tom mourned.

"My hair's been cut off," Tom said distressfully.

"Company should be here in about an hour," Tom guessed.

"Where did you get this meat?" Tom asked hoarsely.

"You dropped a stitch," Tom needled.

"Blow on the fire so it doesn't go out," Tom bellowed.

"I suppose there's room for one more," Tom admitted.

"That's no purebred," Tom muttered.

"I couldn't believe we lost the election by two votes," Tom recounted.

"I'm losing my hair," Tom bawled.

"Measure twice before you cut," Tom remarked.

"Thanks for shredding the cheese," Tom said gratefully.

"Please put some folds in these trousers," Tom pleaded.

"I've located the dog star," Tom said seriously.

"You look like a goat," Tom kidded.

"I used to own that gold mine," Tom exclaimed.

"Another plate of steamers all around!" Tom clamored.

"I memorized the whole thing," Tom wrote.

"That's the last time I'll pet a lion," Tom said offhandedly.

"No thanks to that Frenchman," said Tom mercilessly.

"You're not a real magician at all," Tom said, disillusioned.

"I've never had a car accident," said Tom recklessly.

"It's made the grass wet," said Tom after due consideration.

The real winner: Simon Cowell earned $22,000 per minute as an *American Idol* judge in 2009.

BRAND NAMES

You already know these names. Here's where they came from.

Q-TIPS. In the early 1920s, the owner of the Gerstenzang Infant Novelty Company noticed that his wife cleaned their daughter's ears by wrapping cotton around a toothpick. Inspired, he built a machine that made "ready-to-use cotton swabs." At first he called the product Baby Gays. In 1926 they became Q-Tips ("Q for Quality") Baby Gays…and finally just Q-Tips.

FORMULA 409. The two scientists who invented the "all-purpose cleaner" in the late 1950s didn't get the formula right until their 409th attempt.

LEE JEANS. At the turn of the 20th century, Henry D. Lee was one of the Midwest's biggest wholesalers of groceries, work clothes, and other items. In 1911, because he wasn't getting shipments of work clothes on time, he decided to build his own factory. In 1924 he started making jeans for cowboys. In 1926 Lee made the first jeans with zippers.

TURTLE WAX. In the early 1940s, Ben Hirsch mixed up a batch of car wax in a bathtub. He called it Plastone Liquid Car Wax and started selling it around the country. Several years later while walking along Turtle Creek in Beloit, Wisconsin, he began thinking about how his product gave cars a hard shell like a turtle's. "Plastone" became "Turtle Wax."

CONVERSE ALL-STARS. Named for Marquis M. Converse, who founded the Converse Rubber Company in 1908. He introduced the canvas-topped All-Star—one of the world's first basketball shoes—in 1917.

SARAN WRAP. In 1933 Dow researchers discovered a plastic called *monomeric vinylidene chloride*. They called it VC Plastic. In 1940 a salesman suggested they rename it Saran (the name of a tree in India). Dow liked the new name because it had only five letters and had no negative connotations. During World War II, Saran was used in everything from belts to subway seats. After the war, it was marketed as a plastic film called Saran Wrap.

---

4 of the 6 largest European cities have 6-letter names. (Moscow, London, Berlin, Madrid.)

READING TOMBSTONES

In centuries past, families had special symbols carved into gravestones to tell something about their loved ones, to express their grief, or to reflect their faith or belief in eternal life. So, next time you're strolling through a cemetery, look around—the dead are talking to you.

Anchor: Steadfast hope

Tree trunk: The brevity of life

Birds: The soul

Snake in a circle: Everlasting life in heaven (also called *ouroboros*)

Cherub: Divine wisdom or justice

Broken column: An early death

Cross, anchor, and Bible: Faith, hope, and charity

Cross, crown, and palm: Trials, victory, and reward

Crown: Reward and glory

Horseshoe: Protection against evil

Gourds: Deliverance from grief

Lamb: Innocence (usually on a child's grave)

Swallow: Motherhood

Hourglass: Time and its swift flight

Arch: Rejoined with partner in heaven

Ivy: Faithfulness, memory, and undying friendship

Laurel: Victory

Lily: Purity and resurrection

Mermaid: Dualism of Christ—half God, half man

Conch shell: Wisdom

Oak: Strength

Palms: Martyrdom

Shattered urn: Old age

Peacock: Eternal life

Poppy: Eternal sleep

Column: Noble life

Garland: Victory over death

Rooster: Awakening, courage, vigilance

Shell: Birth and resurrection

Six-pointed star: The creator

Olive branch: Forgiveness

Heart: Devotion

Dolphin: Salvation, bearer of souls across water to heaven

Skeleton: Life's brevity

Broken sword: Life cut short

Crossed swords: Life lost in battle

About 1 in 4 American employees say they're always angry on the job.

THE GARBAGE VORTEX

*A lonely plastic bag blows across a parking lot. It tumbles down a hill
and into a creek, where the water carries it downstream to a river.
Down the river it goes until it's swept out to sea. Day after
day it floats in the expanse until, there in the distance—
another plastic bag! And another, and another…and
millions of others. What is this strange place?*

ALARMING DISCOVERY

In the late 1990s, a sea captain and ocean researcher named Charles Moore entered a yacht race in Hawaii. As he was sailing back home to California, he came upon an odd sight: "There were shampoo caps and soap bottles and plastic bags and fishing floats as far as I could see. Here I was in the middle of the ocean, and there was nowhere I could go to avoid the plastic."

Around the same time, oceanographer Curtis Ebbesmeyer was researching ocean currents by tracking debris that had washed up on beaches around the world. When he heard of Moore's discovery, he named it the Eastern Garbage Patch (EGP).

Moore put together a team to survey the area in August 1998. Onboard the research ship *Alguita*, they pulled all sorts of strange objects out of the ocean: an inflated volleyball dotted with barnacles, a picture tube for a 19" TV, a truck tire on a steel rim, and even a drum of hazardous chemicals. But most of what they saw was plastic…and something else. Moore described it as a "rich broth of minute sea creatures mixed with hundreds of colored plastic fragments—a plastic-plankton soup." But there was six times more plastic than there was plankton.

TROPIC OF PLASTIC

Just how large is the Eastern Garbage Patch? No one knows for sure—it's growing all the time, and the translucent plastic floats just below the water's surface. "It's one of the great features of the planet Earth, but you can't see it," said Ebbesmeyer. Estimates, however, say that it's larger than the state of Texas. And that's just on the surface. Much of the

---

Most-common trash items found on the beach: cigarette butts, bottle caps, and plastic bags.

debris—up to 30%—sinks to the ocean floor and lands on top of animal and plant life.

Just how fast is the EGP growing? In a survey conducted in 2007, Moore found that in less than a decade the "patch" had become a "super-highway of junk" running between San Francisco and Japan. He believes that the amount of plastic could now be 10 times higher than it was in 1998; some of the samples he gathered have as much as 48 parts plastic to 1 part plankton.

IN THE DOLDRUMS

How did all that garbage accumulate there? The answer is ocean currents. The EGP is located in an area known as the North Pacific Subtropical Gyre, about 1,000 miles from any landmass. The Gyre is formed by air and water currents that travel between the coasts of Washington, Mexico, and Japan. The clockwise currents form a vortex in the center, just as if a giant soup spoon were constantly stirring it or, as Moore says, "the same way bubbles gather at the center of a hot tub."

The Gyre is part of the Doldrums—an area named by ancient sailors for its weak winds. For centuries sailors avoided it for fear of stalling there, and fishermen knew there was nothing there to catch but plankton or jellyfish. The Gyre has always accumulated marine debris such as drift-wood, as well as "flotsam and jetsam"—stuff that washes offshore from beaches or falls overboard from ships and is caught by the currents and pulled into the middle, where it swirls continuously. But the difference in the last century is that the never-ending influx of trash has made it larger and larger. A plastic bag that flows into the ocean from a California river will ride the currents for up to a year before finally making it to the EGP. And because ocean currents travel only about 10 miles per day, depending on where a object enters the ocean, it could float for much longer—even decades.

REVENGE OF THE NURDLES

Most garbage breaks down over time, but plastic is different. No one really knows how long it takes for plastic to biodegrade because, so far, none of it has. Instead of biodegrading, plastic *photodegrades*—the sun's UV rays cause it to become brittle, which breaks it down into small pieces...and then into minute particles that resemble tiny confetti.

Sailors call these plastic bits "mermaid tears," but the technical term is *nurdles*. They're light enough to float in the air (think of tiny packing peanuts and how impossible it is to keep them from spilling everywhere). Everything made out of plastic is made out of nurdles, and every year 5.5 quadrillion of them are manufactured around the world. Just how many end up in the oceans is anyone's guess, but it's a huge amount.

Moore has another name for nurdles: "poison pills." They absorb oily toxic chemicals called *persistent organic pollutants*, or POPs, which include DDT and PCBs. Though many of these chemicals were banned in the 1970s, they still linger in the environment and attach themselves to plastic debris. Japanese environmental researchers found that nurdles can absorb one million times their weight in POPs from surrounding water.

Even more troubling: The "poison pills" resemble plankton in how they seem to "swim" near the surface. Jellyfish and "filter feeder" fish that strain their food out of the water—and who have been eating plankton for eons—are now eating the nurdles instead. And then fish eat the nurdle-eaters. And then those fish are caught by fishing boats…which means there's a good chance you're getting more plastic in your diet than you realize. And not just plastic, but all of those toxic chemicals it absorbed.

NO END IN SIGHT
The problem might not be so severe if the EGP were the only garbage patch in the world. But each major ocean has its own gyre, and each gyre has its own vortex of swirling garbage. There are five major patches in all, covering 40% of the world's oceans. "That corresponds to a quarter of Earth's surface," Moore says. "So 25% of our planet is a toilet that never flushes."

The question now becomes: How do you get rid of millions of tons of tiny bits in the middle of the sea? "Any attempt to remove that much plastic from the oceans—it boggles the mind," Moore says. "There's just too much, and the ocean is just too big." So chances are that the garbage patches will be here for a very long time. About the only thing we can do right now is to stop adding to them.

How long does it take a major-league fastball to reach home plate? About 4/10ths of a second.

LET'S PLAY GORUFU!

*Golf isn't just popular in England, Scotland, and
the United States—it's loved all over the world.*

DOMO ARIGATO
Before World War II, there were 23 courses in all of Japan. Today,
the number exceeds 3,000—in a country slightly smaller than
California. Despite the volume of courses and their distance from urban
centers (most are an hour's drive or more), the courses are almost always
busy. Although available tee times are scarce, the clubs compete so
fiercely that all kinds of specials abound, such as free caddies, or, more
commonly, half-price greens fees on Monday. And that's a generous discount, as Japanese golf (or *gorufu*) is very expensive—18 holes might
cost $400. Even the driving ranges are expensive: it can cost 50 cents to
hit a *single ball.*

Only the very wealthy can afford country club memberships. The
price of joining a club costs the equivalent of about five years of a middle-
class worker's salary. The most prestigious clubs charge several million
dollars. However, Japanese golfers view a membership as an investment as
well as a status symbol—they can be bought, sold, transferred, and passed
down. At the peak of the Japanese inflation crisis in the late 1980s, country club memberships accounted for roughly 10 percent of Japan's gross
domestic product.

LAND OF THE RISING GREENS FEES

It's pricey, but Japanese golfers get a lot for their money. Courses are so
meticulously manicured that it's virtually impossible to lose a ball, even in
the rough. Clubhouses are lavishly decorated with marble. Even daily fee-
paying golfers are treated well, with access to saunas, baths, and high-end
restaurants. Refreshing hot towels are provided at the 7th and 16th holes,
and you can get a robot caddie to carry your gear.

Links are so crowded that playing nine holes can take up to three
hours, but golfers are given a 45-minute lunch break after the front nine
(in Japan, you're assigned a tee time for each set of nine holes). And after
the round, there is a traditional bath followed by drinks and coffee, while
clothes and shoes are left to dry in special heated lockers.

Fewer than 50 pilgrims survived their first winter in America.

Some other notable golf hot spots (and cold spots) around the world:

• **ICELAND:** There are only 15 golf clubs in this tiny island nation, but the population is so small, the number of golf courses per capita is comparable to that of the United States. The Akureyri Golf Club is the northernmost course in the world. Each June it hosts the Arctic Open Golf Championship. The sun doesn't completely set for six months of the year in arctic regions, so tee off is at midnight and play continues until 6 a.m. On the other side of the country, the Westman Island Golf Club is set inside a volcanic crater adjacent to the Atlantic Ocean. The bumpy lava formations and unrelenting ocean winds make for a challenging round of golf.

• **INDIA:** One of the first golf clubs outside of the British Isles—the Royal Calcutta—was established in India in 1829. The first national competition, the All-India Amateur Championship, was established in 1892, making it the world's second-oldest open championship after the British Open. British golfers dominated the All-India until 1949, when Mohinder Bal became the first native-born Indian to win it.

• **AUSTRALIA:** Australians have golfed since the mid-1800s, when it was still a British colony. Today, there are plenty of elegant, highly manicured courses near the cities along the coast, but Australia also has huge expanses of largely uninhabited land in its interior. The Outback is mostly grass-free, hot desert, but that doesn't stop course developers from building nine-hole courses of oiled sand. Natural hazards: grazing kangaroos, wombat holes, and snakes.

• **MALAYSIA:** Summer temperatures hover around 90 degrees. Golf is popular there, but how do golfers avoid the extreme heat and humidity? Night golf under high-powered floodlights.

• **IRAN:** In 1979 Iran's pro-Western government was overthrown and replaced by a strict Muslim theocracy that viewed golf as a useless and decadent Western activity. Teheran's once prestigious Imperial Golf Club quickly fell into disrepair; five holes have even been confiscated by the government for their real estate value. Golf is now starting to regain popularity, though, and one politician heads a program that provides funds and equipment to schools with golf programs. Golf is most popular among Iranian women, despite the requirement that on the course they be covered from head to toe and cannot play at the same time as men.

Scientific term for foul-smelling breath (worse than "bad" breath): *ozostomia.*

I'D LIKE TO THANK THE ACADEMY...

Every year, Hollywood puts on the movie industry's biggest party. But there's more to the Academy Awards than sealed envelopes, gold statues, and acceptance speeches. Here are a few little-known facts about the Oscars.

An Oscar isn't really called an "Oscar." It's not even officially called an Academy Award. The award's full title is the Academy Award of Merit. The "Academy" refers to the Academy of Motion Pictures Arts and Sciences, formed in 1927 by film-industry employees to arbitrate labor disputes, provide a forum for teaching movie-making techniques and innovations, and improve the industry's image. In 1929, almost as an afterthought, it began giving out awards for achievement. Most people now associate the Academy only with the awards, but it also continues its other functions (except that it ended its involvement with labor disputes in 1937).

• **At the first ceremony, only 14 awards were given out.** The original award categories were: Actor, Actress, Art Direction, Cinematography, Directing (Comedy), Directing (Drama), Engineering Effects, Unique and Artistic Picture, Writing (Adaptation), Writing (Original), Writing (Title Writing), Outstanding Picture (which went to *Wings*), and two "special achievement" awards. The ceremony lasted 15 minutes; admission was $5.

• **The winners' names were not always closely guarded secrets.** The 1929 ceremony was an unpretentious dinner in the Blossom Room of the Hollywood Roosevelt Hotel. Everyone already knew who had won; the results had been announced nearly three months earlier. The following year, the Academy gave the press the names of the winners ahead of time—on the condition that they wouldn't print the results until after the ceremony. That tradition continued until 1939 when, during a heated race for Best Picture among heavyweight contenders such as *Stagecoach*, *The Wizard of Oz*, *Gone With the Wind*, and *Mr. Smith Goes to Washington*, the *Los Angeles Times* printed the name of the winner (*Gone With the Wind*) in its early evening edition—a few hours before the ceremony, ruining the suspense. Since then, the winners are revealed *only* at the ceremony.

Popular pizza topping in Brazil: green peas.

LET'S DANCE!

More origins of booty-shaking crazes. (For Part I, turn to page 53.)

THE TWIST

You can thank Dick Clark for this dance craze—as host of TV's *American Bandstand*, he was always on the lookout for the next big fad. In 1959 he heard a little-known Hank Ballard b-side called "The Twist." Clark loved the song and urged Ballard to perform it on *Bandstand*, but Ballard wasn't interested. So Clark searched around Philadelphia (where the show was based) and found a part-time chicken plucker named Ernest Evans who was known for his ability to mimic popular singers. Before Evans could perform, however, Clark insisted he find a good stage name. Clark's wife, Barbara, suggested modeling it after Fats Domino: "Fats" became "Chubby," and "Domino" became "Checker." So the newly christened Chubby Checker sang "The Twist" on *Bandstand* and it was an immediate hit. The single shot to #1, and *the* dance craze of the 1960s was born. So why was the Twist so popular? First, as a non-contact dance, it was novel and rebellious enough to appeal to teenagers, but safe enough for the conservative media. Second, the Twist is easy—even non-dancers (like Uncle John) could do it. "It's like putting out a cigarette with both feet and wiping your bottom with a towel," explained Checker.

Typecast: "The Twist" turned Checker into a star. He followed it up with a string of successful dance songs (to this day, he's the only recording artist to have had five albums in the Top 12 at the same time). Yet the song also took a toll on Checker's artistic dreams. "In a way, 'The Twist' really ruined my life," he lamented years later. "I was on my way to becoming a big nightclub performer, and 'The Twist' just wiped it out. It got so out of proportion. No one ever believes I have talent."

THE WALTZ

Even people who can't dance (like Uncle John) can recognize the familiar 1-2-3, 1-2-3 rhythm of the waltz. Although these days it's associated with high society, when the waltz was introduced in European ballrooms in the early 1800s, it was shunned by "respectable" people. For one, the music came from peasant yodeling melodies of Austria and Bavaria. Worse yet: the close proximity of the two dance partners. Even poet Lord

Byron, a notorious rake, claimed that the "lewd grasp and lawless contact" of the waltz "does not leave much to mystery to the nuptial night."

Nevertheless, the waltz caught on and became the standard dance of the upper classes in Europe and the United States. Most of the credit for that goes to Austrian composer Johann Strauss. In the mid-1800s, he reworked the peasant melodies and turned them into layered compositions which were embraced by Viennese royalty. This made Strauss the "waltz king." He toured Europe with his orchestra, taking the music (as well as the dance) to Germany, Poland, and Russia. It soon found its way to England, then the United States…and eventually into Earth's orbit.

Revolver: Perhaps the most wisely recognized waltz is Strauss's 1867 work, "The Blue Danube"—it was so popular in Austria that it became the country's unofficial anthem. The piece also became a staple of American pop culture when Stanley Kubrick used it in his 1969 film *2001: A Space Odyssey* to accompany the delicate dance of a passenger shuttle orbiting a space station as it prepares to dock—which makes sense, as the word "waltz" comes from the German *walzen*, meaning "to revolve."

MORE WAYS TO SHAKE YOUR GROOVE THING

The Macarena: The song by Los del Río about a sensuous Spanish woman took the U.S. by storm in 1996. VH1 called it the "#1 Greatest One-Hit Wonder of All Time."

Hully Gully: A popular line dance from the 1960s, popularized by the 1960 song "Hully Gully," by the Olympics. John Belushi dances the hully gully in the 1980 film *The Blues Brothers*.

Electric Slide: A disco line dance created by the famous disco dancer Ric Silver in 1976. It came from a song called "Electric Boogie," written by Bunny Wailer (from Bob Marley's band).

Charleston: Though it's associated with white "flappers" in speakeasies of the 1920s, the dance actually came from the song of the same name by African-American pianist James P. Johnson.

Achy-Breaky: The 1992 song made Billy Ray Cyrus a country superstar and ushered in a new era of line dancing—not just in America, but all over Europe as well. And it's still going strong today.

Limbo: Created in Trinidad in the 1950s, the name comes from the word "limber," which you must be in order to do this dance. It became a fad in 1962 thanks to Chubby Checker's "Limbo Rock."

…in a car accident three blocks from Dead Man's Curve in Los Angeles.

TONGUE TWISTERS

Try to say these three times fast. And pay no attention to the person banging on the bathroom door, wondering what's going on in there.

Who washed Washington's white woolens when Washington's washerwoman went west?

Lesser leather never weathered wetter weather better.

Shave a cedar shingle thin.

Which wristwatches are Swiss wristwatches?

A thin little boy picked six thick thistle sticks.

Flee from fog to fight flu fast!

The bootblack bought the black boot back.

We surely shall see the sun shine soon.

Miss Smith's fish sauce shop seldom sells shellfish.

Which wicked witch wished which wicked wish?

I slit the sheet, the sheet I slit, and on the slitted sheet I sit.

Give papa a cup of proper coffee in a copper coffee cup.

Imagine an imaginary menagerie manager managing an imaginary menagerie.

The epitome of femininity.

Fred fed Ted bread, and Ted fed Fred bread.

Many an anemone sees an enemy.

Any noise annoys an oyster but a noisy noise annoys an oyster most.

Brooke Shields, Teri Garr, and John Travolta all appeared in 1970s Band-Aid commercials.

THE EARTH IS FLAT!

For centuries, scientists have been able to prove that the Earth is round, but that hasn't stopped people from developing their own unique—and entertaining—theories about its shape.

THE EARTH IS FLAT

Who Says So: The International Flat Earth Research Society

What They Believe: The world is a big flat disc, with the North Pole at the center. What is mistakenly believed to be the South Pole is actually a 150-foot-high mass of ice that forms a big square around the Earth-disc (the way an album cover makes a square around a record). People who think they're sailing around the world are actually sailing in a circle on the surface of the disc.

Flat-Earthers believe the Bible must be interpreted literally. Passages like Revelation 7:1 and 20:8, which refer to "the four corners of the earth," are all the proof they need.

History: In 1849 an English "itinerant lecturer" named Samuel Birley Rowbotham resurrected the flat-Earth theory (which had been widely discredited by the eighth century). The flat-Earth movement grew sporadically over the next 70 years, finally peaking in the 1920s when Wilbur Glen Voliva organized a flat-Earth religious community with several thousand followers in Zion, Illinois. Voliva owned one of the country's first 100,000-watt radio stations, and used it to preach the flat-Earth gospel to folks in the American Midwest. Today the movement lives on in Charles Johnson's Flat Earth Society, which published *Flat Earth News*...until Johnson's house burned down in 1995, incinerating the 3,500-person mailing list. No word on what he's doing now.

THE EARTH IS HOLLOW

Who Said So: Captain John Cleves Symmes, a hero of the War of 1812

What He Believed: Earth has four layers, like a big onion. Each is a "warm and rich land, stocked with vegetables and animals, if not men." What we perceive as the surface of the Earth is actually the fifth and outer layer. And the North and South poles aren't just poles, they're also *holes* leading to the four interior worlds.

John F. Kennedy's rocking chair was auctioned off for $453,500.

History: In 1823 Symmes managed to get a bill introduced in the U.S. Congress to finance a steamship voyage to the "North Hole" and to the inner worlds beyond. When the bill received only 25 votes, Johnson talked President Adams's secretaries of the Navy and the Treasury into outfitting three ships for a voyage to the middle of the earth. But before it got underway, Andrew Jackson became president and scuttled the trip. Symmes died in 1829, unfulfilled, but his theory remained popular with unconventional thinkers until 1909, when Robert Peary set foot on the North Pole (or at least came close)…and found no hole.

Even after 1909, the hollow-Earth theory had its admirers—including Adolf Hitler. Today, a few diehard hollow-Earthers believe that Hitler survived World War II, escaped to an interior world under the South Pole, and may still be hiding there, mingling with "a race of advanced hollow-Earth beings who are responsible for the UFO sightings throughout history."

THE EARTH IS SHAPED LIKE THE INSIDE OF AN EGG

Who Said So: Cyrus Reed Teed, in the late 1860s

What He Believed: Instead of living on the outside of a solid round ball, we're on the inside surface of a hollow one. The rest of the universe— sun, stars, etc.—is where the yolk would be.

Background: For years, Teed grappled with the notion of an infinite universe…but just couldn't accept it. Then one night in 1869, he had a dream in which a beautiful woman explained everything:

> The entire cosmos is like an egg. We live on the inner surface of the shell, and inside the hollow are the sun, moon, stars, planets, and comets. What is outside? Absolutely nothing! The inside is all there is. You can't see across it because the atmosphere is too dense. The shell is 100 miles thick.

The woman in Teed's dream also said he would be the new Messiah, and he took it to heart. In the 1890s, he bought land outside Fort Meyers, Florida, and founded a community called The New Jerusalem that he preached would one day be the capital of the world. He expected 8 million residents, but only got 200. In 1908 Teed died from injuries suffered during a run-in with the local marshal; his dwindling community held on until the late 1940s, when the last of his followers disbanded following a property dispute.

Favorite candy of the Netherlands: *drop.* What is it? Salty licorice.

FOOD A MILLENNIUM AGO

*What could the average medieval peasant expect to find on the dinner
table after a hard day's work? Here's the grueling tale.*

I'M STARVING! WHAT'S FOR LUNCH?

For most people in the year A.D. 1000, finding enough food to eat was
a constant problem. There were long periods, particularly in winter,
when no fresh food was available. During the 10th century alone, Europe
suffered 20 famines. As a result, people tended to gorge themselves whenever food was abundant because they never knew what the next season
would bring. The staple of Joe Peasant's diet was gruel—what we'd call
oatmeal—which nutritionists say was probably healthier than our modern
meat-heavy diet. When vegetables were in season, people ate cabbage,
carrots, peas, and various garden greens. They picked apples, pears, and
nuts right off the trees.

FUNGAL FEVER

Another medieval staple was bread made from whole-grain wheat, rye, or
barley flour. That may sound healthy, but unsanitary kitchens and ovens
introduced other ingredients that weren't so wholesome, including insects
and mold. The mold brought another problem: outbreaks of *ergotism*, a
fatal illness caused by a substance called ergotamine found in a fungus
that often infected rye grain. When baked into bread, the ergotamine
chemically transformed into a deadly hallucinogen. Victims experienced
tingling, dizziness, hallucinations, psychosis and, eventually, death. The
symptoms of ergotism, according to some theories, may have caused some
sufferers to be accused of witchcraft.

WOULD YOU LIKE HORSE WITH THAT?

A millennium ago, horses were just beginning to replace oxen as the
quintessential farm animal. But they were still a valuable food source and
were eaten with gusto. Meat was prepared with salt, pepper, cloves, and
other spices, which not only preserved the food but also masked the rotten taste after it had spoiled. In addition to horses and the odd rabbit or
pig, birds were eaten with regularity. People ate cranes, storks, swans,

Feeding dyes to hens will change the color of their eggs' yolks.

crows, herons, loons, and blackbirds, sometimes served in a pastries like the "four and twenty blackbirds baked in a pie" from the well-known English nursery rhyme.

MINIMALISM, MEDIEVAL-STYLE

Setting the medieval table was fairly simple—because there were no plates. Even nobles, who generally spread out tablecloths for their meals, went without plates. Instead, meals were served on round, flat slabs of bread. Bread plates had the dual advantages of soaking up drippings and being edible. When plates eventually came into vogue, it was customary to share your plate with the person sitting next to you.

Guests were invited to bring their own knives; spoons and forks weren't widely used in Europe until much later. In the eastern Mediterranean, two-pronged forks had been in use for centuries, but they didn't come to Europe until 1071, when a Greek princess brought the custom to Venice. Rich Venetians took it up as the fashion, but forks stayed in Venice for centuries before the rest of Europe caught on.

GROG: BREAKFAST OF CHAMPIONS

A thousand years ago, alcoholic beverages were a diversion and comfort to households among all classes. Wine was the favorite drink of the nobility and wealthier middle class. But everyone drank beer, even for breakfast, and the alcoholic content was three to four times higher than today's brews. Mead, a kind of beer made from fermented honey, was popular in northern Europe and packed an even stronger wallop—it could have an alcohol content of up to 18 percent. Beer was such a prized commodity that one Swedish king chose, among several prospective brides, the one who could brew the best beer.

*   *   *

FREE RANGE

Leonardo da Vinci, an avowed vegetarian, was so opposed to people eating animals that he often purchased live poultry and then set the birds free. He wrote, "I have, from an early age, abjured the use of meat, and the time will come when men such as I will look on the murder of animals as they now look on the murder of men."

An Atlanta, Georgia, law forbids "smelly people" from riding on public streetcars.

THE MISSING MOM

Here's a nightmare: You set off on a simple trip, only to end up more than 1,000 miles away from everyone you've ever known, with no way to get home. It happened to a woman who became known as "Auntie Mon."

LANGUAGE BARRIER

In 1982 Jaeyaena Beuraheng left her home in the Narathiwat Province of southern Thailand to take one of her regular shopping trips across the border in Malaysia. After she was done at the markets, Beuraheng, 51 years old and a mother of seven, accidentally boarded the wrong bus. She fell asleep. When she woke up, she found herself in Bangkok…700 miles north of her home. Unfortunately for Beuraheng, she couldn't speak Thai, and her Malay dialect, Yawi, is spoken by very few people in Bangkok. In fact, to the people in Bangkok whom she asked for directions, it sounded like the woman was speaking gibberish. Without the ability to read signs or ask directions, Beuraheng boarded another bus—one that she thought was headed south. Instead, it took her another 430 miles north and she ended up in the city of Chiang Mai. Beuraheng was now more than 1,100 miles from home, she didn't know where she was, and she'd run out of money.

Meanwhile, back in her hometown, Beuraheng's family told the authorities that their mother was missing and were informed that a woman matching her description had been hit by a train and killed. Beuraheng's son went to identify the body—which was difficult—but he said that it could have been her. So, believing their mother was dead, they stopped searching for her. Beuraheng was on her own. With no other options, she resorted to begging in the street to survive.

A SHELTERED LIFE

Five years later, Beuraheng, now 56, was arrested in a section of the city where begging was not allowed. The police couldn't understand the woman's words, so they took her to a homeless shelter in nearby Phitsanulok. The staff at the shelter deduced that the woman was insane. Still, she seemed nice, so there she stayed. Mostly, Beuraheng sat in a chair and sang a song that no one could understand. They called her "Auntie Mon" because the song reminded them of the language spoken by the ethnic Mon people, who live on the Burma-Thailand border. They even brought in someone who could speak Mon to try and discern if that's what it was, but it wasn't. Everyone who tried to understand Auntie Mon only heard gibberish.

Twenty years passed.

THE POWER OF SONG

In 2007 three university students from Narathiwat were studying the homeless problem in Phitsanulok. As they were touring the shelter, one of the students asked about the old woman singing the song. "That's Auntie Mon. We can't understand her words, but we like the song," said one of the staff workers. The student replied that he could—it was Yawi, a dialect spoken near his hometown. He approached her, smiled, and asked her for her name. It was the first time Beuraheng had understood anything that anyone had said in 25 years. Overjoyed, she told the students about her ordeal—how she took the wrong bus, how she ended up at the shelter, how much she missed being able to speak to anyone, and how much she missed her family.

HOME AT LAST

Beuraheng's family was shocked to receive the news that their mother was alive. Her youngest son and eldest daughter traveled to the shelter to bring her home. She recognized her daughter, but not her son, who was just a small child when she last saw him. They flew back to Narathiwat…and took the *correct* bus home to their village. A two-day celebration ensued, during which Beuraheng—often crying tears of joy—told her amazing story to the press. "I didn't tell anybody where I was going on that day, because I went there quite often. I thought I would die in Phitsanulok. I thought about running away many times, but then I worried I would not be able to make it home. I really missed my children."

Beuraheng, now 79 years old, has a much larger family than when she left (there are many grandchildren). As in the shelter, she still spends much of her time sitting in her chair and singing her song. Only now, those around her can understand the words.

"If all you have is a hammer, every problem looks like a nail." —proverb

SUPPOSEDLY SAID

*Because quoting what other people say is often like playing a game of "telephone,"
what ends up in our collective memory often isn't exactly what the speaker said.*

TARZAN

He supposedly said: "Me Tarzan, you Jane."

...But actually: This line was never uttered in any Tarzan film, nor in the original Edgar Rice Burroughs novel. The quote stems from an interview in which Tarzan actor Johnny Weissmuller made up the line as a comment on the films' simplistic dialogue.

KARL MARX

He supposedly said: "Religion is the opiate of the masses."

...But actually: "Religion is the sigh of the oppressed creature, the heart of a heartless world and the soul of soulless conditions. It is the opium of the people," is what Marx really said. The misquote implies that Marx believed religion "drugs" people. The full quote suggests that Marx had a better understanding of why many people flock to religion.

JOHN KERRY

He supposedly said: "Who among us doesn't like NASCAR?"

...But actually: This quote was well circulated during the 2004 presidential election, often characterizing Senator Kerry as awkward, out of touch, and pandering to blue-collar voters. Turns out that when *New York Times* columnist Maureen Dowd mocked Kerry for the quote in a March 2004 column, it was the first time the quote had ever appeared. Dowd had just made it up.

SGT. JOE FRIDAY (Jack Webb)

He supposedly said: "Just the facts, ma'am."

...But actually: The no-nonsense cop said, "All we want are the facts, ma'am." Satirist Stan Freberg spoofed he show on the 1953 hit record "St. George and the Dragonet," in which he says, "I just want to get the facts, ma'am." It was Freberg's line, not Webb's, that became synonymous with the show.

The Pacific giant octopus grows from the size of a pea to 150 lbs. in 2 years...and then it dies.

MARIE ANTOINETTE

She supposedly said: "Let them eat cake."

...But actually: The queen was said to have made this sarcastic remark when told that many people in France had no bread to eat. In reality, French revolutionaries spread the rumor to stir up hatred for the monarch and support for overthrowing the crown.

ADM. DAVID FARRAGUT

He supposedly said: "Damn the torpedoes! Full speed ahead!"

...But actually: According to *The Yale Book of Quotations*, the Civil War admiral never uttered this famous rallying cry at the Battle of Mobile Bay in 1864. It appeared in print in 1878, but news reports and accounts of the battle make no mention of the phrase.

JAMES CAGNEY

He supposedly said: "You dirty rat!"

...But actually: It's commonly assumed to be a line from Cagney's film *Public Enemy Number One*, but the line isn't in that movie...nor in any others. Where the misquote originated is unknown.

THE KING JAMES BIBLE

It supposedly said: "Money is the root of all evil."

...But actually: Money is not evil; loving it is. The full quote is: "For the love of money is the root of all evil" (1 Timothy 6-7).

LORD ACTON

He supposedly said: "Power corrupts. Absolute power corrupts absolutely."

...But actually: The 19th-century British historian really wrote, "Power tends to corrupt. Absolute power corrupts absolutely. Great men are almost always bad men."

WILLIAM CONGREVE

He supposedly said: "Hell hath no fury like a woman scorned."

...But actually: Close, but not quite. In his 1697 poem "The Mourning Bride," Congreve wrote: "Heaven has no rage like love to hatred turned/ Nor hell a fury like a woman scorned."

Tanzania has a postage stamp featuring Michael Jackson.

COURT TRANSQUIPS

We're back with one of our regular features. Check out these real-life exchanges that were actually said in court, recorded word for word.

Lawyer: "Okay, we've talked at length about how the accident happened, is there anything we haven't covered that you can think of, anything in your mind that you're thinking about how the accident happened that I haven't asked you and you're thinking 'he hasn't asked me that' and 'I'm not going to tell him because he hasn't asked me,' is there anything?"

Witness: "Have you lost your mind?"

Judge (to jury): "If that be your verdict, so say you all."

Two jurors: "You all."

Defendant: "You know, I hate coming out here at seven in the morning and sitting downstairs with a bunch of criminals."

Judge: "I have to do the same thing every day."

Defendant: "Yeah, but you don't have to sit down in a holding tank with 'em."

Judge: "Every day I come in and I meet the dregs of society, and then I have to meet their clients."

Q: "Why do you handle the family finances?"

A: "Because my mom and sister ain't that bright."

Q: "Are you being selective about what you remember and what you don't remember as to the details of your previous record?"

A: "I don't remember."

Q: "Now doctor, isn't it true that when a person dies in his sleep, he doesn't know about it until the next morning?"

Q: "She had three children, right?"

A: "Yes."

Q: "How many were boys?"

A: "None."

Q: "Were there any girls?"

Q: "Is there a difference between a reconditioned and rebuilt piece of equipment in your mind, if you have one?"

Q: "The youngest son, the twenty-year old, how old is he?"

I WALK THE LAWN

Some facts about America's favorite pastime—lawn care. (And when you're done with this page, get out there and start mowing.)

• An average lawn has six grass plants per square inch. That's 850 per square foot—which can contain as many as 3,000 individual blades of grass.

• There are 50 million lawn mowers in use in the U.S.

• About 65% of all water used in American households goes to watering lawns. (In summer, that's about 238 gallons per person per day.)

• According to the Environmental Protection Agency, as much as 5% of all polluting exhaust in urban areas is from lawn mowers.

• The first lawn-care book: *The Art of Beautifying Suburban Home Grounds*, published in 1870.

• The average lawn absorbs water six times more effectively than a wheat field.

• You can get a degree in lawn maintenance from Penn State University (but they call it "Turf Grass Science").

• The most popular lawn ornament: the pink flamingo (250,000 are sold every year).

• There are about 40 million acres of lawn in the United States—three times the acreage planted with irrigated corn.

• AstroTurf was patented in 1967. It was originally named Chemgrass.

• Before mowers were invented, lawns were cut with scythes (or sheep).

• A lawn absorbs 10 times more water on a hot day than it does on a cloudy day.

• A 150-pound man can burn 380 calories in a half hour of mowing with a push-mower.

• The average lawn grows at a rate of about 3 inches per month.

• A recent study found that about 65,000 people per year are hospitalized with lawnmowing-related injuries.

Q: Why are tennis balls fuzzy? A: To slow them down.

GOLDEN-AGE RADIO TREASURES

Uncle John loves old-time radio shows.
Here are some of his favorites.

DRAGNET (NBC, 1949–57)
If you like to watch *CSI* or any other police "procedural" show, you have Jack Webb—*Dragnet's* Sergeant Joe Friday—to thank for it. Webb came up with the idea for *Dragnet* after playing a forensic scientist in the 1948 movie *He Walked by Night*. Other cops-and-robbers radio shows were mostly flights of fancy, but Webb, the creator and producer of the show as well as its star, was a stickler for authenticity. He rode along with police officers on patrol and sat in on classes at the police academy, soaking up details that he put to good use in his show. Even the ring of the telephones and the number of footsteps between offices were exactly as they were at LAPD headquarters.

Things to Listen For: Controversial subject matter. *Dragnet* was the first police show to tackle taboo topics, such as sex crimes, drug abuse, and the deaths of children. The grim storyline of the 1949 Christmas episode: An eight-year-old boy is shot and killed by the .22 rifle his friend got for Christmas. Gritty realism and attention to detail helped make *Dragnet* one of the most popular and long-lasting police dramas on radio. It has influenced nearly every police show—on radio and TV—since.

Note: Good writing is one of the things that makes *Dragnet* so much fun to listen to; *bad* writing is what gives another Jack Webb radio detective show, *Pat Novak for Hire* (ABC, 1946–47), its appeal. The endless stream of cheesy similes ("When Feldman hit me I went down like the price of winter wheat," and, "She was kind of pretty, except you could see somebody had used her badly, like a dictionary in a stupid family") pile up like cars on the freeway at rush hour.

MY FAVORITE HUSBAND (CBS, 1948–51)
If you're a fan of *I Love Lucy*, give *My Favorite Husband* a listen. Lucille Ball stars as Liz Cooper, the screwy wife of George Cooper, played by

---

Role reversal: The all-male Japanese Kabuki theatre style was invented by a woman.

Richard Denning. The show was so successful that CBS decided to move it to television in 1951. Lucy agreed on one condition: Her real-life husband, Cuban bandleader Desi Arnaz, was to play her husband.

YOURS TRULY, JOHNNY DOLLAR (CBS, 1949–62)

Detective series were commonplace during the golden age of radio. This one set itself apart from the pack by making Johnny Dollar a freelance investigator for insurance companies (instead of a typical gumshoe) and structuring the narration of the story as if Johnny was itemizing his expense account in a letter to his client. Each story began with "Expense account item one," followed by another item or two to get the story rolling. The show ended 30 minutes later with the last item on the account, followed by the signature—"Yours truly, Johnny Dollar." The gimmick worked: the show became one of the longest-running detective shows in radio.

INNER SANCTUM (NBC/ABC/CBS, 1941–52)

Before *Inner Sanctum*, the hosts of horror shows were as deadly serious and spooky as the stories themselves. Then came Raymond Edward Johnson, a.k.a. "Your host, Raymond," who introduced each story with bad jokes and one morbid pun after another. He was the inspiration for all the smart-aleck horror hosts that followed, including *Tales from the Crypt*'s wisecracking Crypt-keeper.

Things to Listen For: The squeaking door that opened and closed each broadcast—probably the most famous sound effect in radio history. The sound was actually created by a squeaky office chair…except for the time that someone fixed the squeak without realizing its importance. That forced the sound man to make the squeak with his voice until the chair returned to "normal." Also, do you like tea with your nightmares? For a time Raymond was paired with Mary Bennett, the singleminded spokeswoman for Lipton Tea, who rarely approved of his jokes and always found a way to insert Lipton Tea and Lipton Soup into their conversations. Listening to how she does it is one of the best parts of the show.

THE LONE RANGER (Mutual, 1933–54)

The Lone Ranger was one of the most popular radio shows of all time. It was targeted at children, but more than half of the listeners were adults.

If you listen you'll understand why—crisp storytelling and vivid characters make the show a treat. Earle Graser, who played the Masked Man from 1933 until 1941, delivers a wonderfully over-the-top performance—sometimes he sounds like a crazy man who only *thinks* he's the Lone Ranger.

Things to Listen For: Tragedy struck the show in 1941, when Graser was killed in an automobile accident. For the next five shows, the Lone Ranger spoke only in a whisper until the producers found a replacement—Brace Beemer, the show's longtime announcer, who played the Ranger until the series ended in 1954.

THE GREEN HORNET (Mutual/ABC, 1936–52)

The Lone Ranger was such a huge hit that the show's creators, Fran Striker and George Trendle, decided to create a second show by bringing the formula into the 20th century. Like the Lone Ranger, the Green Hornet wore a mask and had an ethnic sidekick (his valet, Kato, a Filipino of Japanese ancestry). The Lone Ranger had a horse named Silver; the Green Hornet drove a car called the Black Beauty. Trendle and Striker even made the Green Hornet the Lone Ranger's great nephew.

Things to Listen For: The show had several announcers over the years. One of them was Mike Wallace, who later became a correspondent for the CBS-TV show *60 Minutes*. One more thing: In the early episodes, the announcer claims that the Green Hornet goes after crooks "that even the G-men (FBI agents) couldn't reach." In later shows that line was dropped, after J. Edgar Hoover complained that *no* criminals were beyond the Bureau's reach.

CHALLENGE OF THE YUKON (ABC/Mutual, 1938–55)

Why stop at *The Green Hornet*? In 1938 Trendle and Striker reworked the *Lone Ranger* format a third time, this time moving it to the Alaskan Gold Rush of the late 1890s, and combining the hero's sidekick and his animal companion into a single character, that of Yukon King, Sergeant Preston's lead sled dog.

Things to Listen For: Yukon King's astonishing insight into the human condition: He growls and barks at the bad guys before they are revealed to be bad guys, and whimpers in sympathy when murder victims are discovered. "That's right, King, he's dead!"

...being expected to take it home with me." —Frank A. Clark

FLUBBED HEADLINES

*These are 100% honest-to-goodness headlines. Can
you figure out what they were trying to say?*

Factory Orders Dip

SUN OR RAIN EXPECTED TODAY,
DARK TONIGHT

PSYCHICS PREDICT WORLD
DIDN'T END YESTERDAY

CAPITAL PUNISHMENT BILL CALLED
"DEATH ORIENTED"

CHICAGO CHECKING ON
ELDERLY IN HEAT

TIPS TO AVOID ALLIGATORS:
DON'T SWIM IN WATERS
INHABITED BY LARGE ALLIGATORS

Here's How You Can Lick
Doberman's Leg Sores

Coroner Reports on Woman's Death
While Riding Horse

CHEF THROWS HIS HEART INTO
HELPING FEED NEEDY

CINCINNATI DRY CLEANER
SENTENCED IN SUIT

High-Speed Train Could
Reach Valley in Five Years

FISH LURK IN STREAMS

**KEY WITNESS TAKES FIFTH
IN LIQUOR PROBE**

JAPANESE SCIENTISTS GROW
FROG EYES AND EARS

SUICIDE BOMBER STRIKES AGAIN

DONUT HOLE,
NUDE DANCING ON
COUNCIL TABLE

POLICE NAB STUDENT
WITH PAIR OF PLIERS

**MARIJUANA ISSUE SENT
TO JOINT COMMITTEE**

*Girl Kicked by Horse
Upgraded to Stable*

KILLER SENTENCED TO
DIE FOR SECOND TIME
IN TEN YEARS

COURT RULES BOXER SHORTS
ARE INDEED UNDERWEAR

**Nuns Forgive Break-in,
Assault Suspect**

ELIMINATION OF TREES
COULD SOLVE CITY'S
LEAF-BURNING PROBLEM

According to race car drivers, peanuts and the color green are unlucky.

WHAT IS SPAM?

Everybody's tried it and hardly anyone says they like it…but 30% of all American households have a can on hand. So how much do you know about SPAM? How much do you want to know? Not much, probably. Too bad—we're going to tell you about it anyway.

MAKING A SILK PURSE OUT OF A SOW'S EAR
It's a question as timeless as the pork-packing industry itself: Once you've removed all the choice meat from the carcass of a pig, what do you do with all the pig parts nobody wants?

That's the question the folks at the George A. Hormel Company faced in 1937. Their solution: Take the parts that nobody wants and make them into a loaf nobody wants. Jack Mingo describes the historic moment in his book *How the Cadillac Got Its Fins*:

> Seeing thousands of pounds of pork shoulders piling up in the Hormel coolers in 1937 gave one of the company's executives an idea: Why not chop the meat up, add some spices and meat from other parts of the pig, and form it into small, hamlike loaves? Put it in a can and fill the excess space with gelatin from the pig's leftover skin and bones—you could probably keep the meat edible for months without refrigeration. They tried it. It worked. Hormel's Spiced Ham quickly found a niche in the market. It was inexpensive, savory, and convenient, and it didn't need refrigeration.

PORCINE PLAGIARISM
But pig parts were piling up just as high at other pork packers, and as soon as they saw Hormel's solution they began selling their own pig loafs. Afraid of being lost in the sow shuffle, Hormel offered a $100 prize to anyone who could come up with a brand name that would make its pork product stand out from imitators. The winner: A brother of one of the Hormel employees, who suggested turning "*Sp*iced H*am*" into "SPAM."

PIGS AT WAR
Described by one writer as "a pink brick of meat encased in a gelatinous

coating," SPAM seems pretty gross to folks who aren't used to it (and even to plenty who are). It probably wouldn't have become popular if it hadn't been for World War II.

Because it was cheap, portable, and didn't need refrigeration, SPAM was an ideal product to send into battle with U.S. GIs It became such a common sight in mess halls (where it earned the nickname "the ham that didn't pass its physical") that many GIs swore they'd never eat the stuff again. Even General Dwight Eisenhower complained about too much SPAM in army messes.

THEIR SECRET SHAME

American G.I.s *said* they hated SPAM, but evidence suggests otherwise. Forced to eat canned pork over a period of several years, millions of soldiers developed a taste for it, and when they returned home they brought it with them. SPAM sales shot up in supermarkets after the war.

Laugh if you want (even Hormel calls it "the Rodney Dangerfield of luncheon meat—it don't get no respect"), but SPAM is still immensely popular: Americans consume 3.8 cans of it every second, or 122 million cans a year. That gives SPAM a 75% share of the canned-meat market.

SPAM FACTS

• More than five billion cans of SPAM have been sold around the world since the product was invented in 1937. "Nowhere," says Carolyn Wyman in her book *I'm a SPAM Fan*, "is SPAM more prized than in South Korea, where black-market SPAM regularly flows from U.S. military bases and locally produced knockoffs, such as Lospam, abound. In fact, young Korean men are just as likely to show up at the house of a woman they are courting with a nine-can gift pack of SPAM as wine or chocolate."

• SPAM may have helped defeat Hitler. Nikita Khrushchev, himself a war veteran, credited a U.S. Army shipment of SPAM with keeping Russian troops alive during World War II. "We had lost our most fertile, food-bearing lands," he wrote in Khruschev *Remembers*, "Without SPAM, we wouldn't have been able to feed our army."

• SPAM isn't as gross as legend would have you believe. There aren't any lips, eyes, or other pig nasties in it—just pork shoulder, ham, salt, sugar, and the preservative sodium nitrate.

PREDICTIONS
FOR THE YEAR 2000

*For a century, people speculated about what life would be
like way off in the future—in the year 2000. Now that
it's come and gone, we can see just how bizarre
some of those predictions were.*

THE DREAM HOUSE OF 2000
"[Using] wonderful new materials far stronger than steel, but lighter than aluminum...houses [in the year 2000] will be able to fly....The time may come when whole communities may migrate south in the winter, or move to new lands whenever they feel the need for a change of scenery."

—**Arthur C. Clarke,**
***Vogue*, 1966**

"Keeping house will be a breeze by the year 2000. Sonic cleaning devices and air-filtering systems will just about eliminate dusting, scrubbing and vacuuming. There may be vibrating floor grills by doors to clean shoes, and electrostatic filters will be installed in entrances to remove dust from clothes with ultrasonic waves."

—**Staff of the *Wall Street Journal*,**
***Here Comes Tomorrow!* (1966)**

"When [the housewife of 2000] cleans house she simply turns the hose on everything. Why not? Furniture—(upholstery included), rugs, draperies, unscratchable floors—all are made of synthetic fabric or waterproof plastic. After the water has run down a drain in the middle of the floor (later concealed by a rug of synthetic fiber), [she] turns on a blast of hot air and dries everything."

—**Waldemarr Kaempfert,**
***Popular Mechanics*, 1950**

The first TV news helicopter was used by KTLA Channel 5 in Los Angeles, in 1958.

COMMUTING

"[In 2000], commuters will go to the city, a hundred miles away, in huge aerial buses that hold 200 passengers. Hundreds of thousands more will make such journeys twice a day in their own helicopters."

—Waldemar Kaempfert,
Popular Mechanics, 1950

"[Commuters will] rent small four-seater capsules such as we find on a ski lift. These capsules will be linked together into little trains that come into the city. As the train goes out towards the perimeter of the city, the capsule will become an individual unit. One can then drive to wherever he may want to go."

—Ulrich Frantzen,
Prophecy for the Year 2000 (1967)

"A Seattle executive might board his reserved-seat air-cushion coach at 8:15 A.M. It would lift off the roadbed, whirl around an 'acceleration loop' and plunge into the main tube running from Seattle to San Diego. Little more than half an hour later, the car would peel off onto the 'deceleration loop' in downtown Los Angeles. By 9 a.m. the executive would be at his desk."

—Mitchell Gordon,
Here Comes Tomorrow! (1966)

THE WORLD OF WORK

"By 2000 the machines will be producing so much that everyone in the U.S. will, in effect, be independently wealthy. With government benefits, even nonworking families will have, by one estimate, an annual income of \$30,000–\$40,000 (in 1966 dollars). How to use leisure meaningfully will be a major problem."

—*Time,* February 25, 1966

"By the year 2000, people will work no more than four days a week and less than eight hours a day. With legal holidays and long vacations, this could result in an annual working period of 147 days [on] and 218 days off."

—*The New York Times,*
October 19, 1967

The rough, bumpy surface of certain types of glass (such as your shower door) is called *crizzle.*

THE *OTHER* SOPRANOS

*If you're a man, perhaps you need a little reminder
that your life is pretty good. Well, just be glad you
weren't born in Italy in the 1700s. (Now cross
your legs and read this story.)*

THE ULTIMATE SACRIFICE

Who were the *castrati*? They were boys who were castrated in an effort to fill the Catholic Church's need for singing talent. The practice appeared in Europe as early as the 1500s, but historians estimate that between 1720 and 1730 (the height of the craze), 4,000 boys between the ages of nine and twelve who showed even vague musical promise were castrated each year. By that time, the practice was limited almost entirely to Italy, but its seeds had been planted years earlier when the Church, having banned women from singing in choirs (religious officials thought women's voices were too seductive for the church) turned to young boys, whose sweet tones were preferable to the shrill soprano falsettists.

Castration prevented puberty, and without the male hormone *testosterone*, a castrato's vocal cords remained small and immature throughout his lifetime, which kept his voice high. And because his bone joints didn't harden, he also grew unusually tall and developed a large chest cavity, which gave him extra lung capacity. With rigorous training, the combined effect was tremendous vocal flexibility, a high range, pure tone, and extraordinary endurance. The very best could hold a note for up to a minute without taking a breath.

THE GOOD LIFE

Many poor parents willingly sacrificed their sons to this cause in the hope that they'd find fame and fortune. Cardinals, church fathers, choir directors, and composers signed up the castrati for shows and performances. The boys dedicated their youth to a rigorous musical and vocal training regime. But only a few went on to stardom. The rest made careers in cathedrals, church choirs, and the theater.

Many historians consider the castrati who did make it "the original

Christmas trees were introduced to the U.S. by Hessian troops during the Revolutionary War.

pop stars." Women swooned for them onstage and off; one young castrato was welcomed to the city of Florence by the town's wealthiest and most influential citizens. And though their voices were as high as a soprano's, they rarely played women's roles in operas—they were cast instead as the brave young heroes. (Male sopranos played the female roles until women were allowed on the stage in the late 18th century.)

BEST OF THE BEST

At their peak the castrati were employed by all of Europe's opera houses and church choirs, and the century's biggest composers, such as George Frideric Handel and Christoph Willibald von Gluck, wrote operas and vocal music specifically with castrato voices in mind. And the singers demanded enormous annual salaries: Records show some being paid as much as £1,500 (the equivalent of about $245,000 today).

The most famous castrati of them all: Carlo Maria Broschi (1705–82)—known on the stage as Farinelli. He was hired by the king of Spain, Ferdinand VI, for an undisclosed (but assumed to be very large) sum of money to serenade the king every night beneath his bedroom window. Ferdinand credited the youthful-sounding singer with single-handedly lifting his depressed spirits and helping him find the mental strength to attend to his affairs of state. Farinelli worked for the royal family for the next 25 years.

DOWNFALL OF THE DRAMA QUEENS

The reign of the castrati waned in Italy by the mid-1800s. The Catholic Church had long condemned the practice (and threatened to excommunicate participants), and, bowing to public opinion, the Italian government made castration illegal in 1870.

But historians say that it was largely the conceit of the castrati themselves that brought about their demise. Most of the performers became spoiled and egotistical; they often changed the scores to highlight their voices. Leading composers Rossini, Wagner, and Verdi all grew frustrated with their tampering and simply stopped writing for them. At the same time, the devoted but temperamental opera-loving public lost interest in the castrati, turning instead to the female soprano, whose timbre had become fashionable. Alessandro Moreschi, the world's last professional castrato and director of papal music for the Vatican, died in 1922. (Recordings of him are still widely available.)

Technically, you can drown without dying. "Drowning" refers to taking water into the lungs.

OL' JAY'S BRAINTEASERS

*Supersleuth and BRI stalwart Jay Newman has come up
with another batch of his simple yet compelling
puzzles. Answers are on page 284.*

1. BRIGHT THINKING

Uncle John gave Amy this challenge: "In the hallway there are three light switches," he said. "And in the library there are three lamps. Each switch corresponds to one of the lamps. You may enter the library only once—the lamps must be turned off when you do. At no time until you enter can you open the door to see into the library. Your job is to figure out which switch corresponds to which lamp."

"Easy," said Amy.

How did she do it?

2. MYSTERY JOB

Brian works at a place with thousands of products, some of them very expensive. People take his products without paying for them—as many as they can carry—and then just walk out. All that Brian requests of his customers is that they keep their mouths shut.

Where does Brian work?

3. SIDE TO SIDE

Uncle John stood on one side of a river; his dog, Porter, stood on the opposite side. "Come here, Porter!" said Uncle John. Although there were no boats or bridges, Porter crossed the river without getting wet. How?

4. SPECIAL NUMBER

Math usually stumps Thom, but when Uncle John showed him this number, he knew right away what makes it unique. Do you?

8,549,176,320

5. TIME PIECES

"Everyone knows that the sundial is the timepiece with the fewest moving parts," Jay told Julia. "Do you know what timepiece has the *most* moving parts?" She did. Do you?

6. WORD PLAY

"Weird Nate sent me this list of words," said Uncle John. "He says there's something unusual about them. But what?" Ol' Jay figured it out. Can you?

**revive, banana, grammar,
voodoo, assess, potato,
dresser, uneven**

In some parts of England, rum is used to wash a baby's head for good luck.

DEATH CUSTOMS

The treatment and disposal of a dead body is a sacred ritual
in every culture, but each one does it a little bit differently.

IN INDIA, custom calls for a body to be burned on a funeral pyre near a riverbank and a temple; the ashes are thrown into the river. Some adherents to Zoroastrianism place bodies atop towers; after the flesh is eaten by vultures, the bones are thrown into a pit at the center of the tower.

IN THE SOLOMON ISLANDS of the South Pacific, a body was traditionally placed on a reef where it would be eaten by sharks.

INUIT PEOPLE constructed small igloos around a corpse (like an "ice tomb"). The cold protected and preserved the body (unless a polar bear found its way in).

THE NAVAJO feared being haunted by the dead, so the body was burned and the deceased's house was destroyed. On the way back from the funeral, relatives took a long, circuitous route to confuse the spirit into not following them.

A VIKING FUNERAL: At sunset, the dead man was placed on a small boat. As it drifted out to sea, it was lit on fire. If the color of the sunset was the same as that of the fire, it meant the deceased was bound for Valhalla (Viking heaven).

MUSLIMS do not use caskets (unless required by law). The body is washed three times, wrapped in a white shroud, and placed directly in the ground with the head pointed toward Mecca.

THE IROQUOIS buried corpses in shallow graves, but exhumed them after a few months. Relatives then placed the bones in a community burial plot.

IN MODERN JAPAN, bodies are washed in a Buddhist temple, dressed (men in suits, women in kimonos), and put in a casket with a white kimono, sandals, and six coins, all for the spirit's crossing into the afterlife. After a funeral, the body is cremated. Relatives pick bones out of the ash, put them in an urn, and bury it.

WEIRD MEXICO

The odd, the weird, the strange, and the crazy—south of the border.

WORMING AROUND

One of the most lucrative products (and exports) in Mexico is mescal, a liquor similar to tequila, and most commonly packaged with a worm in every bottle. Legend says that eating the worm triggers powerful hallucinations. In 2005 the Mexican government considered banning worms from mescal. Because of the hallucinations? Nope. The worm is too high in fat, they claim. (The proposal failed; the worm remains.)

El LOCO

In 1993 Gerardo Palomero went on an animal-rights crusade, invading Mexico City slaughterhouses and yelling at meat cutters to treat animals more humanely. While workers respected his message, they found Palomero hard to take seriously because he was dressed in the brightly colored spandex costume of his professional wrestling character, "Super Animal."

THE OLDEST PROFESSION

In 2005 women's groups in Mexico City raised funds to build a home for elderly prostitutes. The city government even donated a building. But it's not a retirement home—it's a brothel. Hopeful "resident" Gloria Maria, 74, said, "I can't charge what the young ones do, but I still have two or three clients a day."

SHE KNOWS WHAT SHE'S TALKING ABOUT

In December 1998, newly elected Mexico City mayor Rosario Robles Berlanga was preparing to give an inauguration speech in which she planned to announce a crackdown on crime. Just hours before Berlanga was to speak, her top aide was mugged in a taxi. The thief stole the briefcase containing the mayor's tough-on-crime speech.

Most bullets travel faster than the speed of sound...you'd be hit before you heard the shot.

CRAZY EIGHTS

This page originally explained the meaning of life, but our dog eight it.

THE KIDS ON *EIGHT IS ENOUGH*

Mary
(Lani O'Grady)
Joanie
(Laurie Walters)
Nancy
(Dianne Kay)
Elizabeth
(Connie Needham)
Susan
(Susan Richardson)
David
(Grant Goodeve)
Tommy
(Willie Aames)
Nicholas
(Adam Rich)

DEFUNCT OLYMPIC SPORTS

Tug-of-war, Golf,
Rugby, Croquet, Polo,
Lacrosse, Waterskiing,
Power boating

THE IVY LEAGUE

Harvard, Brown, Yale,
Cornell, Dartmouth,
Princeton, Columbia.
University of
Pennsylvania

U.S. PRESIDENTS FROM VIRGINIA

George Washington
Thomas Jefferson
James Madison
John Tyler
James Monroe
Zachary Taylor
Woodrow Wilson
William H. Harrison

LONGEST RIVERS IN NORTH AMERICA

Missouri
(2,500 miles)
Mississippi
(2,330 miles)
Rio Grande
(1,885 miles)
Colorado
(1,450 miles)
Yukon
(1,265 miles)
Mackenzie
(1,250 miles)
Columbia
(1,152 miles)
Churchill
(1,000 miles)

GR8 MUSICIANS WHO NEVER WON A GRAMMY

The Doors
Diana Ross
Led Zeppelin
Jimi Hendrix
Chuck Berry
Patsy Cline
The Beach Boys
Sam Cooke

MOST POPULAR ICE CREAM FLAVORS

Vanilla
Chocolate
Butter pecan
Strawberry
Neapolitan
Chocolate chip
French vanilla
Cookies and cream

THE PARTS OF SPEECH

Noun, Verb,
Adjective, Adverb,
Pronoun, Preposition,
Conjunction,
Interjection

Hailey Jo Bauer was born on August 8, 2008 (8/8/08) at 8:08 a.m. She weighed 8 lb., 8 oz.

THE ♻ SYMBOL

How cool would it be to have this tidbit on your resume?
"1970: designed a symbol that millions of people
around the world see every day."

THINKING OUTSIDE THE BOX

The first Earth Day, celebrated by 20 million people in April 1970, not only led to the formation of the Environmental Protection Agency, it also launched an unusual contest. A Chicago-based cardboard-box company called Container Corporation of America (CCA), a pioneer in manufacturing recycled products, was looking for a simple design to print on all of their recycled boxes. Inspired by the success of Earth Day, Bill Lloyd, the graphic designer at CCA, decided to advertise the contest nationally at America's high schools and colleges. "As inheritors of the Earth, they should have their say," he said.

In Lloyd's grand vision, the winning design would be more than a symbol printed on CCA's boxes; it would serve as a symbol to promote the nationwide recycling movement. First prize: a $2,500 scholarship to the winner's choice of colleges. More than 500 entries came in from students all over the nation.

TWISTED

The winner: Gary Anderson, a 23-year-old graduate student at USC. He drew his inspiration from 19th-century mathematician August Ferdinand Möbius, who noted that a strip of paper twisted once and joined at the tips formed a continuous one-sided surface. Commonly referred to as a "Möbius strip," the geometric shape has since shown up in engineering (conveyor belts that last twice as long) and in popular art, such as M. C. Escher's fantasy-based woodcuts "Möbius Strip I" and "Möbius Strip II (Red Ants)."

It was that combination of practicality and art—along with the recycling-friendly notion that everything eventually returns to itself—that put Anderson's design at the top of the contest finalists. "I wanted to suggest both the dynamic—things are changing—and the static equilibrium, a permanent kind of thing," he later recalled. (After the design was chosen as the winner, Bill Lloyd altered it slightly; he darkened the edges and rotated the arrows 60 degrees so the interior of the symbol resembled a pine tree. In Anderson's version, one of the pointy ends faced down.)

CCA attempted to trademark the recycling symbol, but after they allowed other manufacturers to use it for a small fee, the trademark application was held for further review. Rather than press the matter, Lloyd and the CCA decided that a petty legal battle over such a positive message was a bad idea. So they dropped the case and allowed Anderson's creation to fall into the public domain. The three arrows have since come to represent the three components of conservation: Reuse, Reduce, Recycle.

SYMBOLOGY

Although anyone is free to use the recycling symbol as part of an advertising campaign (or as a graphic on a page…like in a *Bathroom Reader*), its use to advertise a commercial product's recycling properties is strictly regulated by the Federal Trade Commission's "Guides for the Use of Environmental Marketing Claims." There are several variations, but here are the symbol's two main classifications:

• **Recycled:** If the arrows are surrounded by a solid black circle, then the product is made from previously recycled material. A percentage displayed in the center of the symbol denotes how much of the product was made from recycled material. (If no percentage is denoted, it is 100% recycled.)

• **Recyclable:** If the arrows are not surrounded by a circle, then the product is recyclable, but only if the "regulations and/or ordinances of your local community provide for its collection."

STILL AT IT

Four decades later, Gary Anderson remains active in the green movement. After earning his Ph.D. in geography and environmental engineering from Johns Hopkins University in 1985, the architect-by-trade has spent the bulk of his career as an urban planner with a focus on controlled growth. When asked how it feels to have created one of the most popular symbols in the world, Anderson tries to downplay his accomplishment, but admits that it's "pretty neat."

In Old Testament times, the Mediterranean Sea was called the Great Sea.

SAY GOODNIGHT, GRACIE

With her husband George Burns, Gracie Allen was a star of vaudeville, radio, movies, and television…and one of the funniest women of the 20th century. Here are some of her one-liners and comedy bits.

George: Gracie, let me ask you something. Did the nurse ever happen to drop you on your head when you were a baby?
Gracie: Oh, no, we couldn't afford a nurse. My mother had to do it.

George: Gracie, what day is it today?
Gracie: Well, I don't know.
George: You can find out if you look at that paper on your desk.
Gracie: Oh, George, that doesn't help. It's yesterday's paper.

"They laughed at Joan of Arc, but she went right ahead and built it."

George: This letter feels kind of heavy, I'd better put another three-cent stamp on it.
Gracie: What for? That'll only make it heavier.

Gracie: The baby my father brought home was a little French baby. So my mother took up French.
George: Why?
Gracie: So she would be able to understand the baby.

Gracie: On my way in here, a man stopped me at the stage door and said, "Hiya, cutie, how about a bite tonight after the show?"
George: And you said…?
Gracie: I said, "I'll be busy after the show but I'm not doing anything now," so I bit him.

Harry Von Zell: Gracie, isn't that boiling water you're putting in the refrigerator?
Gracie: Yes, I'm freezing it.
Harry: You're freezing it?
Gracie: Mmm-hmm, and then whenever I want boiling water, all I have to do is defrost it.

"This recipe is certainly silly. It says to separate two eggs, but it doesn't say how far to separate them."

Gracie: Don't give up, Blanche. Women don't do that. Look at Betsy Ross, Martha Washington—they didn't give up. Look at Nina Jones.
Blanche Morton: Nina Jones?
Gracie: I've never heard of her either, because she gave up.

The Wright Brothers tested their first airplane in a wind tunnel before flying it.

A MUSICAL IS BORN

Some musicals are so famous that they are familiar even to people who never go to plays. Here are the origins of some favorites.

SHOWBOAT (1927)

Oscar Hammerstein, Jerome Kern, and producer Florenz Ziegfeld were sick of the light, upbeat musicals that had made them famous. They wanted to do something with adult themes like alcoholism, interracial relationships, and marital troubles—even if no one came to see it. But they needn't have worried. Their adaptation of Edna Ferber's novel about life on a riverboat opened in 1927 to rave reviews and sold out so often that Ziegfeld considered staging a second production in a nearby theater to handle the overflow. So far, the show has had five Broadway revivals, more than any other musical in history.

GREASE (1972)

This show got its start as a five-hour rock 'n' roll musical written by two amateur writers for a Chicago community theater. A producer bought the rights and had it trimmed by more than half before taking it to New York. Interesting sidelight: George Lucas's film *American Graffiti* is usually credited with starting the 1950s nostalgia boom, but *Grease* opened off-Broadway on February 14, 1972—a year before *American Graffiti* premiered. It ran for 3,388 performances, and the 1978 film version was the #1 box-office film of the year.

WEST SIDE STORY (1957)

In 1949 Arthur Laurents and Jerome Robbins came up with an idea to do a modern New York slums-set musical version of *Romeo and Juliet* about a forbidden love amongst racial gangs called *East Side Story*. The plot was about a teenage Catholic American boy who falls in love with a Jewish Israeli girl. By 1950, they shelved the idea after a Broadway play called *Abie's Irish Rose* had a similar plot. Laurents and Robbins decided to revisit it in 1954 after reading an article about street riots in Los Angeles. They changed the musical to *West Side Story* and the racial groups from Catholics and Jews to Polish and Puerto Rican immigrants.

Southern Florida is the only place where alligators and crocodiles both live.

They hired 25-year-old composer Stephen Sondheim to write the lyrics and convinced Leonard Bernstein to compose the songs. The result: a dark, violent musical that was deliberately aggressive to reflect the passions of the angry, adolescent teenage characters. It opened on Broadway in 1957. Audiences and critics were stunned by its originality: *West Side Story* was the first musical with a tragic ending (not changed from *Romeo and Juliet*), and the music was technically intricate with atonal melodies and music in minor keys. Nevertheless, it was a hit, running for 985 performances.

OKLAHOMA! (1943)

This blockbuster was based on a play called *Green Grow the Lilacs*, which had a limited run in the 1930–31 Broadway season. A woman who'd helped produce it thought it would make a good musical and approached composer Richard Rodgers with the idea. He was interested, but his partner Lorenz Hart—who'd become an unreliable alcoholic—wasn't. Rodgers's solution: he teamed up with lyricist Oscar Hammerstein…who hadn't had a hit in years and was considered a has-been. Together they wrote a musical called *Away We Go!* When it got to Broadway, it was renamed *Oklahoma!* and played to sellout crowds. It established Rodgers and Hammerstein as a team.

RENT (1996)

Playwright Billy Aronson came up with an idea in 1988 to create a musical based on Puccini's 1896 opera *La Bohème*, but about young artists dealing with AIDS in modern-day Greenwich Village (and not tuberculosis in 19th century Paris). He hired 29-year-old composer Jonathan Larson, who completely took over the project and conceived it as a rock musical. He named it *Rent*. The title refers to the characters' dingy lofts, but it also means "torn apart," fitting for a play in which nearly all the main characters are dying of AIDS. Larson spent three years writing *Rent* and another five developing it with a theater workshop. It debuted on Broadway in April 1996 and caused a sensation. Critics called it the most important musical of the last 20 years and it went on to win the Pulitzer Prize and the Tony for Best Musical. Tragically, Larson never got to see the fruit of his efforts: He died of a brain hemorrhage the night before *Rent* debuted.

PATENTLY ABSURD

*Here's proof that the urge to invent something—anything—
is more powerful than the urge to make sure the invention
is something that people will actually want to use.*

THE INVENTION: Musical Baby Diaper Alarm
WHAT IT DOES: Three women from France marketed this
alarm to mothers in 1985. It's a padded electronic napkin that goes
inside a baby's diaper. When it gets wet, it plays "When the Saints Go
Marching In."

THE INVENTION: The Thinking Cap
WHAT IT DOES: Improves artistic ability by mimicking the effects of
autism. The cap uses magnetic pulses to inhibit the front-temporal, or "left
brain" functions. This, say the two Australian scientists behind the project, creates better access to extraordinary "savant" abilities. They reported
improved drawing skills in 5 of 17 volunteers in a 2002 experiment.

THE INVENTION: Pantyhose x3
WHAT IT DOES: Patented in 1997, they are three-legged panty hose. No,
they're not for three-legged people, they're for women who know what it's
like to get a run in their stockings. Instead of having to carry spares, you just
rotate the legs. The extra leg is hidden in a pocket in the crotch; the damaged leg rolls up to take its place.

THE INVENTION: The Breath Alert
WHAT IT DOES: This pocket-sized electronic device detects and meas-
ures bad breath. You simply breathe into the sensor for three seconds,
then the LCD readout indicates—on a scale of 1 to 4—how safe (or
offensive) your breath is.

THE INVENTION: Weather-Reporting Toaster
WHAT IT DOES: Robin Southgate, an industrial design student at
Brunel University in London, hooked up his specially made toaster to the
Internet. Reading the day's meteorological stats, the toaster burns the
day's predictions into a slice of bread: a sun for sunny days, a cloud with

---

"I never knew an early-rising, hard-working, prudent man, careful of his earnings, and...

raindrops for rainy days, and so on. "It works best with white bread," says Southgate.

THE INVENTION: Separable Pants
WHAT IT DOES: You don't take them off, you take them apart. The zipper goes all the way around the crotch, from the front to the back. That way, you can mix and match the legs with other colors and styles, making your own artistic, customized pants.

THE INVENTION: Vibrating Toilet Seat
WHAT IT DOES: Thomas Bayard invented the seat in 1966. He believed that "buttocks stimulation" helps prevent constipation.

THE INVENTION: Automatic-Response Nuclear Deterrent System
WHAT IT DOES: A relic from the Cold War era, this idea was patented by British inventor Arthur Paul Pedrick in 1974. He claimed it would deter the United States, the USSR, and China from ever starting a nuclear war. How? Put three nuclear warheads on three orbiting satellites. If sensors on the satellites detected that nuclear missiles had been launched, they would automatically drop bombs: one each on Washington, Moscow, and Peking.

THE INVENTION: Lavakan
WHAT IT DOES: It's a washing machine...for cats and dogs. This industrial-strength machine soaps, rinses, and dries your pet in less than 30 minutes. One of the inventors, Andres Díaz, claims that the 5-by-5-foot, $20,000 machines can actually reduce pet stress. "One of the dogs actually fell asleep during the wash," he said. Cats weren't quite as happy about being Lavakanned. "But it's better than having a cat attach itself to your face, which is what can happen when you try to wash one by hand."

*   *   *

MILITARY INDUSTRIAL SIMPLEX
Andorra is a small country between Spain and France. In the 1970s it reported an annual defense budget of $4.90. The money was used to buy blanks to fire on national holidays.

...strictly honest, who complained of bad luck." —Henry Ward Beecher

SMUDGERS & SLEEPERS

A few bits of top-secret spy lingo.

• **Terminated with extreme prejudice:** When a spy agency executes one of its own spies for betraying the agency. (As opposed to just firing—terminating—them.)

• **Fumigating:** Searching a home or office to remove or neutralize any listening devices, or "bugs."

• **The British disease:** A reference to several members of the British upper classes who betrayed their country by becoming spies for the USSR after World War II.

• **Sleeper:** A dormant spy; sometimes an employee of a government agency who won't begin spying until he or she is promoted to a position with access to classified information.

• **Smudger:** A photographer.

• **Case of the measles:** An assassination made to look like a death from accidental or natural causes.

• **Shopworn goods:** Spy information so old or out of date that it's completely useless.

• **Jack in the box:** A fake torso, sometimes inflatable, that's put in a car to fool surveillance teams about how many people are riding in it.

• **Backstopping:** Creating fake background material (employers, phone numbers, etc.) to enhance the credibility of a spy's cover.

• **Spy dust:** Invisible powder the KGB sprinkled on door knobs, inside cars, etc., so that they could track diplomats and suspected spies as they moved around Moscow.

• **Cover:** The fake identity that a spy assumes to blend in with his or her surroundings.

• **Overhead:** Planes or satellites that spy from the sky.

• **Cannon:** Spies are sometimes paid large sums of cash. A cannon is a professional thief hired by an intelligence agency to steal the money back.

• **The Farm:** Camp Peary, the 10,000-acre facility near Williamsburg, Virginia, where CIA agents get their spy training.

If you're average, there's an 80% chance you have oatmeal in your kitchen.

THE AVRO ARROW, PART I

*If you're not from Canada, you've probably never heard of the
Avro Arrow. If you are from Canada, you may never forget
it. Here's the story of the fastest plane that never was.*

HERE WE GO AGAIN

When the Soviet Union tested its first nuclear weapon in 1949,
just four years after the end of World War II, it seemed like the
next world war, this time a *nuclear* war, was just around the corner. The
Soviets were also developing long-range bombers—could they be planning to attack Europe and North America?

Canada's response was to develop jet fighters that could intercept and
destroy any Soviet bombers before they could attack their targets. The
first such aircraft, a jet fighter named the Avro CF-100 Canuck, entered
service in 1953. By then, however, the Soviets were already working on a
new generation of jet-powered bombers, which would be able to fly higher and faster than any they'd built before. The Royal Canadian Air Force
felt they needed a *supersonic* jet fighter to counter the Soviet threat.

DO IT YOURSELF

Specifically, the RCAF wanted a plane that could fly at Mach 1.5 (one
and a half times the speed of sound), climb to 50,000 feet in less than five
minutes, and fly for 300 nautical miles without refueling. There were no
planes in existence or even on the drawing board that could meet those
specifications, so in December 1953 the Canadian government awarded
Avro Canada Ltd., the builder of the Canuck, a $27 million contract to
begin work on developing just such a plane. When completed, it would
be the fastest fighter plane ever built.

Building the Arrow, as the plane was called, was problematic from the
start. Avro's plan was to design the airframe and then buy the engines,
the weapons systems, and the other major components from outside sup-
pliers. But when its first and second choices for jet engines were both dis-
continued, Avro decided to design the engines in-house. The company
encountered similar problems with its choices of missile and firing systems. All these setbacks caused the cost of the Arrow to soar, but the

---

A 30-second commercial costs about as much to produce as a 30-minute sitcom.

RCAF remained committed to the project. While this was happening, the Soviet Union detonated its first hydrogen bomb and rolled out two different kinds of jet-powered bombers. There was no time to waste—in 1955 the Canadian government awarded Avro a $260 million contract to build five test planes, followed by 35 production aircraft.

TURNING POINT

Avro had never built a supersonic aircraft before, yet it managed to design and build one of the world's most sophisticated aircraft in just under four years. But the timing couldn't have been worse: On the very day that the first flyable Arrow was rolled out in front of 12,000 spectators in October 1957, the Soviet Union sent Sputnik, the world's first artificial Earth satellite, into space. If the Soviets were launching satellites, could nuclear-tipped missiles be very far behind? Defense planners wondered if combat aircraft would become obsolete in the missile age. Meanwhile, the Arrow's cost kept climbing.

Earlier that year, Canada and the United States had begun to coordinate their air defense with a $270 million system that called for using nuclear-tipped antiaircraft missiles, not fighter planes, to intercept enemy bombers. Could Canada afford both missiles *and* fighters?

In September 1958, the Canadian Department of Defense calculated that even after having spent $300 million on the Arrow, another $871 million was needed to finish the program. That was an astronomical amount of money in 1958, and Canada had far fewer taxpayers than the U.S. did to shoulder the cost. The government decided that rather than build 40 planes as planned, it would commit only to finishing the handful of airplanes currently under construction. The rest of the program was placed under review.

BLACK FRIDAY

Then, without warning, on the morning of February 20, 1959, the Canadian government announced it was scrapping the Arrow immediately. Avro employees learned of the decision 20 minutes later, and at 4:00 that afternoon it was announced over the P.A. system that all 14,525 of them were out of a job. Another 26,000 Canadians working for Avro subcontractors lost their jobs, too.

For Part II of the story, turn to page 262.

Crazy fact: About one in four U.S. adults will suffer from a diagnosable mental disorder this year.

DIE-HARD CHICKEN

*Readers have been asking us to tell this story for years. It was so
weird even we had a hard time swallowing it…but it's true.*

OFF WITH HIS HEAD!
On September 10, 1945, Mike the rooster was making his usual
rounds in the Olsen farmyard in Fruita, Colorado. He paused for
a moment to join the other Wyandotte chickens as they hunted and
pecked for grain outside the chicken coop. Mike didn't notice the dark
shadow that fell across his path. It was Lloyd Olsen.

Clara Olsen had sent her husband out to the chicken coop on a mission: catch the rooster and prepare him for dinner. Lloyd Olsen grabbed
Mike and put the rooster on the chopping block. Remembering that his
mother-in-law (who was coming to dinner) loved chicken necks, Lloyd
took special care to position the ax on Mike's neck so a generous portion
of neck would remain. He gave that rooster one strong whack and cut off
his head.

Mike the now-headless rooster ran around in circles, flapping his
wings. At this point, most chickens would have dropped dead. Instead,
Mike raced back to the coop, where he joined the rest of the chickens as
they hunted and pecked for food.

Lloyd Olsen was flabbergasted. He kept expecting the rooster to keel
over. It never happened. The next morning he checked again and found
the feathered fellow—minus his head—asleep in the henhouse with the
hens.

ONE FUNKY CHICKEN

Lloyd decided that if Mike was so determined to live, even without a
head, he would figure out a way to give him food and water, so Lloyd used
an eyedropper to drip food and water into Mike's gullet.

When Mike had managed to live an entire week, Lloyd and Clara took
their headless wonder to scientists at the University of Utah to determine
how it was possible for the bird to stay alive without a head. The scientists
determined that the ax had missed the jugular vein, and a clot had kept
Mike from bleeding to death. Although his head was gone, his brainstem

---

Rabbits are more closely related to horses than to rodents.

and one ear were left on his body. Since a chicken's reflex actions are controlled by the brain stem, Mike's body was able to keep on ticking.

MIRACLE MIKE

Sensing that Mike had the possibility of becoming a real cash cow (or chicken), the Olsens hired a manager and took him on a national tour. Audiences in New York, Los Angeles, Atlantic City, and San Diego paid a quarter each to see "Miracle Mike." *Time* and *Life* magazines ran feature articles on the amazing fowl. Mike even made it into *Guinness World Records*. This "Wonder Chicken" was so valuable, he was insured for $10,000.

For 18 months, Mike the headless chicken was a celebrity. Then one night in a motel in Arizona, he started choking on some food. Lloyd tried to save him, but he couldn't find the syringe he had often used to clear Mike's throat. Moments later Mike was dead—this time for real.

Those who knew Mike, which included many of the residents of Fruita, remembered him as a "robust chicken, and a fine specimen, except for not having a head." One recalled that Mike seemed "as happy as any other chicken."

GONE BUT NOT FORGOTTEN

Mike's been dead for almost 70 years, but his spirit lives on in Fruita. In 1999 the Chamber of Commerce was looking for something more interesting than "pioneers" as the theme for Colorado Heritage Week, when someone suggested Mike. Now, every third weekend in May, folks in this town of 6,500 gather to celebrate the remarkable rooster at the "Mike the Headless Chicken Festival."

The two-day-long celebration features the 5K Run Like a Chicken race, egg tosses, Pin the Head on the Chicken, a Cluck Off, Rubber Chicken Juggling, and the Chicken Dance. Chicken Bingo is played with chicken droppings on a grid and there is a Famous Fowl Pet Parade, for which owners dress their dogs, cats, and horses like chickens. Of course, great quantities of chicken—fried or barbecued—are enjoyed by all.

In 2000 Mike was memorialized in a statue made out of rakes, axes, and farm implements by artist Lyle Nichols, who said, "I made him proud-looking and cocky." And he gave the chamber a discount on the sculpture…because it didn't have a head.

The average married Englishwoman living in the 1600s gave birth to 13 children.

WHEN YOUR HUSBAND GETS HOME...

*Here's a bit of advice taken directly from a 1950s Home Economics textbook.
It was sent in by a reader, along with the comment: "Times have changed!"
No kidding. Believe it or not, this was part of a course intended
to prepare high school girls for married life.*

Have dinner ready: "Plan ahead, even the night before, to have a delicious meal—on time. This is a way of letting him know that you have been thinking about him and are concerned about his needs. Most men are hungry when they come home and the prospects of a good meal are part of the warm welcome needed."

Prepare yourself: "Take 15 minutes to rest so you will be refreshed when he arrives. Touch up your makeup, put a ribbon in your hair and be fresh-looking. He has just been with a lot of work-weary people. Be a little gay and a little more interesting. His boring day may need a lift."

Clear away the clutter: "Make one last trip through the main part of the house just before your husband arrives, gathering up school books, toys, paper, etc. Then run a dust cloth over the tables. Your husband will feel he has reached a haven of rest and order, and it will give you a lift, too."

Prepare the children: "Take a few minutes to wash the children's hands and faces (if they are small) comb their hair, and if necessary, change their clothes. They are little treasures and he would like to see them playing the part."

Minimize all noise: "At the time of his arrival, eliminate all noise of washer, dryer, dishwasher or vacuum. Try to encourage the children to be quiet. Be happy to see him: Greet him with a warm smile and be glad to see him."

Some don'ts: "Don't greet him with problems or complaints. Don't com-

---

The point where your nose meets your forehead is called the *nasion*.

plain if he's late for dinner. Count this as minor compared with what he might have gone through that day."

Make him comfortable: "Have him lean back in a comfortable chair or suggest he lie down in the bedroom. Have a cool or warm drink ready for him. Arrange his pillow and offer to take off his shoes. Speak in a low, soft, soothing and pleasant voice. Allow him to relax—unwind."

Listen to him: "You may have a dozen things to tell him, but the moment of his arrival is not the time. Let him talk first."

Make the evening his: "Never complain if he does not take you out to dinner or to other places of entertainment. Instead, try to understand his world of strain and pressure, his need to be home and relax."

*　　　*　　　*

THE BEST & WORST TIPPERS

According to a poll in *Bartender* magazine:

• Lawyers and doctors are the worst tippers. Normally, doctors are the #1 tightwads. In rougher times, it's lawyers. The reason: "There are more lawyers and less work."

• The biggest tippers are bartenders and "service personnel."

• As smoking gets more restricted, cigar and cigarette smokers—who are, in some states, allowed to smoke in the bar instead but not at restaurant tables—are becoming notably good tippers.

• Other leading tightwads: teachers, software engineers, musicians, professional athletes, and pipe smokers.

• Other top tippers: hairstylists, mobsters, tavern owners, regular customers.

• Vodka drinkers are good tippers. People who order drinks topped with umbrellas are bad tippers.

• Democrats tip better than Republicans.

No plant on Earth has an absolutely black blossom.

JESUS IN SHINGO

An unusual legend, and a fascinating place to visit.

THE ROYAL TOMB

If you're visiting the tiny village of Shingo in the far north of Honshu island in Japan, you can take a path up into the woods until you come to a dirt burial mound. Rising above it is a large wooden cross. This, says local legend, is the final resting place of Jesus Christ.

The legend claims that Jesus' brother took his place on the cross, allowing Jesus to escape from Israel. He made his way across Siberia, then traveled into what is now Alaska, and finally ended up in Japan. There, the legend continues, he married a Japanese woman named Miyuko, had three daughters, and lived to the ripe old age of 106. Many people in Shingo believe the legend is true—and the "Christ Museum" next to the tomb claims it has the proof.

The story seems to have started somewhere around 1935, when a priest in the area discovered what he claimed were ancient scrolls. The 1,900-year-old documents were Christ's last will and testament, he said, indicating that Shingo is the location of Jesus' grave. According to a local museum, the original scrolls were destroyed in World War II and all that exist now are copies. But other evidence supposedly supports the claim:

• Although the tomb was never opened, rods thrust into the dirt around it confirm it is lined by stones, an honor only bestowed on people of great importance.

• For hundreds of years it has been a local tradition to draw charcoal crosses onto babies' foreheads, a practice found nowhere else in Japan.

• Many ancient kimonos from Shingo have been found decorated with what appears to be a Star of David.

No serious historian believes the legend, but more than 40,000 people make the trip to the "Tomb of Christ" every year, and many visit with the garlic farmer who owns the land on which the tomb sits—a man who is reputed to be a direct descendant of Jesus. He, like a surprising number of other people in the area, has blue eyes.

Pop Quiz: What was the real name of Larry from *The Three Stooges*? A: Louis Feinberg.

OSCAR'S BLOOPERS

Some goofs from Best Picture winners.

Movie: *The English Patient* (1996)
Scene: During a flashback, Almásy (Ralph Fiennes) writes a note that ends with "December 22, 1938."
Blooper: When Hana (Juliette Binoche) reads the note in the present, it ends with "December 22." What happened to the year?

Movie: *Rain Man* (1988)
Scene: Raymond (Dustin Hoffman) is spouting off air-travel statistics, stating that QANTAS is the only major airline to have never had a fatal crash.
Blooper: Between 1927 and 1951, QANTAS had eight fatal crashes. (QANTAS, by the way, was the only major airline that didn't delete this scene for its in-flight movie version.)

Movie: *The Godfather, Part II* (1974)
Scene: Toward the end of the movie, the characters are talking about Pearl Harbor and how it happened on "Pop's birthday."
Blooper: The Japanese attacked Pearl Harbor on December 7. According to the tombstone from the end of *The Godfather*, Pop's birthday is April 29.

Movie: *Gladiator* (2000)
Scene: During the Battle of Carthage in the Colosseum, one of the chariots flips over.
Blooper: Look closely when the dust settles and you can see that this ancient Roman chariot was equipped with a gas tank.

Movie: *The Lord of the Rings: The Return of the King* (2003)
Scene: After defeating the big spider, Sam (Sean Astin) rushes over to Frodo (Elijah Wood), who has been paralyzed.
Blooper: When Frodo is lying on the ground unconscious, his eyes are

Some asteroids have other asteroids orbiting them.

open. When Sam picks him up, Frodo's eyes are closed. When he's on Sam's lap, his eyes are open again.

Movie: *Amadeus* (1984)
Scene: Mozart (Tom Hulce) is watching a parody of his operas.
Blooper: When the last little person pops through the paper backdrop with a toy horse, a member of the film crew—wearing blue jeans—can be seen walking backstage.

Movie: *Ben-Hur* (1959)
Scene: The famous chariot race.
Blooper: Do the math: Nine chariots start the race, six of them crash, but somehow four finish.

Movie: *Schindler's List* (1993)
Scene: Oskar (Liam Neeson) is in a car with Jewish investors.
Blooper: Look at the passenger window and you can see the reflection of a movie camera and its operator. (Though it's not entirely clear, the reflection may belong to director Steven Spielberg, wearing his famous "Class of '61" hat.)

Movie: *Rocky* (1976)
Scene: While Rocky (Sylvester Stallone) is training, he does several one-arm push-ups.
Blooper: A careful look reveals that Stallone did only one push-up—the shot was then looped to make it look like he did a lot.

Movie: *Casablanca* (1943)
Scene: Rick (Humphrey Bogart) is driving through France.
Blooper: He's driving on the left; the French drive on the right.

Movie: *Million Dollar Baby* (2004)
Scene: Maggie (Hilary Swank) is driving to the new home she just bought for her mother.
Blooper: The house is supposed to be in Missouri, so why are there palm trees on the side of the road?

There are more pets per person in France than in any other country in the world.

NATURE'S REVENGE

What happens when we start messing around with nature, trying to make living conditions better? Sometimes it works…and sometimes nature gets even. Here are a few instances when people intentionally introduced animals or plants into a new environment…and regretted it.

Import: Kudzu, a fast-growing Japanese vine

Background: Originally brought into the southern U.S. in 1876 for use as shade. People noticed livestock ate the vine and that kudzu helped restore nitrogen to the soil. It seemed like a perfect plant to cultivate. So in the 1930s, the U.S. government helped farmers plant kudzu all over the South.

Nature's Revenge: By the 1950s, it was out of control, blanketing farmers' fields, buildings, utility poles and—often fatally—trees. Today, utility companies spend millions of dollars annually spraying herbicides on poles and towers to keep them kudzu-free. And instead of helping plant kudzu, the government now gives advice on how to get rid of it.

Import: The mongoose

Background: The small Asian mammals famous for killing cobras were brought to Hawaii by sugar planters in 1893. Reason: They thought the mongooses would help control the rat population.

Nature's Revenge: The planters overlooked one little detail: The mongoose is active in the daytime while the rat is nocturnal. "In Hawaii today," says one source, "mongooses are considered pests nearly as bad as rats."

Import: The starling, an English bird

Background: In 1890 a philanthropist named Eugene Schieffelin decided to bring every type of bird mentioned in Shakespeare's plays to New York City's Central Park. He brought in hundreds of pairs of birds from England. Unfortunately, most (like skylarks and thrushes) didn't make it. Determined to succeed with at least one species, Schieffelin shipped 40 pairs of starlings to Central Park and let them loose just before the mating season on March 6, 1890.

The Mason-Dixon line had nothing to do with slavery. It was surveyed in 1767…

Nature's Revenge: There are now more than 50 million starlings in the U.S. alone—all descendants from Schieffelin's flock—and they have become a major health hazard. They fly in swarms, littering roads and highways with their droppings, which carry disease-bearing bacteria that are often transmitted to animals and people. They've also become pests to farmers, screeching unbearably and destroying wheat and cornfields.

Import: The gypsy moth

Background: In 1869 Leopold Trouvelot, a French entomologist, imported some gypsy moth caterpillars to Massachusetts. It was part of a get-rich-quick scheme: He figured that since the caterpillars thrive on oak tree leaves, which are plentiful there, he could crossbreed them with silkworm moths, and create a self-sustaining, silk-producing caterpillar. He'd make a fortune!

Unfortunately, the crossbreeding didn't work. Then one day, a strong wind knocked over a cage filled with the gypsy moth caterpillars. They escaped through an open window and survived.

Nature's Revenge: At first, the moths spread slowly. But by 1950, gypsy moths could be found in every New England state and in eastern New York. They've since spread to Virginia and Maryland—and beyond. Populations have become established as far away as Minnesota and California, probably due to eggs unknowingly transported by cars driven from the Northeast to those regions. They're not a major threat, but can cause severe problems: In 1981, for example, they were reported to have stripped leaves from 13 million trees.

Import: Dog fennel

Background: At the turn of the 19th century, Johnny Appleseed wandered around the Ohio territory, planting apples wherever he went. It's not widely known that he also he sowed a plant called dog fennel, which was believed to be a fever-reducing medicine.

Nature's Revenge: It's not only not medicine, it's bad medicine; farmers are sick of it. "The foul-smelling weed," says the *People's Almanac*, "spread from barnyard to pasture, sometimes growing as high as fifteen feet. Today, exasperated midwestern farmers still cannot rid their fields of the plant they half-humorously call 'Johnnyweed.'"

...to settle a border dispute between British colonies.

YOU'RE MY INSPIRATION

More stories about the inspirations behind cultural milestones.

POPEYE

Was there a real Popeye? Apparently so. E. C. Segar's character was based on a beady-eyed, pipe-smoking, wiry old barroom brawler named Frank "Rocky" Feigle—a legend in Segar's hometown of Chester, Illinois, around 1915. Feigle was reputed never to have lost a fight. But he was no sailor; he earned his drinking money by sweeping out the local saloon.

Note: There was a real Olive Oyl, too: Dora Paskel, a shopkeeper in Chester. She was tall and skinny, wore her hair in a bun, and even wore tall, button-up shoes.

ROCKY

In March 1975, Chuck Wepner fought Muhammad Ali for the heavyweight boxing title. Wepner, a second-rate fighter from Bayonne, New Jersey, was considered a joke; Ali didn't even bother training full-time for the match. But to everyone's surprise, Wepner lasted 15 rounds with the champ, and even knocked him down. Sly Stallone saw the fight on TV, and was inspired to write his Oscar-winning screenplay about Rocky Balboa.

STAGE NAMES

• Nicolas Coppola always admired a comic book character named "Luke Cage, Power Man." So he changed his name to Nicolas Cage.

• Roy Scherer got his stage name by combining two geographical spots: the Rock of Gibraltar and the Hudson River: Rock Hudson.

THE SHINING

Inspired by John Lennon...or at least the term was. Stephen King came up with the idea of the "shining" as a description of psychic power after hearing Lennon's tune "Instant Karma." King recalls: "The refrain went, 'We all shine on.' I really liked that, and used it. The book's name was originally *The Shine*, but somebody said, 'You can't use that because it's a pejorative word for Black'...so it became *The Shining*."

In 1920 *Billboard* became the 1st national magazine to give regular coverage to black musicians.

FART FACTS

You won't find trivia like this in any ordinary book.

THE NAME

The word *fart* comes from the Old English term *foertan*, to explode. *Foertan* is also the origin of the word *petard*, an early type of bomb. *Petard*, in turn, is the origin of a more obscure term for fart—*ped*, or *pet*, which was once used by military men. (In Shakespeare's *Henry IV*, there's a character whose name means fart—Peto.)

WHY DO YOU FART?

Flatulence has many causes—for example, swallowing air as you eat and lactose intolerance. (Lactose is a sugar molecule in milk, and many people lack the enzyme needed to digest it.) But the most common cause is food that ferments in the gastrointestinal tract.

• A simple explanation: The fats, proteins, and carbohydrates you eat become a "gastric soup" in your stomach. This soup then passes into the small intestine, where much of it is absorbed through the intestinal walls into the bloodstream to feed the body.

• But the small intestine can't absorb everything, especially complex carbohydrates. Some complex carbohydrates—the ones made up of several sugar molecules (beans, some milk products, fiber) can't be broken down. So they're simply passed along to the colon, where bacteria living in your intestine feed off the fermenting brew. If that sounds gross, try this: The bacteria then excrete gases into your colon. Farting is how your colon rids itself of the pressure the gas creates.

FRUIT OF THE VINE

So why not just quit eating complex carbohydrates?

• First, complex carbohydrates—which include fruit, vegetables, and whole grains—are crucial for a healthy diet. "Put it this way," explains Jeff Rank, an associate professor of gastroenterology at the University of Minnesota. "Cabbage and beans are bad for gas, but they are good for you."

• Second, they're not the culprits when it comes to the least desirable aspect of farting: smell.

• Farts are about 99% odorless gases—hydrogen, nitrogen, carbon dioxide, oxygen, and methane (it's the methane that makes farts flammable). So why the odor? Blame it on those millions of bacteria living in your colon. Their waste gases usually contain sulfur molecules—which smell like rotten eggs. This is the remaining 1% that clears rooms in a hurry.

AM I NORMAL?

• Johnson & Johnson, which produces drugs for gas and indigestion, once conducted a survey and found that almost one-third of Americans believe they have a flatulence problem.

• However, according to Terry Bolin and Rosemary Stanton, authors of *Wind Breaks: Coming to Terms with Flatulence*, doctors say most flatulence is healthy. What's unhealthy is worrying about it so much.

NOTABLE FARTERS

• Le Petomane, a 19th-century music hall performer, had the singular ability to control his farts. He could play tunes, as well as imitate animal and machinery sounds rectally. Le Petomane's popularity briefly rivaled that of Sarah Bernhardt.

• A computer factory in England, built on the site of a 19th-century chapel, is reportedly inhabited by a farting ghost. Workers think it might be the embarrassed spirit of a girl who farted while singing in church. "On several occasions," said an employee, "there has been a faint girlish voice singing faint hymns, followed by a loud raspberry sound and then a deathly hush."

• Josef Stalin was afraid of farting in public. He kept glasses and a water pitcher on his desk so that if he felt a wind coming on, he could mask the sound by clinking the glasses while pouring water.

• Martin Luther believed, "On the basis of personal experience, farts could scare off Satan himself."

*　　　*　　　*

"Why doesn't Tarzan have a beard?" —**George Carlin**

The average car has about 3,000 feet of electrical wiring.

UNIQUELY PRESIDENTIAL

You may know that Richard Nixon was the only U.S. president to resign or that Grover Cleveland was the only president to serve two non-consecutive terms. But there are many more presidential anomalies than that.

The president: Jimmy Carter
Notable achievement: Only president to write a children's book. Carter wrote *The Little Baby Snoogle-Fleejer*, which was illustrated by his daughter Amy, and published in 1995. The plot: A crippled boy named Jeremy meets a repulsive sea monster who turns out to be quite friendly.

The president: Abraham Lincoln
Notable achievement: Only president to earn a patent. In 1849 Lincoln invented a type of buoy. Lincoln is also the only U.S. president to have worked as a bartender.

The president: Theodore Roosevelt
Notable achievement: Only president to be blind in one eye. Roosevelt took a hard punch to his left eye in a boxing match. It detached the retina, leaving Roosevelt blind in his left eye for the rest of his life. The boxing match occurred in 1908, while Roosevelt was president.

The president: Richard Nixon
Notable achievement: Only president to have been a carny. When he was a teenager, Richard Nixon was a midway barker at the Slippery Gulch Rodeo in Arizona.

The president: Gerald Ford
Notable achievement: Only president to survive two assassination attempts in the same month. In September 1975, former Charles Manson follower Lynette "Squeaky" Fromme tried to shoot Ford when he reached out to shake her hand in a public meet-and-greet. She pulled the trigger, but the gun's chamber was empty. Just three weeks later another woman, Sara Jane Moore, fired on Ford in a similar crowd situation, but a bystander knocked her arm away.

In Seattle, Washington, a dog must pay full bus fare if it weighs more than 25 pounds.

JAWS, JR.

*They're just little fishes, but piranhas can turn you into a
skeleton in a few seconds flat. Nice thought, huh?*

THE NAME. The word "piranha" comes from the Tupi language of South America and means "toothed fish." In some local dialects of the Amazon region, the name for common household scissors is also "piranha."

NOT A SHARK. A piranha only has one row of upper and lower teeth, not several, as many sharks do. But its teeth are sharper than almost any shark teeth. When the piranha snaps them together, says one expert, "the points in the upper row fit into the notches of the lower row, and the power of the jaw muscles is such that there is scarcely any living substance save the hardest ironwood that will not be clipped off." Natives often use the teeth as cutting blades.

FISHING TIP. Piranhas are capable of biting through a fishing net. If caught on a hook, they usually die from the injury. So a good way to "bring them in alive" is to throw a chunk of meat in the water. The fish will bite into it so hard that you can lift bunches of them out of the water before they let go.

BEHAVIOR. Some things that attract piranhas are blood and splashing. Experts disagree over whether the fish will attack a calm, uninjured person, but piranhas are definitely territorial. That's why Amazon fishermen know that if they catch a piranha, they'd better try another spot if they expect to catch anything else.

DEADLY DIET. Surprisingly, only a few species of piranha are meat-eaters; many eat fruits and other plants that fall into the river. But those meat-eaters can do exactly what you think they can. In the 19th century, for example, Teddy Roosevelt wrote about his adventures along the Amazon. He claimed to have seen piranhas quickly make a skeleton of a man who had fallen off his horse and into the river.

THE FIRST…

A bunch of musical firsts.

…pop album with printed lyrics: The Beatles' *Sgt. Pepper's Lonely Hearts Club Band*, 1967.

…singer to refuse a Grammy: Sinéad O'Connor won Best Alternative Album prize in 1990 for *I Do Not Want What I Haven't Got*. She declined the award to protest the Grammys' "extreme commercialism."

…foreign-language #1 pop song: "Volare," by Italian singer Domenico Modugno. It went to the top of the Billboard charts in 1958.

…double album: Benny Goodman's *Live at Carnegie Hall*, 1938. First rock double album: Bob Dylan's 1966 *Blonde on Blonde*.

…American pop band to tour the Soviet Union: the Nitty Gritty Dirt Band, in 1977.

…musical guest on *Saturday Night Live*: Billy Preston. He beat the debut show's other guest, Janis Ian, by about 20 minutes.

…recorded yelling of "Free Bird!" at a concert: 1976, at the Fox Theater in Atlanta. The show was being taped for Lynyrd Skynyrd's live album, *One More From the Road*.

…music book published in the United States: *Seven Songs for Harpsichord or Forte-Piano*, by Francis Hopkinson, in 1788.

…first African-American recording artists: Pianist Willie "The Lion" Smith of Newark, New Jersey, who played on the 1920 song "Crazy Blues" by Mamie Smith's Jazz Hounds.

…British musician with a #1 single in the United States: It's not the Beatles—it's Mr. Acker Bilk, whose clarinet instrumental "Stranger on the Shore" topped the American charts in 1962.

…band to rock Antarctica: Nunatuk, a band made up of resident British researchers, who performed in Antarctica as part of a series of environmental awareness concerts in 2007.

…album released on CD: ABBA's 1981 album *The Visitors*.

Dolly Parton's first single: "Puppy Love" (1960). She was 13.

CASTLE IN THE DESERT

*How a cowboy named "Death Valley Scotty" conned his way into
fame, fortune…and a big house that didn't belong to him.*

HOT PROPERTY

In a desolate canyon in Death Valley National Park sits a 33,000-square-foot Spanish-Mediterranean castle with 14 bathrooms, 14 fireplaces, 4 kitchens, a solar water heating plant, a hydroelectric generating system, a gas station, stables for dozens of horses, and a 56-foot clock tower complete with 25 chimes. The main house has a rock wall fountain, is decorated with European antiques, hand-painted tiles, and hand-crafted ironwork, and features a theater organ with 1,121 pipes and a 250-foot unfinished swimming pool. The castle sits on 1,500 acres and is surrounded by a 45-mile-long fence. It cost $2 million to build in the 1920s.

Walter Scott lived there in high style for decades. He claimed the castle as his own and said that it sat atop a gold mine. But the truth was he didn't have a cent.

A DRIFTING GRIFTER

Walter Scott was born in Kentucky in 1872. He left home at 11 to become a cowboy in Nevada and, at 13, got a job working as a water boy for the Harmony Borax Works in Death Valley. By the time he was 18, he was such a skilled rider that Buffalo Bill Cody offered Scott a role in his Wild West Show. For 12 years Scott traveled and performed throughout the United States and Europe. In 1901 he arrived in New York City, where he was supposed to ride into town with the other performers. But he went out drinking instead. Buffalo Bill saw Scott standing drunk (and cheering) along the parade route and fired him on the spot.

He was out of work but not out of ideas. Scott had (unsuccessfully) worked a gold mine for one winter in Colorado, so, well versed in the art of publicity from his days with the Wild West Show, he invented a tale about a gold mine in Death Valley, one of the most remote areas of the country and the perfect place to hide a fictitious gold mine. Scott lured several New York investors with tales of the lucrative mine and convinced them to give him money to excavate the ore in exchange for a percentage of the profits.

A PRO AT CONS

There was no mine, but Scott took the money anyway and headed to California. Once there, he lived it up in the towns around Death Valley and in Los Angeles. He stayed in expensive hotels and tipped in large bills.

Even though none of the money went to mining equipment, he continued spinning his tale and investors continued to give him money. When his backers asked why they hadn't seen any ore or profits from the mine, Scott put them off, saying there had been a mule stampede, a flash flood, or a run-in with bandits.

ENTER ALBERT JOHNSON

One investor, though, started to distrust Scott's excuses. Born in 1872, Albert Johnson had made a fortune in zinc mining but also made several bad investments. In 1906 Johnson invested in Scott's gold mine.

Three years passed before Johnson began to doubt Scott's tales, but in 1909, he traveled to California to see for himself the Death Valley Mine whose riches never seemed to materialize. Scott agreed to take Johnson to the mine, believing the trip would prove too difficult for the Easterner and that Johnson would back out before they ever reached the "site." But Johnson loved the desert. Ten years earlier, he'd been injured in a train crash, and he still suffered the ill effects of a broken back. The dry climate and the adventure in Death Valley made him feel better than he had in years.

It didn't take long for Johnson to realize there was no mine, but he had such a good time in Death Valley that he didn't care that he'd been duped. He kept returning to the area and eventually bought 1,500 acres in Grapevine Canyon. When his wife, Bessie, began accompanying him on his trips and grew tired of the tents and rude shack that served as accommodations, Johnson decided to build a permanent home.

HOME ON THE RANGE

In 1925 Albert Johnson approached Frank Lloyd Wright to design a house, to be called the "Death Valley Ranch." But Wright's design wasn't grand enough for Johnson, so he hired a second architect, C. Alexander MacNeiledge. Over the next five years, the castle started to take shape.

The word *eclair* means "lightning" in French.

And because the home was so elaborate, its construction revived the rumors of Scott's gold strike, rumors that neither Scott nor Johnson did anything to quiet. In fact, Scott (who by this time had earned the nickname "Death Valley Scotty") bragged to reporters about the castle and said it belonged to him. Johnson perpetuated the lie and would say only that he was "Scotty's banker." So Death Valley Ranch became known as "Scotty's Castle."

In 1931 construction on the castle stopped. The 1929 stock market crash had cost Johnson most of his fortune, and he could no longer afford to keep building. The castle stood unfinished.

DEATH (VALLEY) AND TAXES

In the early 1930s, the federal government began surveying Death Valley in preparation for making it a national monument and discovered that Albert Johnson didn't actually own the land on which he'd built the castle—the boundary for Johnson's land was one mile away. It took four years for Johnson to get permission from the government, but in 1937, he bought the land he thought he already owned for $1.25 an acre.

Death Valley officially became a national monument in 1933 and the tourists began pouring in. Johnson, still needing money, opened up the castle for guided tours and paying guests. He and his wife moved to a house in Los Angeles, but Scotty remained at the castle, where he entertained visitors with jokes and stories of the Wild West.

Scotty also continued to brag about the gold mine, which brought some unwelcome attention in the early 1940s. The Internal Revenue Service wanted to know why Scotty had never paid any income taxes on this supposedly fabulous wealth. Finally, Albert Johnson had to admit that he owned the castle and Scott never had a gold mine in Death Valley.

END OF AN ERA

Albert Johnson died in 1948, but Death Valley Scotty lived at the ranch until his death in 1954. After that, a charitable organization called the Gospel Foundation inherited the castle and maintained it. In 1970 the National Park Service bought the site for $850,000.

Today, 200,000 people visit the ranch annually. Park officials wear authentic 1930s garb and regale tourists with the tale of Death Valley Scotty and the legend he built on a lie.

Nails the landing! One in 25 babies is born feet first.

TOY FADS

The Federal Communications Commission used to have a rule banning
children's TV shows based on existing commercial characters or toys.
The reasoning was that kids are impressionable, and such TV shows
would just be long ads. But in 1982, the FCC repealed the ruling.
Result: TV shows designed to sell toys...lots of toys.

TEENAGE MUTANT NINJA TURTLES

Description: Radioactive ooze turns four pet turtles into human-size crime-fighting, pizza-eating, jive-talking teens named Leonardo, Raphael, Michelangelo, and Donatello.

A Fad Is Born! In 1984 cartoonists Peter Laird and Kevin Eastman self-published *Teenage Mutant Ninja Turtles*, a violent but darkly funny comic book. They printed 50,000 copies, all of which sold out in a few weeks. After that, the comic was published regularly for two years but garnered little interest beyond comic book fans. In 1986 advertising executive Mark Freedman discovered the comic and bought the rights from Laird and Eastman, figuring the Turtles could be a cultural phenomenon if they were marketed to kids, rather than older comic-book collectors. A newer, more kid-friendly comic was introduced, along with a TV cartoon series and lots and lots of Ninja Turtle toys. Freedman was right: In 1989, $250 million worth of toys were sold; in 1990, a live-action movie earned $140 million; and in 1991, a Burger King promotion sold 200,000 Turtle videos per week. But all fads are destined to die. Sales plummeted in 1992, and the cartoon was cancelled. A grittier, back-to-basics comic book was released, but it bombed. New cartoons and new toys were released in 2003, but they flopped too. A big failure? Hardly. Since 1984 the Ninja Turtles have generated $6 billion in revenue.

TRANSFORMERS

Description: Giant robots that can "transform" into vehicles crash land on Earth from outer space, and wage battle for "energon" cubes.

A Fad Is Born! In 1982 Hasbro Toys scoured the world for toys on which they could base cartoons, which they could then use to sell more toys. They bought the rights to three Japanese toy lines: Takara Toys' Car Robots and Micro Change, and Bandai's Machine Men. The toys were all die-cast metal robots that, with a few twists and turns, became toy planes, cars, or other objects. Nearly 20 million of these toys had been sold around the world—but would they sell in the United States? Industry insiders predicted that Hasbro's "Transformers" would flop—complicated Japanese toys were untested and parents would balk at paying $10 for a toy car, they said. But the insiders were wrong. Kids loved the strange new toys and action-packed cartoon. (It didn't hurt that kids could figure out how to make the toys "transform," while their parents couldn't.) By the end of 1985, $380 million worth of Transformers had been sold. Sales and interest declined after that, but various versions of the show have been on the air since 1985 and related toys still sell well, with further help from the two recent *Transformers* films. The success of the toy line helped make Hasbro the second-largest toymaker in the world.

MIGHTY MORPHIN POWER RANGERS

Description: With the help of huge robot dinosaurs, six teenagers use ninja skills to fight giant monsters sent to Earth by an evil witch who lives in a dumpster on the moon.

A Fad Is Born! The most popular kids show and toy line of the 1990s is an unlikely success story. In 1986 TV producer Haim Saban had an idea: take footage of the robot dinosaurs from the Japanese action show *Kyoryu Sentai Zyuranger* (Dinosaur Squadron Beast Ranger) and combine it with newly shot scenes of American teenagers. The special effects from the Japanese show were cheap and sloppy, mixing miniature models, marionettes, and stuntmen in rubber suits. It took Saban seven years to sell it to a network, but Fox finally agreed to air it. Good move. It was an instant hit in the fall of 1993, becoming the #1 kids show on TV. Bandai was contracted to make toys based on the teenagers and robots, but didn't anticipate the high demand. How high? Twelve million toys were sold in 1993. By 1996 the show had exhausted all the available *Kyoryu* footage, so it had to start stealing from other Japanese shows. Now, each fall, *Power Rangers* changes its entire premise and cast. New heroes, monsters, robots, villains—and toys—are introduced. To date, Bandai has sold over 160 million Power Ranger toys.

Burn it off: Your body temperature rises slightly when digesting a large meal.

SCOTLAND'S DISH

Back in the 1950s, the BRI's future food historian, Jeff Cheek, took a
trip to Scotland while on one of his clandestine missions with the CIA.
(He won't tell us why he was there.) But he did write this story of
haggis for us—the origin, the tradition, and the elusive
hunt for a wee, tiny beastie

WASTE NOT, WANT NOT

Scotland has given the world many gifts: plaid, golf, the poetry of Robert Burns, and Scotch whisky. They have also offered us their national dish—*haggis*—but there are few takers…once they find out what haggis is made of. It is the offal (the waste parts) of a slaughtered sheep, minced and then boiled in the sheep's stomach. The dish and name most likely came from the Vikings—the Swedes have a similar dish, *hagga*, but they use choice cuts of meat to make it. The frugal Scottish farmers, however, wasted nothing, so instead of discarding the lungs, heart, and liver, they used these along with homegrown oats to make haggis. And the Scots have revered it for centuries.

In his "Address to a Haggis," 18th-century poet Robert Burns called the dish "the Great Chieftain of the Pudding Race." And it has become a Scottish tradition to serve haggis on Burns Night, January 25, to celebrate the poet's birthday. Loyal Scotsmen are also supposed to eat haggis on November 30, St. Andrew's Day, to honor Scotland's patron saint.

DOWN THE HATCH

Another tradition may explain the dish's lasting popularity: you don't eat the haggis by itself—it must be served with "neeps, tatties, and a dram." Translation: turnips, mashed potatoes, and Scotch whisky. (Possible rationale: everything tastes better if you wash it down with whisky.)

As you might imagine, most non-Scots (and many natives) are quick to reject a dish of innards, so many of the restaurants in Scotland prepare a more palatable version of haggis for their squeamish visitors: it's cooked in pots instead of stomachs and uses choice cuts of meat instead of the awful offal.

The world record for "haggis hurling" is held by Alan Pettigrew: 180'10".

HAGGIS HUNTING

Now *you* know where haggis comes from, but gullible tourists are told a different tale by the Scots: The haggis is actually a "wee beastie" that lives in the bogs and glens of Scotland. It's easy to recognize these little creatures—their legs are shorter on one side than the other. Why? From scurrying sideways up the steep Scottish hills, of course. It's very difficult to find a haggis, as they only come out at night. And they have very sensitive ears.

"So if ye go huntin' for the haggis, don't wear anything under ye kilt. The sounda ye underwear rubbin' against ye plaid will send 'em divin' for cover, laddie! And another thing: Before ye go, ye've gotta drink lots and lotsa Scotch to mask ye human odor. Them haggis have very sensitive noses, too, ye know!"

Result: Scores of happy, half-naked, inebriated tourists wandering around the countryside after midnight, drinking whisky and swearing that they just saw a real, live haggis…but it got away. "If ye com' back next year," you'll be told, "perhaps ye'll catch one of them wee, tiny beasties."

Here is a recipe for traditional haggis.

Ingredients:

- 1 pound sheep liver
- 1 large onion, chopped
- 2 pounds dry oatmeal
- 1 sheep stomach, scraped and cleaned
- 1 pound suet, chopped
- 3 cups meat stock
- $1/2$ teaspoon each cayenne pepper, salt, and black pepper

Preparation: Boil liver and onion until liver is done. Mince together. Lightly brown oatmeal in a hot skillet, stirring constantly to prevent burning. Mix all ingredients. Fill stomach with mixture, pressing to remove the air. Sew stomach securely, then prick several times with needle so it won't burst. Slow boil for four hours. Serve with "neeps, tatties, and a dram."

Something to chew on while waiting for the haggis to cook: A Scottish chef, John Paul McLachlan, created the world's most expensive haggis for Burns Night in 2005. He marinated Scottish beef in Balvenie cask 191, a 50-year-old Scotch (only 83 bottles exist), and then boiled it in a sheep's stomach. Cost: $5,500.

Physics fact: If all the empty space around all the atoms in the world disappeared, the entire…

CLOSE ENCOUNTERS OF THE CREDIBLE KIND

Investigations into 99% of UFO sightings have resulted in rational and very Earthly explanations. But then there are those few that simply have no explanation. Here are three cases that still have the experts baffled.

STRANGE BALL

In 1783 a London, England, man named Tiberius Cavallo, Fellow of the Royal Society, witnessed something that was unlike anything he'd ever seen before. "Northeast of the Terrace," he wrote in his memoirs, "in clear sky and warm weather, I saw appear suddenly an oblong cloud nearly parallel to the horizon. Below the cloud was seen a luminous body, brightly lit up and almost stationary." Cavallo described the object as a "strange ball" that was faint blue when he first saw it but then grew brighter and brighter. At one point, it flew high up into the air, then back down, and flew low across the horizon. After a few minutes, "it changed shape to oblong, acquired a tail, and seemed to split up into two bodies of small size." The object then disappeared over the horizon in a flash, and the last thing Cavallo heard from it was a "loud rumble like an explosion." Thinking the object may have crashed, Cavallo and other witnesses searched the area, but couldn't find a craft or an impact crater. One possible explanation: The "explosion" may have been a sonic boom, created when an object goes faster than the speed of sound...but this happened more than 150 years before humans had invented any type of vehicle that could break the sound barrier.

STS 48

While stationed in Earth orbit in September 1991, the Space Shuttle *Columbia*'s aft-mounted TV camera recorded video of several unidentified objects that seemed to be "swimming around." The camera was focused on an experimental tether 44 miles away, and beyond that was the horizon of the Earth. The glowing white objects intermittently entered the frame, and then turned and swam around, like microbes swimming in a petri dish. After a few minutes, a white flash appeared in the bottom left corner of the screen and suddenly, as if on cue, the little white objects all turned in unison and zoomed out of the frame. A few seconds later, a streak of light entered the frame and seemed to pause. Then, inexplicably, the camera rotated down toward the cargo bay, which was completely out of focus, then rotated back up...and the lights were gone.

NASA has dismissed the objects as "normal ice and debris" that sometimes float around ships in orbit. But these weren't floating; they were moving independently of each other and changing direction. And the occasional "debris" NASA referred to is usually found close to the ship. The camera was focused miles away on the long tether, and some of the objects appeared to fly *behind* the tether. So what were these things? No one knows for sure. They are truly unidentified flying objects.

FLAMING ARROW

On the night of June 30, 2002, a UFO was sighted across nearly all of central China. It was first seen over the eastern province of Jiangsu, then moved west, over Henan province, then Xiaxi province, and then Sichuan. "At 10:30 p.m., an object resembling a flaming arrow appeared in the night sky," wrote Henan's *City Morning Post* the next day. "Then the tail of the fiery arrow opened up like a fan, which emitted bright light. The light-emitting section then changed into a crescent. A fireball on top of the crescent glowed brilliantly. Five minutes later, the UFO disappeared."

Dozens of other newspapers reported the event, based on thousands of eyewitness accounts. The government had no explanation, except to say that it was definitely not a Chinese craft. Wang Sichao, a well-respected astronomer at Nanjing's Zijinshan Astronomy Center, studied the reports and photographs, and offered this conclusion: "It is a dimensional flying machine. But whether it is of human origin or extraterrestrial, whether it is controlled inside or remotely, are still unknown. Maybe we will not be able to uncover the truth for many years, but human curiosity will never let us stop searching."

TO TELL THE TRUTH, PART II

Lie detectors have come a long way since the days of "trial by red-hot poker" (see page 120). But are the modern gizmos foolproof?

BEATING THE SYSTEM

Modern-day lie detectors are pretty sophisticated, but they have the same flaw that the ancients methods did—they all assume that liars, out of guilt or fear of discovery, will have some kind of involuntary physical response every time they lie. But that isn't necessarily the case, according to most experts. "I don't think there's any medical or scientific evidence which tends to establish that your blood pressure elevates, that you perspire more freely, or that your pulse quickens when you tell a lie," prominent defense lawyer William G. Hundley once said.

Still, many people believe that the polygraph is a useful tool when used in concert with other investigative methods, especially when they're used on ordinary people who don't know how to cheat. "It's a great psychological tool," says Plato Cacheris, another defense lawyer. "You take the average guy and tell him you're going to give him a poly, and he's concerned enough to believe it will disclose any deception on his part." (Cacheris is famous for having represented Aldrich Ames, a CIA spy who passed a lie detector test in 1991 and then went on to sell more than $2.5 million worth of secrets to the Russians before he was finally caught in 1994.)

FAKIN' IT

Two tricks to help you beat a lie detector:

• Curl your toes or press your feet down against the floor while answering the "innocent" questions. It can raise the polygraph readings to the same range as the "guilty" questions, which can either make you appear innocent or invalidate the results.

• Stick a tack in your shoe and press your big toe against the sharp point during the "innocent" questions.

Both toe-curling and stepping on a tack during the innocent questions have the same effect: they raise the stress level of your body.

The buttoned flaps on the back pockets of Levi's jeans are called *arcuates.*

VIDEO TREASURES

Ever found yourself in a video store staring at thousands of films you've never heard of, with no idea what to rent? It happens to us all the time—so we decided to offer a few recommendations.

COMFORT AND JOY (1984) *Comedy*

Review: "Quirky, fun little comedy. When a mild-mannered Scottish disc jockey's girl moves out on him, his world begins to fall apart. He decides to find more meaning in his life by throwing himself into a noble struggle to reconcile two groups battling over territorial rights for their ice cream trucks. Full of dry wit and subtle humor. Sophisticated viewers are more likely to find this good fun." Music by Mark Knopfler of Dire Straits. (*Illustrated Guide To Video's Best*) *Stars:* Bill Paterson, Eleanor David. *Director:* Bill Forsyth.

THE FOUNTAIN (2006) *Science-Fiction*

Review: "A present-day medical researcher works on a cure for cancer. Meanwhile, a 15th century conquistador searches out the Tree of Life. Finally, in 2500, a man tries to regenerate the Tree in the heart of a star. At heart, this is a simple fable about love and death, but keeps viewers enthralled from Mayan temples to space nebulae. A complex and gorgeous mini-epic." (*Empire* magazine) *Stars:* Hugh Jackman, Rachel Weisz. *Director:* Darren Aronofsky.

SCOTLAND, PA (2001) *Comedy/Thriller*

Review: "In this darkly comic and faithful adaptation of *Macbeth*, Joe 'Mac' McBeth and his frighteningly ambitious wife both work at a hamburger joint. Mac is full of ideas about the future of fast food, but his boss isn't listening. When he passes over Mac to give the manager position to his son, Mac's thoughts turn to murder." (*TV Guide's Movie Guide*) *Director*: Billy Morrissette.

RUN, LOLA RUN (1999) *German/Drama*

Review: "A quick stop for cigarettes derails the normally prompt Lola, and now she has 20 minutes to save her boyfriend Manni. The movie mixes film, video, and animation to show how Lola's journey affects those she encounters during her mad dash. A flawless, 81-minute love story perfect for a generation raised on Sega and MTV." (*Roughcut Reviews*) *Stars:* Franka Potente and Moritz Bleibtreu. *Director:* Tom Tykwer

BORN INTO BROTHELS (2004) *Documentary*
Review: "Two American photographers went to Calcutta to film prostitution and hit upon the idea of giving cameras to the children of prostitutes, asking them to take photos of the world in which they lived. The filmmakers bring out the innate intelligence of the children as they use their cameras to see their world in a different way. (There are no scenes that could be described as explicit, because filmmakers did not want to exploit their subjects.) The movie is a record by well-meaning people who try to make a difference for the better." (Roger Ebert) *Directors:* Zana Briski and Ross Kaufman.

THE MAN WHO WOULD BE KING (1975) *Adventure*
Review: "Old-fashioned adventure and derring-do. Two British soldier-pals try to bamboozle high priests of remote Kafiristan into turning over their riches by convincing them that one of them is a god. The acting is ideal, the script is superb, and the film is entertaining." (*Leonard Maltin's Movie & Video Guide*) *Stars:* Sean Connery, Michael Caine. *Director:* John Huston.

LAST NIGHT (1998) *Drama/Science-Fiction*
Review: "A film about the end of the world that paints a bittersweet picture. The world will end at midnight precisely and we meet a small group of people as they try to face the end with a certain grace and dignity. As the final hour approaches for the characters, there are moments of startling poignancy." (*Roger Ebert's Movie Yearbook*) *Stars:* Don McKellar, Sandra Oh. *Director:* Don McKellar.

SHALL WE DANCE? (1996) *Foreign/Drama*
Review: "This film proves that Japanese filmmakers can fashion charming, feel-good movies every bit as effective as their Hollywood counterparts. The film uses ballroom dancing to explore one man's struggle for freedom from the suffocating repression of Japanese society. This is a film for anyone who prefers to leave the theater smiling. Winner of 13 Japanese Academy Awards." (*ReelViews*) *Director:* Masayuki Suo.

Singer Dave Matthews emigrated to the U.S. to avoid service in the South African military.

I TOAST YOU!

On a recent trip to Ireland, Uncle John spent many an evening going from pub to pub collecting traditional toasts (and many a morning after, begging for aspirin). Here are some favorites.

May you have food and clothing, a soft pillow for your head; May you be forty years in heaven, before the devil knows you're dead.

For every wound, a balm. For every sorrow, a cheer. For every storm, a calm. For every thirst, a beer.

May the roof above us never fall in, and may we friends gathered below never fall out.

Here's health and prosperity, to you and all your posterity, And them that doesn't drink with sincerity, That they may be damned for all eternity!

Gentlemen, start your livers!

May we live to learn well, and learn to live well.

May your right hand always be stretched out in friendship and never in want.

Here's to warm words on a cold evening, A full moon on a dark night, And the road downhill all the way to your door.

Success to the lover, honor to the brave, health to the sick, and freedom to the slave.

May the Lord keep you in His hand, And never close His fist too tight on you.

Old wood to burn, old books to read, old wine to drink, old friends to trust.

May misfortune follow you the rest of your life, but never catch up.

Champagne to our real friends, and real pain to our sham friends.

May you live as long as you want, and never want as long as you live.

May I see you gray, combing your grandchildren's hair.

May the people who dance on your grave get cramps in their legs.

Health and long life to you, The woman of your choice to you, A child every year to you, Land without rent to you, And may you die in Ireland.

The 1937 Oscar, awarded to Spencer Tracy, was mistakenly engraved to "Dick Tracy."

I CURSE YOU!

*Save these classic curses to use against
people who refuse to toast you.*

May the curse of Mary Maline and her nine blind children chase you so far over the hills of Damnation that the Lord himself won't find you with a telescope.

May your daughter's beauty be admired by everyone in the circus.

May the devil cut the head off you and make a day's work of your neck.

Six horse-loads of graveyard clay upon you.

May I live just long enough to bury you.

May you be afflicted with the itch and have no nails to scratch with.

All your teeth should fall out except one, and you should have a toothache in that one.

May the seven terriers of hell sit on the spool of your breast and bark in at your soul-case.

May you be transformed into a chandelier, to hang by day and burn by night.

May you win a lottery and spend it all on doctors.

May the devil swallow you sideways.

May you live in a house of 100 rooms, and may each room have its own bed, and may you wander every night from room to room, and from bed to bed, unable to sleep.

May you go stone-blind so that you can't tell your wife from a haystack.

Your nose should grow so much hair it strains your soup.

May fire and brimstone never fail to fall in showers on you.

May you have devoted children to chase the flies off your nose.

May you back into a pitchfork and grab a hot stove for support.

May those who love us love us. And those that don't love us, may God turn their hearts, and if He cannot turn their hearts, may He turn their ankles so we'll know them by their limping.

FAMILIAR PHRASES

*Here's one of our regular features—the origins
of some common terms and phrases.*

THE BALL'S IN YOUR COURT

Meaning: It's your turn; it's up to you

Origin: "This term comes from tennis, where it signifies that it is the opponent's turn to serve or play the ball. A British equivalent is 'the ball's at your feet,' which comes from football (soccer), and has been in use much longer. How much longer? Lord Auckland used it figuratively in a letter written in about 1800: 'We have the ball at our feet.'" (From *Southpaws & Sunday Punches*, by Christine Ammer)

TO BEAR DOWN

Meaning: To put pressure on someone or something

Origin: "For centuries sailors used the word *bear* in scores of expressions to describe a ship's position in relation to the wind, the land, or another ship. Most are still used by sailors today. *Bear up*, for instance, means to head the ship into the wind. *Bear off* means to head away from the wind, a phrase sailors came to use figuratively whenever they wanted anything thrust away from their person. *Bear down* in the original nautical sense meant to approach from the weather, or windward, side. It later came to mean to approach another ship rapidly, pressuring them to yield." (From *Scuttlebutt*, by Teri Degler)

BY THE SKIN OF ONE'S TEETH

Meaning: By an extremely narrow margin; just barely

Origin: "A literal translation of a biblical phrase from Latin. The biblical source is the passage where Job is complaining about how illness has ravaged his body: 'My bone cleaveth to my skin and to my flesh, and I am escaped with the skin of my teeth.' The point is that Job is so sick that there's nothing left to his body. The passage is rendered differently in other translations; the Douay Bible, for example—an English translation of the Vulgate (St. Jerome's fourth-century translation)—gives: 'My bone hath cleaved to my skin, and nothing but lips are left about my teeth.'

The phrase first appeared in English in a mid-16th-century translation of the Bible. It did not become common until the 19th century." (From *Jesse's Word of the Day*, by Jesse Sheidlower)

TO EAT ONE OUT OF HOUSE AND HOME

Meaning: To eat large quantities of someone else's food

Origin: "Its first recorded use in English was by William Shakespeare, who used it in his play *Henry IV*, written in 1597–98. In Act II, Hostess Quickly of the Boar's Head Tavern is complaining about Sir John Falstaff, who has been lodging with her, eating huge quantities of food, and avoiding paying his bill: 'He hath eaten me out of house and home, he hath put all my substance into that fat belly of his…' The phrase *out of house and home* was in use as early as the 13th century, and during the 15th century people often said 'he hath eaten me out of house and harbor.' Shakespeare combined the two phrases." (From *Inventing English*, by Dale Corey)

NOT UP TO SNUFF

Meaning: Below standard

Origin: "Englishmen were so fond of finely powdered tobacco, or snuff, that its use was nearly universal throughout the kingdom. Connoisseurs would pride themselves on knowing their snuff. One derided as *not up to snuff* was considered an amateur at judging powdered tobacco. But soon the phrase expanded to any person or product considered to be less than discerning." (From *Everyday Phrases*, by Neil Ewart)

TO PAY THE PIPER

Meaning: To accept the consequences

Origin: "Street dancing was a common form of amusement during medieval times. Strolling musicians, including flute players, would play for a dance wherever they could gather a crowd.

"Frequently a dance was organized on the spur of the moment. Persons who heard the notes of a piper would drop their work and join in the fun. When they tired of the frolic, they would pass the hat for the musician. It became proverbial that a dancer had better have his fun while he could; sooner or later he would have to pay the piper." (From *I've Got Goose Pimples*, by Marvin Vanoni)

Japan has .25% of the world's land mass, but 10% of the world's active volcanoes.

THE JOY OF SECTS: A QUIZ

And by that, we mean religious sects—particularly the ones that thrive in Pennsylvania. Here's a quiz to help you avoid embarrassing gaffes the next time you're visiting the Keystone State. (Answers on page 285.)

1. You see a group of girls in old-fashioned clothes. They're probably…

A. Mennonites

B. Quakers

C. Amish

D. Moravians

2. One weekend, you notice men moving benches into a home that has dark green window shades. You should…

A. Call the police to report a bizarre case of burglary, in which thieves are putting furniture *into* the house.

B. Check the entertainment guide in the local paper to see if a concert is scheduled.

C. Realize it's basketball season, buy some pretzels and beer, knock on the door, and ask if you can watch the game.

D. Ignore the whole thing, unless you're Amish.

3. You're invited to a "Love Feast" at the local Moravian church. You should…

A. Bring all your souvenir buttons from Woodstock.

B. Practice your musical scales.

C. Bake a pie.

D. Make sure the iPod is charged up because there's likely to be a long, boring sermon.

4. You're at an all-day religious service with non-stop sermons. The preachers don't pause, even when the listeners get up to eat. At the end of it all, people pair off and wash each other's feet. Who are these people?

A. Quakers

B. Amish

C. Schwenkfelders

D. Moravians

5. A Mennonite, a Quaker, an Amish, and a Moravian walk into a bar. Which one orders tea?

Q: What are a meatball, a Captain Hook, and a gopher ball? A: Types of baseball pitches.

Q & A:
ASK THE EXPERTS

*Everyone's got a question they'd like answered—basic stuff,
like "Why is the sky blue?" Here are a few questions,
with answers from the nation's top trivia experts.*

WEIGHTY QUESTION

Q: *Why doesn't pound cake weigh a pound?*

A: "Traditionally, it was made with a pound of flour, a pound
of sugar, and a pound of butter. That would make three—enough to shatter the pound barrier and cause a crash landing directly on your hips. Incidentally, the same name game is played with cupcakes. The original recipe called for one cup of each ingredient. And you thought it was because they're baked in those cute little paper cups." (From *Crazy Plates*, by Janet Podleski)

SICK OF IT ALL

Q: *Why do people get sick more often in the winter?*

A: "It is not cold feet and wet heads that are the problem, disease experts say, but the fact that human beings are warmth-loving social animals. At least in cold climates, widespread outbreaks of diseases like colds and influenza tend to start in winter months, when people spend more time together indoors in close quarters with the windows shut. The cold months also bring children, those well-known vectors of bacteria and viruses, together in the classroom, where they can pick up infections and take them home to the rest of the family." (From *The New York Times Second Book of Science Questions and Answers*, by C. Claiborne Ray)

GET A LEG UP

Q: *Why do male dogs lift their leg up to urinate?*

A: "It isn't to avoid 'missing' and squirting their legs by mistake. It's to mark territory. Most dogs are compulsive in their habits and have favorite 'watering holes.' By lifting a leg, the urine flows up and out much farther, extending the boundaries of the male's territory. From a dog's point of view, evidently, the bigger the territory, the better." (From *Why Do Dogs Have Wet Noses?*, by David Feldman)

THERE'S THE RUB

Q: *How does an eraser erase pencil marks?*

A: "Look at a pencil mark under a microscope. You'll see that it's not continuous; it's made up of individual black particles, a few ten-thousandths of an inch big, clinging to the paper fibers. The eraser's job is to pluck them out. It can do that because (a) it is flexible enough to reach in between the fibers and (b) it is sticky enough to grab onto the black particles. But while the eraser is rubbing the paper, the paper's fibers are also rubbing off pieces of the rubber. The rubbed-off shreds of rubber roll up their collected black particles into those pesky crumbs that you have to brush away." (From *What Einstein Told His Barber*, by Robert L. Wolke)

TASTES LIKE...SPLEEN?

Q: *What's really in a hot dog?*

A: "All manufacturers must list their ingredients on the label. 'Beef,' 'pork,' 'chicken,' 'turkey,' etc. can only be used if the meat comes from the muscle tissue of the animal. If you see the words 'meat by-products' or 'variety meats,' the hot dog may contain snouts, stomachs, hearts, tongues, lips, spleens, etc. Frankfurters once contained only beef and pork but now can legally contain sheep, goat, and up to 15% chicken. Hot dogs are made by grinding the meat with water, seasoning, sweeteners, preservatives, salt, and binders." (From *Why Does Popcorn Pop?*, by Don Voorhees)

CAN I DRIVE 55?

Q: *When a speed limit sign is posted, does that speed take effect when the driver sees it or when the driver passes it?*

A: "Speed limit signs, whether decreasing or increasing the speed limit, take effect at the time that you pass the sign and not a car length sooner. Yellow speed limit signs are there to warn drivers of potentially dangerous situations, such as sharp curves, requiring a reduction in speed. They are considered 'advisory,' but should you crash while maneuvering through one of these areas, you may be cited for reckless driving." (From *First Coast News*, by Linda Mock)

A pigeon can fly up to 600 miles—the distance from Detroit to Providence, RI—in a single day

A BARREL OF LAUGHS

This letter is a classic piece of American humor. It's been around in various forms for nearly a century, appearing in dozens of books and movies, and even in a Saturday Night Live sketch in 2004. This version is a memo to an insurance company, but there are many others. The tale has now been passed around so often that it's achieved urban legend status—in other words, some people believe it's true. It's not. In fact, it was written in 1902 by Will Rogers. (Not really; we just thought we'd add to the legend.)

Dear Sir:

I am writing in response to your request for additional information in Block 3 of the accident report form. I put "poor planning" as the cause of my accident. You asked for a fuller explanation, and I trust the following details will be sufficient.

I was alone on the roof of a new six-story building. When I completed my work, I found that I had some bricks left over which, when weighed later, were found to be slightly more than 500 pounds. Rather than carry the bricks down by hand, I decided to lower them in a barrel by using a pulley that was attached to the side of the building on the sixth floor.

I secured the rope at ground level, climbed to the roof, swung the barrel out, and loaded the bricks into it. Then I climbed back down and untied the rope, holding tightly to ensure a slow descent of the bricks.

You will notice in Block 11 of the accident report form that I weigh 135 pounds. Due to my surprise at being jerked off the ground so suddenly, I lost my presence of mind and forgot to let go of the rope. Needless to say, I proceeded at a rapid rate up the side of the building.

Somewhere in the vicinity of the third floor, I met

The little flap of cartilage at the opening of your ear is called a **tragus.**

the barrel, which was now proceeding downward at an equally impressive speed. This explains the fractured skull and the broken collar bone, as listed in section 3 of the accident form.

Slowed down slightly, I continued my rapid ascent, not stopping until the fingers on my right hand were two knuckles deep into the pulley.

Fortunately, by this time I had regained my presence of mind and was able to hold tightly to the rope—in spite of beginning to experience a great deal of pain. At approximately the same time, however, the barrel of bricks hit the ground and the bottom fell out of the barrel. Now devoid of the weight of the bricks, the barrel weighed approximately 50 pounds.

(I refer you again to my weight.)

As you can imagine, I began a rapid descent down the side of the building. Somewhere in the vicinity of the third floor, I met the barrel coming up. This accounts for the two fractured ankles, the broken tooth, and the lacerations of my legs and lower body.

Here my luck began to change slightly. The encounter with the barrel seemed to slow me enough to lessen my injuries when I fell on the pile of bricks; fortunately, only three vertebrae were cracked.

I am sorry to report, however, that as I lay there on the pile of bricks—in pain and unable to move—I again lost my composure and presence of mind and let go of the rope; I could only lay there watching as the empty barrel begin its journey back down towards me. This explains the two broken legs.

I hope this answers your questions.

Sincerely,
Thomas L.

Only 22 percent of Canadians own guns, as opposed to 49 percent of Americans.

RAMBO, STARRING AL PACINO

Some roles are so closely associated with a specific actor that it's hard to imagine he or she wasn't the first choice. But it happens all the time. Can you imagine, for example...

GENE HACKMAN AS HANNIBAL LECTER (*The Silence of the Lambs*, 1991). Hackman wanted to direct the film, star, and write the screenplay, so Orion Pictures bought the rights to the novel. Then Hackman realized how violent the film would be and dropped out. Director Jonathan Demme signed Anthony Hopkins for the part without telling Orion head Mike Medavoy, who was furious that "an Englishman" would play Lecter. Medavoy agreed on one condition: that Jodie Foster be cast as FBI agent Clarice Starling instead of Meg Ryan. Demme agreed; Foster won her second straight Oscar.

GOLDIE HAWN AND MERYL STREEP AS THELMA AND LOUISE (*Thelma and Louise*, 1991). Streep wanted to test her comedic talents; Hawn's film *Private Benjamin* had made $100 million at the box office. They seemed perfect for the film, and wanted to work together. But their schedules were full. "We weren't available right then," Hawn says, "and the director, Ridley Scott, wouldn't wait." Michelle Pfeiffer and Jodie Foster turned down the film; so did Cher. So Scott gave the parts to Geena Davis and Susan Sarandon.

ELVIS PRESLEY AS JOE BUCK (*Midnight Cowboy*, 1969). Desperate to be taken seriously as an actor, the King went shopping around for "a more serious movie role." The part of the male prostitute in *Midnight Cowboy* was one of the parts he considered, but he ultimately turned the film down and did one called *A Change of Habit* instead. Reason: "Since it was about a doctor (Elvis) and a nun (Mary Tyler Moore) in the ghetto, that qualified as being more 'serious.'" *A Change of Habit* was Elvis's biggest box office dud; *Midnight Cowboy* won the Oscar for Best Picture and turned Jon Voight into a star.

AL PACINO AS RAMBO (*First Blood*, 1982). Pacino wasn't the first major star interested in the part of John Rambo. (Clint Eastwood, Robert De Niro, and Paul Newman turned it down.) He wanted Rambo to be "a little more of a madman," and had the script rewritten. But the new draft made the character too dark and nutty, so Pacino passed on the role. So did John Travolta, Michael Douglas, and Nick Nolte. Then Carolco Pictures bought the script and offered it to Sylvester Stallone, who rewrote the insane Vietnam vet into a misunderstood American hero, "kind of like a Rocky movie." *First Blood* was Stallone's first non-*Rocky* film that didn't bomb. It saved his career. The sequel, *Rambo*, established it for good.

DORIS DAY AS MRS. ROBINSON (*The Graduate*, 1967). Day's Hollywood image was "the perennial virgin." "There was something about taking that All-American housewife image and turning it all around," said producer Larry Turman. "I sent the script to her, but we never heard a thing." Day later explained that she read the script, but just couldn't see herself playing the role. So it was offered to Anne Bancroft, who could.

BURT REYNOLDS AS RANDALL P. McMURPHY (*One Flew Over the Cuckoo's Nest*, 1975). When Marlon Brando turned down the part, director Milos Forman had breakfast with Burt Reynolds and told him he was one of two actors being considered for the part. Reynolds was thrilled. "If the other guy isn't Jack Nicholson," he replied, "I've got the part." When Forman stopped eating dead in his tracks, Reynolds knew he wasn't going to get the part. Nicholson got the role, and won the Oscar for best actor.

BURT REYNOLDS AS GARRETT BREEDLOVE (*Terms of Endearment*, 1983). About 10 years after Reynolds was turned down for *Cuckoo's Nest*, director James L. Brooks sent him the script for *Terms of Endearment*. The lead had been created especially for him, but Reynolds rejected it. "I'd promised that I'd star in *Stroker Ace*," he explained later. So Brooks offered the part to Jack Nicholson, who jumped at it. "How many scripts make you cry?" Nicholson said. "I read hundreds of screenplays every year and this one made me think, 'Yeah, I know just how this guy feels.' It was terrific." *Stroker Ace* was one of the more forgettable films of the year; *Terms of Endearment* won Nicholson his second Oscar.

Odds of surviving a jump off the Golden Gate Bridge: 2%. (98% all all jumpers have died.)

"GOING, GOING...GONE!"

You've paid your dues at broadcasting school and have finally worked your way up to becoming a play-by-play announcer in the majors. Congratulations! Now all you need is your own signature home run call. (Just don't use any of these—they're already taken.)

"Holy Cow!"
—Phil Rizzuto, Yankees

"Whoa, boy! Next time around, bring me back my stomach!"
—Jack Brickhouse, White Sox

"Tell it 'Bye-Bye, baby!'"
—Russ Hodges, Giants

"Forget it!"
—Vin Scully, Dodgers

"Going back...at the track, at the wall...SSSEEEEE-YA!"
—Michael Kay, Yankees

"Get up, get outta here, gone!"
—Bob Uecker, Brewers

"It's deep, and I don't think it's playable."
—Keith Olbermann, ESPN

"They usually show movies on a flight like that."
—Ken Coleman, Indians, Red Sox, and Reds

"It's going, going...gone!"
—Harry Hartman, Reds (he coined it in 1929)

"Kiss it goodbye!"
—Bob Prince, Pirates

"Long drive, way back, warning track, wall...you can touch em' all!"
—Greg Schulte, Diamondbacks

"That ball is going and it ain't coming back!"
—Jeff Kingery, Rockies

"To the wall and over the wall! Oh, Doctor!"
—Jerry Coleman, Yankees, Angels, Padres

"Open the window, Aunt Minnie, here it comes!"
—Rosey Roswell, Pirates

"*Bonsoir, elle est partie!*" (French for "So long, she's gone!")
—Rodger Brulotte, Expos

Manufacturing rum was colonial New England's largest and most prosperous industry.

THE WHO?

Ever wonder how rock bands get their names? So do we.
After some digging around, we found these origins.

CHICAGO. They originally called themselves Chicago Transit Authority, but had to shorten it after the city of Chicago sued.

ALICE COOPER. Lead singer Vincent Furnier claims to have gotten his stage name from a Ouija board, through which he met a spirit with that name.

EURYTHMICS. An 1890s system of music instruction that emphasized physical motion.

METALLICA. Drummer Lars Ulrich was helping a friend name a heavy metal magazine. Ulrich's two suggestions: 1) Metal Mania (which the friend used), and 2) Metallica.

THE REPLACEMENTS. They were filling in for another band at the last minute. When the MC asked who the band was, singer Paul Westerberg replied, "The replacements."

WHITE STRIPES. While the band members are named Jack and Meg White, the band is named for Meg's love of red-and-white-striped peppermint candies.

WEEZER. Lead singer Rivers Cuomo got this nickname in grade school. He had asthma.

THE SMITHS. They wanted a generic name that wouldn't suggest anything about the band's kind of music.

XTC. Singer Andy Partridge saw an old movie in which Jimmy Durante said, "That's it, I'm in ecstasy!"

BLACK SABBATH. From a 1963 Boris Karloff horror movie.

DEF LEPPARD. Singer Joe Elliot once drew a picture of a leopard with no ears—a "deaf leopard."

First televised NFL game: the Brooklyn Dodgers vs. the Philadelphia Eagles in...

MOODY BLUES. They named the band in honor of one of their favorite songs—Duke Ellington's "Mood Indigo."

BADFINGER. They were originally called the Iveys. When they signed with the Beatles' Apple Records label, Paul McCartney gave them this name. It was the original title of the Beatles song "A Little Help from My Friends."

FALL OUT BOY. In their early years, they asked an audience what their name should be. Somebody yelled "Fall Out Boy." They liked it and took it, unaware that it was the name of a character on *The Simpsons*. When they found out, they feared they'd be sued. But *The Simpsons*' producers thought the band had the name first, and that *they* were going to be sued. (Neither was.)

DEATH CAB FOR CUTIE. Named after a song written by Monty Python collaborator Neil Innes for his 1960s psychedelic group, the Bonzo Dog Doo-Dah Band.

TLC. It's not what you think. It comes from the first letters of each of the group members' first names: Tionne, Lisa, and Chilli.

EMINEM. The rapper gave himself this stage name using his initials—M and M (for Marshall Mathers)—spelled out phonetically.

NINE INCH NAILS. Nine-inch nails were once used in coffins. Singer Trent Reznor made a list of potential band names and settled on this one because "it still sounded good after two weeks" and could be easily abbreviated.

WINGS. Paul McCartney came up with it while waiting in a hospital *wing* as his wife Linda was giving birth to one of their children.

EVERCLEAR. Named after an extremely strong (190 proof) grain alcohol.

COLDPLAY. They stole it from another band that broke up. The original band got the name from a book by poet Philip Horky, entitled *Child's Reflections, Cold Play*.

WHAT'S FOR BREAKFAST?

Some culinary origins to start your day off right.

WAFFLES. Introduced to the United States by Thomas Jefferson, who brought the first waffle iron over from France. The name comes from the Dutch *wafel*. Waffles owe much of their early popularity to street vendors, who sold them hot, covered in molasses or maple syrup. It wasn't until the 20th century that the electric waffle iron made them an American staple.

ENGLISH MUFFINS. In 1875, Samuel Bath Thomas moved to America from England, bringing with him his mother's recipe for "tea muffins." He started out baking them in New York in 1880. In 1926, he officially named them Thomas' English Muffins.

FRENCH TOAST. Really does have its origins in France, where it's known as *ameritte* or *pain perdu* ("lost bread"), a term that has persisted in Creole and Cajun cooking. Throughout its history in America, it has been referred to as "Spanish," "German," or "nun's toast." Its first appearance in print as "French toast" was in 1871.

GRAPE JUICE. In 1869, Dr. Thomas Welch, Christian, dentist, and prohibitionist, invented "unfermented wine"—grape juice—so that fellow teetotalers would not be forced into the contradiction (as he saw it) of drinking alcohol in church. Local pastors weren't interested, so he gave up and went back to pulling teeth. His son Charles began selling it as grape juice in 1875.

PANCAKES. When the first European settlers landed in the New World, they brought pancakes with them. They met Native Americans who made their own pancakes, called *nokehic*. Even the ancient Egyptians had pancakes; in fact, there are few cultures that don't have pancakes of one kind or another. The first ready-made pancake mix came in 1889, when two men in St. Joseph, Missouri, introduced "Self-Rising Pancake Flour." They named it "Aunt Jemima" after a song from a minstrel show.

Why don't we eat turkey eggs? Mostly because, proportionately, they lay far fewer than chickens

CARD-PLAYING SUPERSTITIONS

Over the centuries, card players have come up with all sorts of strange superstitions to help them win—and elaborate explanations for why they're losing. (Ignoring, of course, the possibility that they're just bad card players.)

GOOD LUCK

• Blow on the cards or spit on them, preferably when no one is looking. (Remember to wipe up any excess spit, so no one knows you've fouled them.)

• Wear an article of dirty clothing when you play cards, especially when you play poker. The dirt helps keep evil at bay.

• Stick a pin in your lapel, or in a friend's lapel.

• There's one lucky card in each deck. If you can figure out which card it is, touch it with your index finger before the game begins.

• If you're sitting at a table made of wood, choose a seat that lets you lay your cards with the grain instead of against it.

• Whenever you're on a losing streak, tilt your chair up on its forelegs and twist it three times. This works best if you twist following the path of the sun—i.e., from east to west.

• If twisting doesn't help, rotate the chair so the back faces the table, then sit astride it so that you're facing the seat back.

• If you're sitting astride your chair and still losing, try sitting on a handkerchief, or walk clockwise three times around the table. (If you still lose, switch to a new deck of cards or consider taking up dominos.)

• If you see a hunchback on the way to your game, that's good luck. Don't touch the hump—just seeing the hunchback is all it takes.

BAD LUCK

• Don't sing or whistle during a card game. It's unlucky (not to mention annoying).

In Britain, judges first began wearing black robes in 1714 to mourn the death of Queen Anne.

• Don't pick up any of your cards until all the cards have been dealt, and when you do pick them up, use your right hand.

• Never, ever let someone hover over you and look at your cards, unless that person never plays cards. If they never play cards, then standing over you may actually bring you luck. People who bring you luck are known as "mascots."

• Don't sit with your legs crossed—it "crosses out your luck."

• Never play cards in a room with a dog in it.

• Never let anyone place their foot on the rung of your chair. On the other hand, if you want to give bad luck to someone who's beating you, put your foot on the rung of *their* chair.

• Never play cards with a cross-eyed man or woman. (This superstition dates back to the days when people thought that cross-eyed people could see the cards of the people sitting next to them.)

MORE BAD LUCK

• Never play cards on a bare table. (Bring felt or a tablecloth, preferably green, with you…just in case.)

• Don't lend money during a card game. Don't borrow it, either.

• If you are dealt a steady succession of black cards, it means that you or someone in your family will die soon.

• If you're a pilot, coal miner, soldier, fisherman, or sailor, you should never carry playing cards on your person. If you do and bad luck occurs—a storm or an enemy attack, for example—throw the cards as far away from you as you can to get rid of the bad luck.

LUCKY AND UNLUCKY CARDS

• The four of clubs is "the devil's bedstead." Discard it unless you absolutely need it. If you're dealt the four of clubs in the first hand of the game, throw down the cards and leave the game—you'll have nothing but bad luck.

• Dropping any card on the floor is bad luck, but dropping one of the black aces is worst of all. If you drop a black ace, leave the game immediately. Nobody recovers from luck that bad.

According to experts, the best badminton shuttlecocks are made from the left wing of a goose.

LADIES, BEHAVE YOURSELVES

Women, you can follow these antique rules of etiquette…or just laugh at them.

"Immoderate laughter is exceedingly unbecoming a lady; she may affect the dimple or the smile, but should carefully avoid any approximation to a horse-laugh."

—The Perfect Gentleman (1860)

"Sending out a letter with a crooked, mangled or upside-down stamp is akin to letting your lingerie straps show."

—Good Housekeeping's Book of Today's Etiquette (1965)

"Fingernails are another source of feminine excess. The woman who goes about her daily avocations with blood-red finger-nails is merely harking back to the days of savagery, when hands smeared with blood were a sign of successful fighting."

—Things That Are Not Done (1937)

"It's a great idea to file your fingernails in the street car, bus, or train. It's certainly making the most of your time. The noise of the filing drowns the unpleasant noise of the wheels. But it is the act of an ill-bred person. Who but an ordinary person would allow her epithelium to fly all over? I think that one might as well scatter ashes after a cremation, around the neighborhood."

—Manners for Millions (1932)

"The perfect hostess will see to it that the works of male and female authors be properly separated on her bookshelves. Their proximity, unless they happen to be married, should not be tolerated."

—Lady Gough's Etiquette (1863)

"No matter what the fashion may be, the gloves of a well-dressed woman are never so tight that her hands have the appearance of sausages."

—The New Etiquette (1940)

"Don't affect a lisp or talk baby talk. Somebody will probably kill you sometime if you do."

—Compete! (1935)

One of the first programs to be broadcast by radio was a British yacht race (1898).

"A lady-punster is a most unpleasing phenomenon, and we would advise no young woman, however skilled she may be, to cultivate this kind of verbal talent."

—*Collier's Cyclopedia of Commercial and Social Information* (1882)

"Girls, never, never turn at a whistle, to see if you are wanted. A whistle is usually to call a dog."

—*Good Manners* (1934)

"A beautiful eyelash is an important adjunct to the eye. The lashes may be lengthened by trimming them occasionally in childhood. Care should be taken that this trimming is done neatly and evenly, and especially that the points of the scissors do not penetrate the eye."

—*Our Deportment* (1881)

"If a man must be forcibly detained to listen to you, you are as rude in thus detaining him, as if you had put a pistol to his head and threatened to blow his brains out if he stirred."

—*The Gentlemen's Book "of Etiquette and Manual of Politeness* (1860)

"Still less say of anything which you enjoy at table. 'I love melons,' 'I love peaches,' 'I adore grapes'—these are school-girl utterances. We love our friends. Love is an emotion of the heart, but not one of the palate. We like, we appreciate grapes, but we do not love them."

—*The American Code of Manners* (1880)

"Never use your knife to convey your food from your plate to your mouth; besides being decidedly vulgar, you run the imminent danger of enlarging the aperture from ear to ear. A lady of fashion used to say that she never saw a person guilty of this ugly habit without a shudder, as every minute she expected to see the head of the unfortunate severed from the body."

—*Etiquette for the Ladies* (1849)

"Certain daring necklines have a paralyzing effect on the conversation and even on the appetite of the other dinner party guests, who hope to see a little more than is already revealed and would love to change places with the waiter, who has a particularly stimulating view."

—*Accent on Elegance* (1970)

"Large hats make little women look like mushrooms."

—*Everyday Etiquette* (1907)

STATUE RATS

They're called "flying carp," "winged weasels," "scum of the sky,"
"park lice," and "winged infestation." Lawyers? No, pigeons.
They don't get much respect, but maybe they should.
There's more to them than you might think.

• Pigeons were first domesticated by the ancient Egyptians more than 5,000 years ago.

• Pigeons can see clearly for 25 miles and hear wind changes hundreds of miles away.

• Pigeons mate for life and share parenting duties. The father sits on the eggs during the day, the mother at night.

• Pigeons are the only birds that don't have to lift their heads to swallow water.

• Passenger pigeons were once the most numerous birds in the world. Ornithologist John J. Audubon recorded seeing a single flock in 1808 that he calculated to be 150 miles long, numbering over two billion birds. By 1914 hunting and deforestation had led to the total extinction of the birds.

• Ever seen a baby pigeon? You probably have: young pigeons grow extremely fast. They may weigh more than their parents by the time they're only four to six weeks.

• In the 17th century, pigeon droppings were used to tan hides and to make gunpowder.

• Homing pigeons were used in both world wars to carry messages between troops and headquarters. They had a 98% success rate in missions flown.

• Racing pigeons have been clocked at 110 mph.

• Only mammals produce milk, right? Wrong. Pigeons make "pigeon milk," an extremely nutritious secretion from the "crop," a chamber at the bottom of the esophagus. Both parents make it and feed their young with it.

• Racing pigeons are bred for speed. In 1992 champion racer *Invincible Spirit* was sold for over $130,000.

• Why do pigeons live in cities? One theory: They are descended from rock doves, cliff dwellers that live near the Mediterranean. Urban structures mimic those ancestral cliffs.

Q: What is the largest animal that ever lived on Earth? A: Not a dinosaur—it's the blue whale.

WHEN CELEBRITIES ATTACK

Stars are often at their funniest when they're attacking other stars.

"I'm not a Julie Andrews fan, no. I'm a diabetic."
—**David Janssen**

"Prince looks like a dwarf that fell into a vat of pubic hair."
—**Boy George, on Prince**

"Marlon [Brando] is the most overrated actor in the world."
—**Frank Sinatra**

"Zsa Zsa the-Bore. Did I spell that right?"
—**Elayne Boosler**

"If Kathleen Turner had been a man, I would have knocked her out long ago."
—**Burt Reynolds**

"Jeremy Irons has no sex appeal....He's perfect for horror movies—or science fiction. He's an iceberg with an accent."
—**Andy Warhol**

"Where else but in America could a poor black boy like Michael Jackson grow up to be a rich white woman?"
—**Red Buttons**

"Charlton Heston—a graduate of the Mt. Rushmore school of acting."
—**Edward G. Robinson**

"Peter O'Toole looks like he's walking around just to save the funeral expenses."
—**John Huston**

"Sylvester Stallone's got two bodyguards who look exactly like him walking around on the beach, so I guess he figures that cuts the odds of being assassinated to one in three."
—**Jack Lemmon**

"I am fascinated by Courtney Love, the same way I am by someone who's got Tourette's syndrome walking in Central Park."
—**Madonna**

"In truth, he's [Michael Caine] an overfat, flatulent, 62-year-old windbag, a master of inconsequence now masquerading as a guru, passing off his vast limitations as pious virtues."
—**Richard Harris**

State with the highest cremation rate: Nevada, at 65%. Lowest: Alabama, at 4.5%.

ASK UNCLE JOHN:
THE HUMAN BODY

*Answers to every question you ever had about physiology, provided
that every question you ever had is one of these three.*

Dear Uncle John: What is all this about "left-brained" and
"right-brained" people? Does it have a basis in reality? Or is it
the new astrology?

The answer is yes to both. The human brain is largely composed of
two hemispheres, the left and the right, each of which is better at certain tasks. Generally, the left side of your brain is the part that handles most of the "logical" aspects of thinking and processing, while the right side handles a lot of the "creative" processes. So, for example, you do math with your left brain, but you do improv dance numbers with your right. People who are better at logical, reality-based thinking are said to be "left-brained," while people who excel at creative tasks are said to be "right-brained." So there is some truth to the "left-brain, right brain" theory. But people tend to grossly oversimplify the concept, which makes it like astrology: Whatever scientific underpinnings there are to their understanding of the subject are overwhelmed by miscomprehension of it.

For one thing, no one is wholly "left-brained" or "right-brained"—almost every human is adept at skills from both sides of the hemispheric menu. In addition, not every brain works the same way. More than 75 percent of people predominately use their left hemisphere for language skills—but that still leaves a large chunk of people who have language skills in the right hemisphere, or in both hemispheres. Also, many people erroneously believe that your "handedness" correlates to which side of your brain predominates—so if you're left-handed, you're right-brained (the hemispheres are in charge of the opposite sides of the body). But that correlation doesn't hold up, either—there are plenty of left-handed math geeks and right-handed artists.

Dear Uncle John: Why is your heart on the left side of your body?
It's not. Crack open an anatomy book (or alternately, if you're a doctor,

---

In Europe, a moose is known as an elk, and an elk is known as a wapiti.

crack open a human chest), and you'll notice that the heart is more or less in the middle of the chest, nestled between the lungs. What makes people think the heart is to the left is that the heart's left ventricle, a chamber that pumps blood, is larger than the right ventricle. This gives the heart its left-leaning shape, so that the heart intrudes farther into the left side of the body than to the right. It also gives the sensation of the heartbeat coming from left of center.

And why is the left ventricle so much larger than the right ventricle? It's because of where the ventricles are pumping blood. The right ventricle receives deoxygenated blood that's just come from the body and sends it off to the lungs to get oxygen. Since the lungs are right next to the heart, it's not a very long trip, and not that much effort is required. The left ventricle, however, is sending the now-oxygenated blood to all the rest of the body, which requires more force to get the blood to where it needs to go.

Dear Uncle John: Do "double-jointed" people actually have two sets of joints?

No. "Double-jointedness"—the ability to bend your thumbs, elbows, or other joints at odd or extreme angles—is a condition known in medical circles as *joint hypermobility syndrome*. It's not that these people have more joints than the rest of us do; it's simply that their joints are more flexible. And while "joint hypermobility syndrome" sounds like a disease, most of the time it's fairly harmless. Doctors say that somewhere between 10 and 15 percent of children have hypermobility (which is something that anyone who has ever been in a classroom of third-graders knows already), and most of these kids will lose their hyperflexibility over time. Hypermobility often runs in families, and occurs more often in women than in men.

In fairly rare cases, joint hypermobility can be a symptom of Ehlers-Danlos Syndrome, a class of ailments that includes weakened connective tissues at the joints, as well as other phenomena such as hyperelastic skin. People who have hypermobile joints may also be more susceptible to pulls, sprains, dislocations, and other more serious ailments such as scoliosis (curvature of the spine). Finally, a recent study published in the *Journal of Rheumatology* suggests that people who are double-jointed may be slightly more susceptible to fibromyalgia (a pain disorder affecting the muscles and bones) and chronic fatigue syndrome.

Kelsey Grammar sings and plays the piano on the theme song to *Frasier*.

NEW PRODUCTS

Just when you think everything that could possibly be invented has already been invented, along comes something like rejection-letter toilet paper.

TRUTH IN ADVERTISING

Say, what's that suspicious looking device? It's the "Suspicious Looking Device!" A darkly humorous response to the increased fears of terrorism in recent years, the SLD is a red metal box with dotted lights, a small screen, a buzzer, and whirring motor. What does it do? Nothing. It's just supposed to *appear* suspicious.

I WISH...FOR AN FTC INVESTIGATION

A company called Life Technology Research International has created the seemingly impossible: a magical wishing machine. You simply speak into the microphone on the Psychotronic Wishing Machine to tell it what you want...then sit back and wait a few days for your wish to come true. Just make sure the machine is on—LTRI says that the wish is far less likely to ever come true if the machine is turned off while the wish is still being "processed." Nevertheless, results are still *not* guaranteed. How does it work? "Conscious human interaction and energy fields." Cost: $499.

GET YOUR MOTOR RUNNIN'

For the cat owner who has everything: A California man has invented the Purr Detector. It's a small motion detector and light embedded inside a cat collar. Whenever the cat purrs, the collar glows. It's only available by mail order, so if you need to know if your cat is purring before the Purr Detector arrives, you can always use your ears.

TASTE IS NOT A FACTOR

The gross-out game show *Fear Factor* is no longer on the air, but it's still going strong with a line of candy based on its most memorable segment: people eating disgusting animal parts. There are lollipops in the shape of a chicken's foot, pig's snout, and cow's heart (flavored lemon, bubblegum, and cinnamon, respectively) as well as candy sheep eyeballs (mango) and "coagulated blood balls" (mmm…cherry!).

POT STICKERS

Many toddlers resist potty training because they're afraid of the toilet. The white porcelain behemoth is supposed to look a lot less imposing with Toilet Buddies: brightly-colored animal stickers that affix to the toilet, making it look kid-friendly enough for the little ones to use it. They're available in Poo P. Bunny, Puddles Puppy, and Ca Ca Cow.

NO, YOU'RE REJECTED!

Most successful writers had a period of frequent rejection letters from publishers (even Uncle John). Now, jilted authors can happily take out their revenge on those who have denied them literary glory with Rejection Letter Toilet Paper. You go to the Web site of a company called Lulu, upload the text of a rejection letter, and the company prints it onto four rolls of toilet paper for you.

ZOMBIE-UTIFUL

A few years ago, friends of Canadian artist Rob Sacchetto asked him to draw pictures of them as zombies to use as decorations for a Halloween party. Now Sacchetto runs a business selling Zombie Portraits. For $80, Sacchetto takes a photograph of you and uses it as the basis for a hand-drawn caricature of you as a zombie, complete with rotting flesh, oozing brains, and sagging eyeballs.

BRUSH YOUR CASTLE

Sarah Witmer had a tradition with her grandchildren: Whenever they lost a tooth, they'd put it under their pillow and the "tooth fairy" (Witmer) took it away. But this tooth fairy was a little different: A couple of days later, the kid would get a small sculpture of a castle made out of sand and the ground-up tooth. Now Witmer makes "Fairy Tooth Castles" professionally. When your child loses a tooth, you can send it to Witmer. She'll grind it up, mix it with sand and a hardening agent, sculpt a nine-inch-tall castle out of it, and send it back to you.

STAGECOACH RULES

Stagecoach travel has been glamorized by Hollywood: a handsome hero in an immaculate white shirt and string necktie, and a neatly coiffured heroine swaying gently as the stage races across the prairie. Romantic? Yes. Truthful? No. Stagecoaches didn't race—good drivers averaged 5 mph. And passengers arrived covered with dust and aching from the bone-rattling journey. These rigorous conditions created discord, so at every station, Wells Fargo posted this list.

Stagecoach Riders' Nine Commandments

1. Abstinence from liquor is requested. If you must drink, share your bottle; otherwise you will appear to be selfish and unneighborly.

2. If ladies are present, gentlemen are urged to forego smoking pipes or cigars, as the odor is repugnant to the gentle sex. Chewing tobacco is permitted, but spit with the wind, not against it.

3. Gentlemen must refrain from using rough language in the presence of ladies and children.

4. Buffalo robes are provided for your comfort during cold weather. Hogging robes will not be tolerated and the offender will be made to ride with the driver.

5. Don't snore loudly while sleeping or use your fellow passenger's shoulder for a pillow. He (or she) may not understand and friction may result.

6. Firearms may be kept on your person for use in emergencies. Do not fire them for pleasure or shoot at wild animals as the sound riles the horses.

7. In the event of runaway horses, remain calm. Leaping from the coach in panic will leave you injured, at the mercy of the elements, hostile Indians, and hungry coyotes.

8. Forbidden topics of discussion are stagecoach robberies and Indian uprisings.

9. Gents guilty of unchivalrous behavior toward lady passengers will be put off the stage. It's a long walk back. A word to the wise is sufficient.

Boris Karloff had a pet pig named Violet.

CELEBRITY LAWSUITS

*Uncle John noticed that a number of the cases in our
"Strange Lawsuits" file involve celebrities of one
sort or another. Here's a sampling.*

THE PLAINTIFF: Mark Twain

THE DEFENDANT: Estes and Lauriat Publishing Co.

THE LAWSUIT: In 1876 the Canadian publishers pirated the text of Twain's book *Tom Sawyer* and put out a low-priced edition. It cut into legitimate U.S. sales and deprived Twain of royalties. When he wrote *The Adventures of Huckleberry Finn* in 1884, he was determined to prevent a recurrence. He decided to publish *Huck Finn* himself…but hold off printing it until he had orders for 40,000 copies. That way, the book pirates wouldn't have a chance to undercut him.

Yet somehow, Estes and Lauriat got hold of a manuscript and started selling a pirated edition two months *before* Twain's authorized edition was available. Livid, Twain sued them.

THE VERDICT: Believe it or not, Twain lost the case. He issued this statement: "[The judge has allowed the publisher] to sell property which does not belong to him but me—property which he has not bought and I have not sold. Under this same ruling, I am now advertising the judge's homestead for sale; and if I make as good a sum out of it as I expect, I shall go on and sell the rest of his property."

THE PLAINTIFFS: Ten people named Jeff Stone, including the mayor of Temecula, California; a guy who works for NASA; and Paul Peterson—who isn't actually a Jeff Stone, but played a character with that name on TV's *Donna Reed Show* from 1958 to 1966

THE DEFENDANT: Jeff Gillooly, Tonya Harding's infamous ex-husband, who served seven months in jail for plotting the 1994 attack on her skating rival, Nancy Kerrigan

THE LAWSUIT: In 1995 Gillooly filed to change his name to Jeff Stone (so he could have some anonymity). Other Jeff Stones announced that they were outraged. Mayor Stone said his "hard-earned good name would be sullied"; Peterson insisted Gillooly was mocking his sitcom; NASA's Stone spread the word that he simply didn't want to share his name with Gillooly. And then they sued to prevent it.

THE VERDICT: In a 10-minute hearing, the judge ruled there was no basis for stopping Gillooly from becoming a Jeff Stone.

THE PLAINTIFF: Saddam Hussein

THE DEFENDANT: *Le Nouvel Observateur*, a French magazine

THE LAWSUIT: In an article about Hussein, the magazine described him as a "monster," "executioner," "complete cretin," and a "noodle." Hussein sued for libel.

THE VERDICT: Case dismissed.

THE PLAINTIFF: A dentist

THE DEFENDANTS: Johnny Carson and NBC

THE LAWSUIT: In the early 1980s, during a broadcast of the *Tonight Show*, Carson mentioned he'd seen a report saying that dentists were closing their offices due to lack of business. "News like this," he quipped, "hasn't made me so happy since I heard the Gestapo disbanded." An angry dentist immediately sued Carson and the station for $1 million for libel.

THE VERDICT: Case dismissed.

THE PLAINTIFF: Dustin Hoffman

THE DEFENDANT: *Los Angeles* magazine

THE LAWSUIT: In its March 1997 issue, the magazine superimposed a picture of Hoffman's face—from the film *Tootsie*, in which he dressed as a woman—on a the body of a model "wearing a smashing gown and smart high heels." The caption: "Dustin Hoffman isn't a drag in a butter-colored silk gown by Richard Tyler and Ralph Lauren heels." Hoffman sued for $5 million, saying they had turned him into "an unpaid fashion model."

THE VERDICT: Calling Hoffman "one of our greatest living treasures," the judge ordered the magazine to pay the actor $3 million.

MANEKI NEKO

There are countless superstitions involving cats, most of
them focused on the bad luck that they supposedly bring.
In Japan and other Asian countries, however,
the cat is a symbol of good fortune.

THE BECKONING CAT

If you've ever walked into a Chinese or Japanese business and noticed a figure of a cat with an upraised paw, you've met Maneki Neko (pronounced MAH-ne-key NAY-ko). "The Beckoning Cat" is displayed to invite good fortune, a tradition that began with a legendary Japanese cat many centuries ago.

According to legend, that cat, called Tama, lived in a poverty-stricken temple in 17th-century Tokyo. The temple priest often scolded Tama for contributing nothing to the upkeep of the temple. Then one day, a powerful feudal lord named Naotaka Ii was caught in a rainstorm near the temple while returning home from a hunting trip. As the lord took refuge under a big tree, he noticed Tama with her paw raised, beckoning to him, inviting him to enter the temple's front gate. Intrigued, the lord decided to get a closer look at this remarkable cat. Suddenly, the tree was struck by lightning and fell on the exact spot where Naotaka had just been standing. Tama had saved his life! In gratitude, Naotaka made the little temple his family temple and became its benefactor. Tama and the priest never went hungry again. After a long life, Tama was buried with great respect at the renamed Goutokuji temple. Goutokuji still exists, housing dozens of statues of the Beckoning Cat.

LUCKY CHARMS

Figures of Maneki Neko became popular in Japan under shogun rule in the 19th century. At that time, most "houses of amusement" (brothels) and many private homes had a good-luck shelf filled with lucky charms, many in the shape of male sexual organs. When Japan began to associate with Western countries in the 1860s, the charms began to be seen as vulgar. In an effort to modernize Japan and improve its image, Emperor Meiji outlawed the production, sale, and display of phallic talismans in 1872.

"If you would be a real seeker after truth, it is necessary that at least once in your life...

People still wanted lucky objects, however, so the less controversial Maneki Neko figures became popular.

Eventually the image of the lucky cat spread to China and then to Southeast Asia. How popular did the Beckoning Cat become? In Thailand, the ancient goddess of prosperity, Nang Kwak, was traditionally shown kneeling with a money bag on her lap. Now she's usually shown making the cat's raised-hand gesture and occasionally sporting a cat's tail.

In Europe and North America, images of Maneki Neko can be found in Asian-owned businesses, such as Chinese restaurants. And back in Japan, a new cat icon adorns clothing, toys, and various objects: Hello Kitty—a literal translation of Maneki Neko, or "Beckoning Cat."

MANEKI NEKO FACTS

• Sometimes Maneki Neko has his left paw up, sometimes the right. The left paw signifies that the business owner is inviting in customers. The right invites in money or good fortune.

• Most Maneki Nekos are calico cats; the male calico is so rare it's considered lucky in Japan. But Maneki Neko may be white, black, red, gold, or pink to ward off illness, bad luck, or evil spirits and bring financial success, good luck, health, and love.

• Maneki Nekos made in Japan show the palm of the paw, imitating the manner in which Japanese people beckon. American Maneki Nekos show the back of the paw, reflecting the way we gesture "come here."

• The higher Maneki Neko holds his paw, the more good fortune is being invited.

*　　　*　　　*

"I don't need a reading lamp in my living room. I don't have a toilet in there."

—**Norm MacDonald**

…you doubt, as far as possible, all things." —René Descartes

UNCLE JOHN'S PAGE OF LISTS

Uncle John has a list of 10 reasons why the Bathroom Reader
should have lists in it. (The list is confidential.)

7 "OFFICIAL" ATTRIBUTES OF THE PILLSBURY DOUGHBOY

1. His skin must look like dough: "off-white, smooth, but not glossy"

2. Slightly luminous, but no sheen

3. No knees, elbows, wrists, fingers, ears, or ankles

4. Rear views do not include "buns"

5. Walks with a "swagger"

6. Stomach is proportional to the rest of his body.

7. He is not portly.

6 MOST COMMONLY MISSPELLED U.S. CITIES

1. Pittsburgh, PA

2. Tucson, AZ

3. Cincinnati, OH

4. Albuquerque, NM

5. Culpeper, VA

6. Asheville, NC

4 SPORTS YOU CAN ONLY WIN BY GOING BACKWARDS

1. Rappelling

2. Rowing

3. Tug-of-war

4. High jump

5 MOST WIDELY ASSIGNED BOOKS IN HIGH SCHOOLS

1. *The Adventures of Huckleberry Finn*

2. *The Scarlet Letter*

3. *To Kill a Mockingbird*

4. *Lord of the Flies*

5. *The Great Gatsby*

7 ANIMALS THAT MATE FOR LIFE

1. Beaver

2. Orangutan

3. Fox

4. Stork

5. Penguin

6. Vulture

7. Pigeon

7 HIGHEST TEMPERATURES RECORDED ON EACH CONTINENT

1. Africa: 136°F

2. N. America: 134°F

3. Asia: 129°F

4. Australia: 128°F

5. Europe: 122°F

6. S. America: 120°F

7. Antarctica: 59°F

6 FLAVORS OF KIT-KAT BARS SOLD IN JAPAN

1. Green tea

2. Red bean

3. Yubari melon

4. Cherry blossom

5. Wine

6. Blood Orange

5 THINGS INVENTED BY MONKS

1. Mechanical clocks

2. Pretzels

3. Roulette

4. The @ sign

5. Munster cheese

EARTH'S GREATEST HITS

*Every so often a hunk of rock hurtles out of the sky and slams
into our planet, creating a gigantic hole and wreaking havoc.
Here are some of the more impressive cosmic splats.*

CHICXULUB, YUCATÁN

About 65 million years ago, a giant meteor six miles wide splashed down in the Caribbean region of Mexico. It probably split in two shortly before impact. The result: *two* craters that are a combined 102 miles in diameter. The meteors fell in a sulfur-rich area of the Yucatán Peninsula, kicking up billions of tons of poisonous dust. The sky all over the world was dark for six months, making global temperatures drop below freezing. That climate change, according to most scientists, caused the extinction of half the Earth's existing species… including the dinosaurs.

GRAND TETONS, WYOMING

In 1972 a 1,000-ton meteor entered the Earth's atmosphere high above the Grand Tetons at a very shallow angle and then skipped back out into space like a stone skipping off the surface of a lake (but not before being recorded by Air Force and tourist photographers). If it had gone all the way through the atmosphere, it would have hit Canada and the impact would have rocked the area with a blast the size of the Hiroshima A-bomb.

TUNGUSKA, SIBERIA

On June 30, 1908, Russian settlers north of Lake Baikal saw a giant fireball streak across the sky. Moments later a blinding flash lit up the sky, followed by a shock wave that knocked people off their feet 40 miles away. The blast was estimated to be more than 10 megatons, toppling 60 million trees over an area of 830 square miles. What was startling about the Tunguska blast was that there was no crater, which led to speculation about the blast: A black hole passing through the Earth? The annihilation of a chunk of antimatter falling from space? An exploding alien spaceship? Research ultimately revealed that the devastation was caused by a meteor about 450 feet in diameter that exploded

---

Rule of tongue: Generally, the smaller the pepper, the hotter it is.

four to six miles above the ground. If it had landed on a city, no one would have survived.

BARRINGER METEOR CRATER, ARIZONA

Located in the middle of the desert, this crater is important be-cause it was the first one on Earth positively identified as the result of a falling meteor. The meteorite that made the crater was about 150 feet in diameter, weighed about 300,000 tons, and was traveling at a speed of 40,000 mph when it landed. The crater is three quarters of a mile wide and was named for D. M. Barringer, the mining engineer who correctly identified it. He also believed that the actual meteorite was still lodged below the Earth's surface and could be mined for its iron content. (He died before studies revealed that it had vaporized on impact.) Scientists say a meteor of this size can be expected to hit the Earth every 50,000 years. Since this one fell to Earth about 49,000 years ago, we could be due for another one soon.

METEOR FACTS

• So far 150 impact craters have been identified on the Earth's surface.

• Oldest crater on Earth: Vredefort Crater in South Africa. It's two billion years old.

• Meteors the size of a basketball hit Earth once a month.

• More than 25,000 meteors bigger than 3.5 ounces hit every year.

• Meteors as large as the one that hit Tunguska impact the Earth every 100 years or so. Bigger explosions, the size of the largest H-bombs, take place about once every 1,000 years.

• Terminology: in space it's a *meteor*; on the ground, it's a *meteorite*.

• A large meteorite is always cold to the touch. The outer layers are burned off from its trip through the atmosphere; the inner layers retain the cold of deep space.

• Preview of the big one? In 1994 the comet Shoemaker-Levy 9 slammed into the atmosphere of Jupiter, generating an explosion the equivalent of 300 trillion tons of TNT. The comet was estimated to be three miles in diameter; the hole it made was larger than Earth. If it had hit our planet instead of Jupiter...well, you do the math.

In an airtight room, you'd die of carbon dioxide poisoning before you'd die of oxygen deprivation

TO SLEEP...OR NOT TO SLEEP?

If you think about it, it's kind of unfair that we have to spend one-third of our entire lives unconscious. But it turns out that if we didn't, our lives would be a lot shorter.

THE NEED FOR SLEEP

Newborn babies sleep about 16 hours a day—adults average half that. Teens, especially girls, are gluttons for sleep (10 hours average), but it's not because they're lazy, as many parents think. Stanford researchers found it was tied to the complex inner labors of puberty. This hunch is underlined by teen girls' need for extra Z's during their periods.

• We sleep best at certain times and if we stray from our required sleep needs, there's no telling what will happen. The nuclear disasters at both Chernobyl and Three Mile Island, as well as the Exxon *Valdez* wreck and *Challenger* shuttle explosion, have been linked to lack of sleep or altered sleep cycles among key people at key moments.

• "Jet lag" shifts our sleep cycle, often creating confusion, mental dullness and a desire to sleep at odd times. The U.S. Army was disappointed to find that troops flown overseas often require a week to overcome their disorientation. This phenomenon is the bane of passenger jet crews. In one instance, for example, all three members of a jetliner crew fell asleep as they reached the end of their overnight New York-to-Los Angeles flight. While air traffic controllers radioed them frantically, the jet flew 100 miles out over the ocean. Finally, one of the crew woke up and saw the sea in every direction. They had just enough fuel to make it back to LAX.

NAPTIME

According to Stanley Coren, in his book *Sleep Thieves*, scientists have identified the two big peaks in our need for sleep—at 3 a.m. and 3 p.m. The first is dead in the center of our sleep cycle, but the second is smack in the middle of our workday. Conclusion: We should be napping in mid-afternoon. At present, only 38% of us do.

75% of women make a birthday wish when they blow out the candles; only 17% of men do.

Who's getting the most sleep? Surveys find:

- In the U.S., Westerners and Southerners sleep longer than Easterners and Midwesterners.

- Women sleep more than men.

- Poor people sleep more than the rich.

- People who work evening or night shifts get far less sleep—about 5.6 hours—than day workers. No matter how hard they try, researchers say, people who sleep out of their normal cycle never fully adjust.

DOES LESS SLEEP = SUCCESS?

- A short sleep cycle is not inherently bad. Some people seek it out and sing its praises. Multi-millionaire magnate Donald Trump boasts of needing only three to four hours a night. Former junk-bond king Michael Milken gets only four to five hours.

- This raises the question: Is there a link between sleep and success? Tufts University researcher Ernest Hartmann found that people who sleep less than 5.5 hours tend to be extroverted, ambitious and efficient, while people who sleep more than 9 hours tend to be anxious, insecure, introverted and indecisive. Other researchers think this is nonsense, noting that short-sleepers tend to be fast-paced, Type-A personalities (thus prone to heart disease), while long-sleepers include society's creative, alternate type thinkers and artists.

- Researchers conducted a survey of the CEO's and chairs of the Fortune 500 companies to settle the question of whether "the early bird really does get the worm." Apparently, it does. They found that 46% of the leaders they surveyed slept an hour less than the national average of 7.5 hours. Fifteen percent slept 5–6 hours and 2% slept 4–5 hours.

THE TRICK OF GETTING MORE SLEEP

Most of us, however, aren't looking for ways to sleep less—our focus is on how to get more. Here are some tips from the experts:

- Go to bed about the same time each night.
- Avoid nightcaps, except warm milk.
- Avoid illuminated clocks (they're a reminder you can't sleep).
- Exercise before going to bed.
- A dark and slightly cool bedroom is best (about 65°F).

J. M. Barrie, author of *Peter Pan*, stopped growing at age 15, at the height of 5 feet.

GAME SHOW GOOFS

Being on a game show may look easy from the comfort of your living room, but under those hot television lights, contestants' mouths sometimes disconnect from their brains.

Anne Robinson: What insect is commonly found hovering above lakes?
Contestant: Crocodiles.
—The Weakest Link

Alex Trebek: If a Japanese *isha* (doctor) asks you to stick out your *shita*, he means this.
Contestant: What is…your behind?
—Jeopardy!

Anne Robinson: Who is the only Marx brother that remained silent throughout all their films?
Contestant: Karl.
—The Weakest Link

Todd Newton: Bourbon whiskey is named after Bourbon County, located in what state?
Contestant: England.
—Press Your Luck

The Puzzle: TOM HANKS AS _ORREST GUMP
Contestant: Tom Hanks as Morris Gump.
—Wheel of Fortune

Richard Dawson: Name something a blind man might use.
Contestant: A sword.
—Family Feud

Eamonn Holmes: Name the playwright commonly known by the initials G.B.S.
Contestant: William Shakespeare?
—National Lottery Jet Set

Steve Wright: What is the capital of Australia? And it's not Sydney.
Contestant: Sydney.
—Steve Wright Radio Show

Bob Eubanks: What is your husband's favorite cuisine?
Contestant: *All in the Family.*
—The Newlywed Game

Kevin O'Connell: What moos?
Contestant: A car.
—Go

Richard Dawson: Name an occupation whose members must get tired of smiling.
Contestant: Game show host.
—Family Feud

The surgical device used to extract bullets is called an *alphonsin*.

THE AVRO ARROW, PT. II

Here's the conclusion of a story that's familiar to many Canadians but, for the rest of the world, was just "the fastest plane that never was." (Part I is on page 197.)

WHAT'S THE PROBLEM?

The irony of the Avro Arrow's cancellation was that in spite of all the problems, Avro had managed to produce a very sophisticated aircraft that had performed exceptionally well in flight testing. At the time the program was cancelled, the company was only two weeks away from fitting the aircraft with improved jet engines that would likely have made it the fastest fighter plane in the world.

Would the Arrow have broken the world speed record? We'll never know for sure, because shortly after the program was cancelled, the Canadian government ordered everything associated with the program—aircraft, models, tooling, spare parts, even blueprints and photographs—to be destroyed to prevent the technology from falling into the hands of Soviet spies. Canadian taxpayers had pumped more than $300 million into the project by then, but had literally nothing to show for it. Avro closed its doors; Canada lost its edge in defense aviation and never built another fighter plane. Many of Avro's top designers and engineers went abroad to find work: Some went to Europe and worked on the Concorde, and more than 30 went to NASA and played leading roles in the effort to land *American* men on the moon.

JET SET

All that survives today are a couple of engines, a cockpit and nose cone, a few diagrams, odd parts, and some historical photos. This near-total destruction of the Arrow, combined with the fact that it was the most advanced fighter of its day, has elevated the plane to mythical status. "Arrow Heads," as fans are known, build replicas, trade conspiracy theories, and dream of what might have been. Wishful thinkers look at the 1959 photo showing the jets lined up outside the factory to be destroyed and note that one plane, RL-202, is not in the picture. Does that mean it's still out there somewhere, waiting to be found? University of Toronto historian Michael Bliss likes to tell his students it's in a barn in Saskatchewan. "It's taken out and flown once a year. By Elvis."

The common garden slug may be soft and slimy, but it does have a shell. It's inside its body.

THE BEST DEAL IN $PORT$ HISTORY

When you hear about how much money sports generates for players, owners, and agents, it can make you feel sick—even fed up with the whole sports establishment. But, for some reason, these guys make us smile.

THE A-B-AWAY

In 1974 textile tycoons Ozzie and Dan Silna paid about $1 million for the struggling Carolina Cougars of the American Basketball Association and moved the team to Missouri, where they renamed it the Spirits of St. Louis. Why did they buy the team? Oddly enough, because they knew the league would be going out of business soon. The ABA, just seven years old at the time, was in terrible shape: They couldn't compete with the growing and much more popular National Basketball Association, and ABA teams were losing money or folding altogether. The Silna brothers felt that a merger between the two leagues was probably in the cards, and that some of the more successful ABA teams would become NBA teams, a potentially lucrative opportunity. So they beefed up the Spirits with great young players—Moses Malone and Don Chaney among them—and waited for the league to collapse. In 1976 it did, and the NBA moved in. One problem: They didn't want the Spirits.

THE DEAL

The ABA was down to just six teams by this point (the NBA had 18), but the bigger league wanted only four of them—the Denver Rockets (later the Nuggets), the Indiana Pacers, the New York (later New Jersey) Nets, and the San Antonio Spurs. The two they didn't want: the Kentucky Colonels and the Spirits. Luckily, that didn't leave the Silnas and the Colonels' owner John Y. Brown powerless: For the merger to go through, every owner had to agree with whatever deal was hammered out. The NBA dealt with the Colonels by offering Brown a $3.3 million "buyout"—and he took it. They offered the same to the Silnas...but they declined. They had other ideas.

Gastromancy is the art of telling the future by the noises in your belly.

On top of the $3.3 million, the Silnas, along with their bulldog of an attorney, Donald Schupak, demanded one-seventh of future television revenues generated by the four former ABA teams. At the time, television revenues for pro basketball games were relatively miniscule—the league had terrible ratings compared to pro baseball and football. So the NBA, after negotiating the lump-sum payment down to $2.2 million, agreed. It was a mistake that they regret to this day.

SPIRITS IN THE MATERIAL WORLD

For the first few years, the Silnas made less than $100,000 per year from the TV deal. That's not bad for doing nothing, but it was about to get a lot better. The legendary rivalry between Larry Bird's Boston Celtics and Magic Johnson's Los Angeles Lakers, starting in 1980, fueled a huge growth in the NBA's popularity—and in TV revenues. By 1982 the Silnas were making almost $200,000 a year. The league offered the brothers $5 million to buy out their contract. They said they'd take $8 million, but the NBA refused—which was probably a dumber move than when it made the original deal. In 1984 Michael Jordan entered the league; by 1988 the Silnas were getting nearly $1 million per year. In 1992 the league offered them $18 million to end the contract. No way. By 1994 their earnings were up to around $4 million annually. And it gets still better.

SLAM DUNK

Business experts have called the Silna brothers' 1976 contract possibly the best in history—and not just in sports, but in all business. And the most significant clause in it: "The right to receive such revenues shall continue for as long as the NBA or its successors continue in its existence."

As of 2010, the former owners of the former team known as the Spirits of St. Louis have raked in about $180 million in total. Over the next eight years, based on the NBA's latest contracts with ABC, TNT, and ESPN, they'll be getting around $130 million *more*. That'll bring their total up to more than $320 million...for an initial investment of about $5 million. "I would have loved to have an NBA team," says 73-year-old Ozzie Silna. "But if I look at it retrospectively over what I would have gotten, versus what I've received now—then I'm a happy camper."

Horses in New York City caused 75% more fatalities per capita in 1900 than cars did in 2000.

VAMPIRES ON BIKINI BEACH

Film historian David Skal writes, "Dracula has been depicted in film more times than almost any fictional being." Here's a look at some of the more unusual vampire movies that have been made.

Dracula Blows His Cool (1982)
"Three voluptuous models and their photographer restore an ancient castle and open a disco in it. The vampire lurking about the castle welcomes the party with his fangs." (*Video Hound's Golden Movie Retriever 2001*)

Little Red Riding Hood and Tom Thumb vs. the Monsters (1960)
"Little Red Riding Hood and Tom Thumb fight a vampire and a witch in a haunted forest! One of three Hood movies made the same year in Mexico and shipped up here like clockwork in the mid-'60s to warp the minds of little kids whose parents wanted to go Christmas shopping." (*The Psychotronic Encyclopedia of Film*)

Planet of the Vampires (1965)
"Some astronauts crash land on a strange planet where the undead kill the living, only to discover that the alien-possessed vampiric survivors are preparing to land on another alien world—Earth!" (*The Essential Monster Movie Guide*)

The Devil Bat (1940)
"Bela Lugosi plays a crazed scientist who trains bats to kill at the scent of a certain perfume." (*Halliwell's Film and Video Guide*)

Haunted Cop Shop (1984)
"When vampires invade a meat-packing plant, the elite Monster Police Squad is brought in to stop them. When the squad botches the job, the Police Commissioner bumps them down to foot patrol until the vampires

attack the county hospital. Impressive special effects." (*The Illustrated Vampire Movie Guide*)

Samson vs. the Vampire Women (1961)

"Sexy vampire women keep muscular male slaves on slabs in their atmospheric crypt. Santo the silver-masked Mexican wrestling hero (called Samson in the dubbed version) defeats them all." (*The Psychotronic Encyclopedia of Film*)

Vampires on Bikini Beach (1988)

"Californians save their beach from undesirable vampires." (Is there some other kind?) (*The Illustrated Vampire Movie Guide*)

Billy the Kid vs. Dracula (1965)

"The title says it all. Dracula travels to the Old West, anxious to put the bite on a pretty lady ranch owner. Her fiancé, the legendary Billy the Kid, steps in to save his girl from becoming a vampire herself. A classic." (*Video Hound's Golden Movie Retriever*)

The Return of the Vampire (1943)

"Bela Lugosi plays Armand Tesla (basically Dracula under another name), who returns to claim a girl after 'marking' her when she was a child. But his assistant, the werewolf-with-a-heart, turns on him and drags him out into the sunlight, where he melts in spectacular fashion." (*Amazon Reviews*)

Atom Age Vampire (1960)

"Badly dubbed Italian timewaster with cheese-ball special effects and a tired premise. A mad professor restores the face of a scarred accident victim." (*Video Movie Guide*)

Haunted Cop Shop II (1986)

"This improved sequel to the 1984 original features non-stop action. The vampire creature is destroyed by the hero relieving himself into a swimming pool and completing an electrical circuit!" (*The Illustrated Vampire Movie Guide*)

Traditionally, Swiss newlyweds make a wish and break a pretzel.

BIERCE-ISMS

Author and newspaper columnist Ambrose Bierce (1842–1914)
often peppered his articles with his own humorous—and cynical
—definitions for common words. Here are a few of our favorites.

Dentist: A magician who, putting metal into your mouth, pulls coins out of your pocket.

Positive: Mistaken, at the top of one's voice.

Acquaintance: A person whom we know well enough to borrow from, but not well enough to lend to.

Dog: An additional Deity designed to catch the overflow and surplus of the world's worship.

Clairvoyant: A person who has the power of seeing that which is invisible to her patron—namely, that he is a blockhead.

Revolution: An abrupt change in the form of misgovernment.

Corporation: An ingenious device for obtaining individual profit without individual responsibility.

Admiration: Our polite recognition of another's resemblance to ourselves.

Saint: A dead sinner, revised and edited.

Alliance: The union of two thieves who have their hands so deeply inserted in each other's pockets that they cannot separately plunder a third.

Responsibility: A detachable burden easily shifted to the shoulders of God, Fate, Fortune, Luck, or one's neighbor.

Appeal: In law, to put the dice into the box for another throw.

Coward: One who in a perilous emergency thinks with his legs.

Famous: Conspicuously miserable.

Friendship: A ship big enough to carry two in fair weather, but only one in foul.

Husband: One who, having dined, is charged with the care of the plate.

Meekness: Uncommon patience in planning a revenge that is worthwhile.

Outcome: A particular type of disappointment.

Love: A temporary insanity curable by marriage.

FOUNDING FATHERS

You already know the names. Here's who they belonged to.

William Colgate. In the early 1800s, making soap at home was a matter of pride with American housewives: That's where 75% of U.S. soap was made (although it smelled terrible). In 1806 Colgate opened a soap business and succeeded by offering home delivery, and by adding perfume to his soap.

Gerhard Mennen. While recovering from malaria in the 1870s, he learned so much about the pharmaceutical trade that he opened his own drug store. He made his own remedies, including Mennen's Borated Talcum Infant Powder—America's first talcum powder.

Dr. William Erastus Upjohn. Until Upjohn invented a process for manufacturing soft pills, prescription pills were literally hard as a rock—you couldn't smash them with a hammer, and they often passed through a person's system without being absorbed by the body. Upjohn's new process changed all that.

John Michael Kohler. A Wisconsin foundry owner in the 1880s. One of his big sellers was an enameled iron water trough for farm animals. In 1883, convinced that demand for household plumbing fixtures was growing, he made four cast-iron feet, welded them to the animal trough, and began selling it as a bathtub.

William Boeing. When he wasn't working for his father, a timber and iron baron, Boeing and a friend named Conrad Westervelt built seaplanes as a hobby. In 1916 the pair founded Pacific Aero Products. When the U.S. entered World War I in 1917, the Navy bought 50 of his planes. He never worked for his father again.

William Rand and Andrew McNally. Rand and McNally printed railroad tickets and timetables. In 1872 they added maps to their line. Other companies used wood or metal engravings for their maps; Rand McNally used wax engravings, allowing them to update and correct maps at a fraction of the cost. By the early 1900s, Rand McNally was one of the largest mapmakers in the country.

Michael Jordan had a specific clause in his contract that permitted him...

NAME THAT COUNTRY

*See if you can guess the name of the country before
reading all the clues. (Answers on page 286.)*

SAVED

1. It was originally inhabited by the Pipil tribe.
2. The Pipil are believed to be direct descendants of the Aztecs.
3. The Pipil were defeated by Spanish explorers looking for gold.
4. The Christian Spaniards named it in honor of Jesus.

Name the country.

NOTHING TO IT

1. The local Nama people call it "an area where there is nothing."

2. The name describes the coastal desert area of the country.

3. It has been governed at different times by the British, the Germans, and the South Africans.

4. It gained independence in 1990 from South Africa.

Name the country.

THE NAMELESS NAME

1. It got its European name long before Europeans knew it existed.

2. Early geographers insisted it must be there—if not, the Earth would "wobble."

3. The early name was Latin for "The Unknown Southern Land."

4. Captain James Cook "discovered" it in 1770.

Name the country.

OVER THERE WHERE THE SUN COMES UP

1. Our word for this country originally comes from China.

2. It combines the words "sun" and "east."

3. Portuguese traders learned the name from Malaysians in the 1500s.

4. Inhabitants of this country call it Nippon.

Name the country.

...to play basketball anytime in the off-season. It's known as a "love-of-the-game clause."

GRECIAN FORMULA

1. Early inhabitants called themselves the Pritani.

2. The Greek sailor Pytheas named it after the inhabitants in 300 B.C.

3. When enemy tribes attacked in the 400s, many inhabitants fled this island, taking the name with them to the mainland.

4. To differentiate between the new "lesser" settlement on the mainland, the word "Greater" was added to the name of the island.

Name the island.

ACUTE COUNTRY, BUT A BIT OBTUSE

1. This country, when grouped with two other countries, is known by another name.

2. When grouped with three other countries, it's known by *another* name.

3. The name comes from a Germanic tribe that invaded the country about 1,500 years ago.

4. It is believed that the tribe's name referred to their homeland in present-day Germany, which was shaped like a fishhook.

Name the country.

WHY DON'T THEY SPEAK GERMAN?

1. This country was also named after an invading Germanic tribe.

2. The tribe's name came from a Latin word meaning "masculine."

3. Their allegiance with Rome, and use of its written Latin language, are two reasons why their language is so different from German.

4. They controlled so much of Europe at one point that the Arabic and Persian words for "European" are based on their name.

Name the country.

OVERCOATIA

1. This country was named by the Portuguese in the 1470s.

2. The name comes from the Portuguese word for an overcoat, *Gabao*.

3. The French gained control of this equatorial country in the late 1800s and helped to end its slave trade.

4. It's in western Africa.

Name the country.

It can take as little as 20 seconds for a child to drown.

LOCAL HERO: LEROY GORHAM

*Here's the story of a man who suffered a family
tragedy and then went on a mission to save
other families from the same fate.*

TERRIBLE LOSS

In the summer of 1946 a fire broke out in LeRoy and Lillian Gorham's house in The Bottom neighborhood of Chapel Oaks, Maryland. It took firefighters a very long time to arrive. Too long. By the time they put out the fire, all three of the Gorhams' children—Ruth, 4, Jean, 3, and LeRoy Earl, 2—had perished in the blaze.

There's no way to know if the Gorham children could have been saved had the fire department arrived sooner, and for that matter, no one knows exactly why it took the fire department so long to get there. But The Bottom is a black community, and residents there claim that the all-white fire departments of surrounding communities were always slow to respond to emergencies in black neighborhoods…if they came at all.

"It's just the way it was," said resident Luther Crutchfield. "If they got a call for a fire in a black neighborhood, they either came or they didn't. Sometimes they came, but they took their time." Further complicating matters, The Bottom didn't have running water in the 1940s, so even when firefighters did respond, there was no place to hook up their hoses. Fires were fought with bucket brigades, using water drawn from nearby wells and streams.

A NEW BEGINNING

Gorham was devastated by the loss of his children. He wanted to do anything he could to see to it that no other families in his neighborhood or the surrounding communities ever had to suffer the same fate. So he and a group of his friends decided to found the Chapel Oaks Volunteer Fire Department, the first all-black volunteer fire company in the state of Maryland.

Tennis balls are mentioned in Shakespeare's *Henry V.*

Less than a year after the fire, the department opened its doors. It wasn't easy—the organizers didn't receive any funding from Prince George's County, so they took up a collection in the surrounding black community and used these funds to buy an old pumper, which they kept in an old garage that served as the fire station. There wasn't enough money for proper firefighting gear, so the Chapel Oaks firefighters made do with surplus helmets, coats, and boots they got from the U.S. military. They had no breathing equipment, either—if the men had to enter burning buildings, they simply held their breath or tied wet handkerchiefs over their mouths. Since they didn't have access to professional training, the volunteers trained themselves by setting fires in abandoned buildings and putting them out.

"We weren't in the county fire association, because they had a white male–only clause," remembers Crutchfield, who joined the department in 1949. And the discrimination continued even when firefighters battled a blaze. "The white firefighters would take our lines out and put theirs in," Crutchfield says. "They wouldn't recognize the authority of our chief on the scene. But we wouldn't play those games. We were professional men who were there to save lives, and that's what we did."

HEALING

Change came slowly in the decades that followed. When a fire destroyed the garage that served as Chapel Oak's first fire station, the volunteers raised enough money from the community to build their first proper fire station nearby and laid the bricks themselves. The county fire association eventually dropped its whites-only clause and Chapel Oaks joined in 1960; then, in 1979, the county built them a new fire station.

Gorham and his wife had three more children. He was a volunteer with the department for 54 years, serving as chief for 17 of those. And when he wasn't at the station, he was listening to his radio scanner. "The only time his scanner wasn't on was when he was at church," his daughter Tanya said.

Even when he became too old to fight fires, Gorham continued to visit the fire station every day, and did so until the day before he died in July 2000. "LeRoy wanted to be sure," his friend and fellow firefighter Roy Lee Jordan remembers, "that no other children died like his did."

A fresh lemon left at room temperature will lose 20% of its Vitamin C in 8 hours.

TEARING DOWN THE WHITE HOUSE

The White House wasn't always a national treasure. A number of
presidents once seriously considered demolishing it or turning it
into a museum and building a new residence somewhere else
But today, that's unthinkable. Here's why.

NOT ENOUGH SPACE

At first, most Americans didn't think there was anything particularly special about the White House. Few had ever seen it or had any idea what it looked like, and even the families who lived there found it completely inadequate.

When it was built, the White House was the largest house in the country (and it remained so until after the Civil War). But it served so many different purposes that little of it was available for First Families to actually live in. The first floor, or "State Floor," was made up entirely of public rooms; and half of the second floor was taken up by the president's offices, which where staffed by as many as 30 employees. The First Family had to get by with the eight—or fewer—second-floor rooms that were left.

By Lincoln's time, the situation was intolerable. Kenneth Leish writes in *The White House*, "The lack of privacy was appalling. The White House was open to visitors daily, and office seekers, cranks, and the merely curious had no difficulty making their way upstairs from the official rooms on the first floor."

THE LINCOLN WHITE HOUSE

Lincoln was so uncomfortable with the situation that he had a private corridor (since removed) constructed. This at least allowed him to get from the family quarters to his office without having to pass through the reception room, where throngs of strangers were usually waiting to see him.

He also received a $20,000 appropriation to improve the furnishings of the White House, which had become, as one visitor put it, "bare, worn

---

The barbiturate sodium thiopental is also known as truth serum.

and spoiled," like "a deserted farmstead," with holes in the carpets and paint peeling off of the walls in the state rooms.

Lincoln was busy with the Civil War, so he turned the matter over to his wife, who spent every penny and went $6,700 over budget. Lincoln was furious, and refused to ask Congress to cover the balance. "It would stink in the nostrils of the American people," he fumed, "to have it said that the President of the United States had approved a bill overrunning an appropriate [amount] for *flub dubs* for this damned old house, when the soldiers cannot have blankets."

The new furnishings didn't last for more than a few years. When Lincoln was assassinated in 1865, the White House fell into disarray. "Apparently," writes The White House Historical Society, "no one really supervised the White House during the five weeks Mrs. Lincoln lay mourning in her room, and vandals helped themselves."

SAVING THE HOUSE

Ironically, at the same time the White House was being ransacked, it was gaining a new respect with Americans, attaining an almost shrine-like status.

National tragedy turned the presidential residence into a national monument. It wasn't just the White House anymore—it was the place where the great fallen hero, Lincoln, had lived. Photography had only been invented about 30 years earlier. Now for the first time, photos of the White House circulated around the country. It became a symbol of the presidency…and America.

The Founding Fathers had assumed that future presidents would add to, or even demolish and rebuild the official residence as they saw fit. But after 1865, no president would have dared to suggest tearing it down.

*　　　*　　　*

HOME, BLEAK HOME

"I'll be glad to be going—this is the loneliest place in the world."
> —President William Howard Taft,
> on leaving the White House

THE ENGLISH LANGUAGE

*If English is your first language, thank your lucky stars
that you didn't have to learn it as a second language.*

"Any language where the unassuming word 'fly' signifies an annoying insect, a means of travel, and a critical part of a gentleman's apparel is clearly asking to be mangled."

—**Bill Bryson**

"It's a strange language in which skating on thin ice can get you into hot water."

—**Franklin P. Jones**

"English has created the word 'loneliness' to express the pain of being alone. And it has created the word 'solitude' to express the glory of being alone."

—**Paul Tillich**

"Not only does the English language borrow words from other languages, it sometimes chases them down dark alleys, hits them over the head, and goes through their pockets."

—**Eddy Peters**

"Introducing 'Lite'—the new way to spell 'Light', but with twenty percent fewer letters."

—**Jerry Seinfeld**

"When I read some of the rules for writing the English language correctly, I think any fool can make a rule, and every fool will mind it."

—**Henry David Thoreau**

"If the English language made any sense, 'lackadaisical' would have something to do with a shortage of flowers."

—**Doug Larson**

"The English language is like a broad river on whose bank a few patient anglers are sitting, while, higher up, the stream is being polluted by a string of refuse-barges tipping out their muck."

—**Cyril Connolly**

"Even if you do learn to speak correct English, whom are you going to speak it to?"

—**Clarence Darrow**

"Do not compute the totality of your poultry population until all the manifestations of incubation have been entirely completed."

—**William Jennings Bryan**

The metal loop that a lampshade sits on is technically known as a "harp."

OOPS!

It's comforting to know that other people are screwing up even worse than we are. So go ahead and feel superior for a few minutes.

LIGHT MY FIRE

JERUSALEM—"It was, to say the least, a very unfortunate mistake. German chancellor Gerhard Schroeder accidentally extinguished Israel's eternal memorial flame for the six million Jews killed in the Nazi Holocaust.

"At a somber ceremony in Jerusalem's Yad Vashem Holocaust Memorial, Schroeder turned a handle that was supposed to make the flame rise. It went out instead. Israeli prime minister Ehud Barak stepped forward to try to help, but was unsuccessful. Finally, a technician used a gas lighter to bring the flame to life again, but by then the damage had been done."

—Reuters

REAL-LIFE LESSON

"A Grand Rapids, Minnesota, SWAT team, scheduled a drill at a local high school with actors and actresses playing the part of terrorists. But they mistakenly stormed another school next door. One of the teachers terrorized in the 'raid' said she was sure she was about to be killed as she was led from the building at gunpoint by the officers, who never identified themselves."

—Bonehead of the Day

SANTA CROOK

PHILADELPHIA—"Construction workers recently did a 'chimney sweep' of a vacant building and found the remains of a serial burglar who had tried to rob the place several years ago. According to Detective Romonita King, workers were knocking down the chimney Saturday when they smelled a foul odor. On closer inspection, they noticed a pair of sneakers, jeans, a Phillies cap, and what appeared to be human remains. The medical examiner's office tentatively listed the cause of death as accidental compression asphyxia. It was reported that the remains could be at least

Only musical instrument that's played without being touched: the theremin.

five years old and it was not known how long the business—ironically, a theft-prevention business—was closed."

—*Bizarre News*

THREE STRIKES, YOU'RE OUT

"Lorenzo Trippi, a lifeguard in Ravenna, Italy, lost his job when three people drowned after he hit them with life preservers. Police said his aim was too accurate."

—*Strange World #2*

HOE NO!

"Leonard Fountain, 68, got so fed up with having his gardening tools stolen from his shed that he rigged a homemade shotgun booby trap by the door. A year later, he was in a hurry to get some pruning done and opened the door, forgetting about the modification. He received severe flesh wounds to his right knee and thigh from the ensuing blast, and was charged with illegal possession of firearms."

—*Stuff*

THE YOUNG AND THE WRESTLESS

TACOMA, Wash.—"A seven-year-old boy practicing wrestling moves he had seen on TV bounced off his bed and tumbled out a second-story window. The boy sustained minor cuts and bruises after smashing through the bedroom window and tumbling two stories onto a cushion of grass. 'He was jumping from the dresser and doing a back-flip to the bed and went straight out the window,' said his mother.

"The boy was treated for minor internal injuries and hospitalized in satisfactory condition Friday. 'It hurts to wrestle,' he said. 'I'm not doing any more wrestling moves.'"

—*CNN Fringe*

*　　*　　*

"I watched the Indy 500 and I was thinking—if they left earlier, they wouldn't have to go so fast."

—*Steven Wright*

The White House owns more than 13,000 knives, forks and spoons.

MY BODY LIES OVER THE OCEAN

When someone passes away and their remains are buried or cremated, it's said they are being "laid to rest." But for some, the journey is just beginning.

DANIEL BOONE

Claim to Fame: 18th-century explorer and American frontiersman

Final Resting Place: Near Charette, Missouri…or maybe Frankfort, Kentucky

Details: If you owned a cemetery and wanted to attract new customers, how would you do it? One trick: a celebrity endorsement. Living celebrity pitchmen are best, but dead celebrities aren't bad either, because they can't complain.

That's how Daniel Boone ended up in Frankfort. When he died in the backwoods of Missouri in September 1820, he was buried in a small graveyard on a farm near Charette, in accordance with his wishes. But in 1845, the Capital Cemetery Company of Frankfort, Kentucky, started looking around for a famous American to bury in its new cemetery in the state capital. Boone was the perfect candidate: He was one of the founders of Kentucky and though he eventually left the state over a land dispute and swore he'd never return, he was still considered a hero.

Boone was also admired in Missouri, so the owners of Capital Cemetery had to act quickly and move the body before anyone could object. They enlisted the support of some of Boone's distant relatives, and then went to the farm and talked the new owner into letting them dig up the body. But the graves were poorly marked, so no one knew for sure which one was Boone's. That didn't matter: they made their best guess, dug up the remains of two bodies—assumed to be Boone and his wife—and spirited them off to Frankfort for reburial.

To this day no one knows for sure whether Boone and his wife are buried in Missouri or Kentucky, and it's doubtful we ever will. After so many years in the ground, there's probably not enough left for a DNA test.

In France, it's illegal to name a pig Napoleon.

LOST IN TRANSLATION

A few years ago, a British company called Today Translations commissioned a worldwide poll of 1,000 professional interpreters to find the world's most difficult-to-translate words. Here's their list of the 10 English words that are the hardest to translate into other languages.

AND THE WINNERS ARE:

10. Kitsch. "An item, usually of poor quality, that appeals to common or lowbrow tastes." (Need examples? Stop by Uncle John's house.)

9. Chuffed. A British word. A variation on the adjective *chuff* ("puffed with fat"), it means "proud, satisfied, or pleased."

8. Bumf. More Brit-speak. A shortened version of *bumfodder*, it once meant "toilet paper," but now refers to paperwork in general.

7. Whimsy. "A quaint or fanciful quality."

6. Spam. The luncheon meat, not the junk e-mail.

5. Googly. A term from the sport of cricket that means "an off-breaking ball with an apparent leg-break action on the part of the bowler." To explain the meaning of googly, you first have to explain the game of cricket—that's what makes this word so difficult to translate. "I am from Lithuania," says translator Jurga Zilinskiene. "We simply do not have googlies in Lithuania."

4. Poppycock. "Nonsense; empty writing or talk." From the Dutch word *pappekak*, which translates literally as "soft dung."

3. Serendipity. Finding something valuable, useful, or pleasant that you weren't searching for; a happy accident.

2. Gobbledygook. Wordy, unintelligible nonsense.

...and the most difficult-to-translate word in English is:

1. Plenipotentiary. "A special ambassador or envoy, invested with full powers to negotiate or transact business."

A group of hummingbirds is called a *hover*; a group of sparrows is a *quarrel*.

THE SAD TALE
OF CENTRALIA

*On Valentine's Day, 1981, eleven-year-old Todd Domboski was walking through
a field in Centralia, Pennsylvania, when a 150-foot-deep hole suddenly opened
beneath his feet. Noxious fumes crept out as the boy fell in. He only survived
by clinging to some newly exposed tree roots until his cousin ran over
and pulled him to safety. What was happening here…and why?*

COAL COUNTRY

Eastern Pennsylvania is anthracite coal country. Back at the turn
of the 20th century, miners were digging nearly 300 million tons
of coal per year from the region, leaving behind a vast subterranean network of abandoned mine shafts. In May 1962, while incinerating garbage
in an old strip mine pit outside of Centralia, one of the many exposed
coal seams ignited. The fire followed the seam down into the maze of
abandoned mines and began to spread. And it kept spreading—and burning—for years.

Mine fires in coal country are actually not all that uncommon. There
are currently as many as 45 of them burning in Pennsylvania alone.
Unfortunately, there's no good way to put them out. But that doesn't stop
people from trying.

• The most effective method to extinguish such a fire is to strip mine
around the entire perimeter of the blaze. That's an expensive—and in
populated areas, impractical—proposition. Essentially, it means digging an
enormous trench, deep enough to get underneath the fires, which are
often more than 500 feet below ground.

• An easier (but not much easier) method is to bore holes down into the
old mine shafts, and then pour in tons of wet concrete to make plugs.
Then more holes are drilled and flame-suppressing foam is pumped into
the areas between plugs. It, too, is a very expensive project, and it doesn't
always succeed.

• The cheapest way to deal with a mine fire by far is to keep an eye on it
and hope it burns itself out. (One fire near Lehigh, Pennsylvania, burned

from 1850 until the 1930s.) After a 1969 effort to dig out the Centralia fire proved both costly and unsuccessful, they admitted defeat and let the fire take its course. By 1980, the size of the underground blaze was estimated at 350 acres, and large clouds of noxious smoke were billowing out of the ground all over town. The ground temperature under a local gas station was recorded at nearly 1,000°F. Residents of the once-thriving mountain town began to wonder if Centralia was a safe place to live.

EXODUS

When the boy fell in the hole and almost died, the fire beneath Centralia became a national news story. The sinkhole—caused by an effect known as *subsidence*, which occurs when mine shafts collapse, possibly because the support beams are on fire—put the town's 1,600 residents in a fix. Their homes were suddenly worthless. They couldn't sell them and move someplace safer—no one in their right mind would buy them.

The townsfolk were given a choice: a $660-million digging project that might not work, or let the government buy their homes. They voted 345 to 200 in favor of the buyout, and an exodus soon began. By 1991, $42 million had been spent buying out more than 540 Centralia homes and businesses.

GHOST TOWN

If you were to visit Centralia today, the first thing you'd notice is that there are more streets than buildings. At first glance, it would seem that someone decided to build a town, but only got as far as paving the roads. If you looked a bit closer, however, you'd notice the remnants of house foundations. Looking still closer, you'd see smoke still seeping out of the ground.

Just after the buyout, nearly 50 die-hard Centralians continued to live in the smoldering ghost town. Since then, the number has dwindled to less than 10. Experts estimate it will take 250 years for the fire to burn itself out.

*   *   *

"Nearly all men can stand adversity, but if you want to test a man's character, give him power."

—Abraham Lincoln

THAT'S ABOUT THE SIZE OF IT

Most people never give a second thought to life's most important questions, such as: How tall should a bowling pin be? Fortunately for them, Uncle John does. Here's a look at the standard sizes of everyday objects.

Soccer Ball: Must measure between 27 and 28 inches in circumference and weigh 14 to 16 ounces.

Napkin (dinner): Should be no less than 183 square inches, unfolded. (A cocktail napkin should be no larger than 100 square inches, unfolded.)

Boulder: An "official" boulder must be at least 256 millimeters (10.07 inches) in diameter.

Pebble: A pebble must be no smaller than 4 millimeters (0.16 inch) and no larger than 64 millimeters (2.51 inches) in diameter.

Bowling ball: Should be 27 inches in circumference and weigh no more than 16 pounds.

Bowling pin: Should weigh between 3 pounds, 2 ounces and 3 pounds, 10 ounces and should be exactly 1 foot, 3 inches tall.

Dart: Cannot be more than 1 foot in length, or weigh more than 50 grams.

Dartboard: Must be hung so that the bull's-eye is 5 feet, 8 inches above the floor. The person throwing the dart must stand 7 feet, 9 $\frac{1}{4}$ inches from the board.

Wash cloth: Should be a square of cloth no smaller than 12 by 12 inches and no larger than 14 by 14 inches.

Compact car: Must weigh at least 3,000 pounds, but no more than 3,500.

Parachute: To slow a 200-pound person to a landing speed of 20 feet per second, a parachute must be 28 feet in diameter.

Golf ball: Must weigh no more than 1.62 ounces, with a diameter no less than 1.68 inches. (A standard tee is 2 $\frac{1}{8}$ inches long.)

King mattress: Must be no smaller than 80 inches long and 76 inches wide.

Jumbo egg: One dozen jumbo eggs should weigh no less than 30 ounces.

"Yesterday's home runs don't win today's games." —Babe Ruth

FINAL THOUGHTS

If you had to pick some last words, what would they be?
Here are a dozen that people are still quoting.

"Don't worry—it's not loaded."
—**Terry Kath, leader of
the band Chicago,
playing Russian roulette**

"I should never have switched
from Scotch to Martinis."
—**Humphrey Bogart**

"How about this for a headline
for tomorrow's paper? French
fries."
—**James French, executed
in the Oklahoma
electric chair, 1966**

"I'll take a wee drop of that. I
don't think there's much fear of
me learning to drink now."
—**Dr. James Cross, Scottish
physicist and lifelong teetotaler**

"Am I dying, or is this my
birthday?"
—**Lady Astor, awaking
to find her relatives gathered
around her bedside**

"And now, I am officially dead."
—**Abram S. Hewitt,
industrialist, after removing
the oxygen tube from his mouth**

"I've had 18 straight whiskeys. I
think that's the record!"
—**Dylan Thomas, poet**

"Why, of course....That's His
line of work."
—**Heinrich Heine,
German poet, on being
told that God would
forgive his sins**

"So little done. So much to do!"
—**Alexander Graham Bell**

"I desire to go to hell and not to
heaven. In the former place I
shall enjoy the company of
popes, kings, and princes, while
the latter are only beggars,
monks and apostles."
—**Niccolo Machiavelli**

"Waiting, are they? Waiting, are
they? Well, let 'em wait."
—**General Ethan Allen,
Revolutionary War hero,
on being told, "The angels
are waiting for you."**

"Either the wallpaper goes, or I
do."
—**Oscar Wilde**

Raw coffee beans, soaked in water and spices, are chewed like candy in some parts of Africa.

ANSWER PAGES

PLOP, PLOP, QUIZ, QUIZ
(Answers for page 25)

1) Maxwell House coffee
2) Allstate insurance
3) Perdue chickens
4) Brylcreem
5) Federal Express
6) Schlitz beer
7) Hebrew National hot dogs
8) Alka-Seltzer
9) Morton's salt
10) American Express
11) Packard
12) Remington shavers
13) Timex
14) AT&T
15) Yellow Pages
16) Energizer batteries
17) Marlboro cigarettes
18) Bactine ointment
19) Milk
20) Cattlemen's Beef Board
21) Delta Airlines
22) Bartles & Jaymes wine coolers
23) Chrysler Cordoba
24) General Foods International Coffees
25) Irish Spring soap
26) Pepsi
27) Motel 6
28) DuPont

OL' JAY'S BRAINTEASERS
(Answers for page 185)

1. BRIGHT THINKING
Standing in the hallway, Amy turned on the first light switch. She waited two minutes and then turned on the second light switch. Then after another minute she turned them both off. When she walked into the library, one was very hot, the other was slightly warm, and the other was cold—making it easy for her to tell Uncle John which switch turned on which lamp.

2. MYSTERY JOB
Brian works at a library.

3. SIDE TO SIDE
The river was frozen.

4. SPECIAL NUMBER
8,549,176,320
When spelled out, it contains

The horns of a male bighorn sheep can weigh up to 30 lbs.—as much as all the bones in its body

each number—zero through nine—in alphabetical order.

5. TIME PIECES

An hourglass. It is filled with thousands of grains of sand.

6. WORD PLAY

If you remove the first letter of each word and place it on the end of the word, it will spell the same word backwards.

THE JOY OF SECTS
(Answers for page 230)

1. A or C. Bravo if you eliminated Quakers and Moravians right away—they don't wear old-fashioned clothes. As for the other two, take another look at the clothes. Color doesn't matter, but patterns do. The Amish wear only solid colors, so anything else suggests the girls are Mennonites.

2. D. Amish communities do not have churches. Instead, they hold Sunday services in different homes each week, so a wagonload of benches is delivered to the designated house. Most Amish homes have dark green window shades. Why the plain, identical window treatments? The Amish community would consider decorative shades or frilly curtains signs of vanity.

3. B. Although a basket of buns and mugs of coffee may be passed around, the Moravian Love Feast is actually a festival that includes the singing of hymns and the playing of devotional music. The practice imitates early Christian celebrations that included prayer and sharing a meal. Moravian Love Feasts are held on holidays, anniversaries, and other special occasions.

4. B. You might see foot washing at a pre-Easter service in a Catholic church, but the Amish hold the only ceremony in which everyone gets their feet cleaned—a special adults-only communion service called Grossgemee in the spring and fall. The service lasts all day, and the adults wash each other's feet to imitate Jesus, who once washed the feet of his disciples.

5. Most likely, the Quaker. That's the only sect of the four that originated in England, and the British are avid tea drinkers. None of these groups approve of drunkenness, but all of them actually do allow moderate drinking. Amish men enjoy beer, and the others have changed their attitudes toward drinking over time. Mennonites in the United States were completely against alcohol during the 19th and early 20th centuries, for instance, but the sect has since relaxed that stance. Today, about 60 percent of Mennonites consider moderate alcohol consumption to be acceptable.

What's a *bipennis*? Surprise! It's a medieval double-sided axe.

NAME THAT COUNTRY
(Answers for page 269)

SAVED: El Salvador. *El Salvador* is Spanish for "The Savior." The Spanish conquered the Pipil, claimed the land, and gave it a new name in 1524.

NOTHING TO IT: Namibia.

THE NAMELESS NAME: Australia. Pre-18th-century maps show a large land mass labeled *Terra Australis Incognita*, Latin for "The Unknown Southern Land." Geographers had never seen the land, but insisted that without it, the Earth would be lopsided.

OVER THERE WHERE THE SUN COMES UP: Japan. In China, *jih* means "sun," *pun* means "east," and since the sun rises in the east, *jih pun* means "sunrise." Referring to the islands east of China, it means "land of the rising sun." *Japan* derived from the Malaysian version of the Chinese name: *Japang*.

GRECIAN FORMULA: Great Britain. Pythaes sailed around this island around 300 B.C., naming it *Pretanic*, after the Pritani, or the Prits. *Pritani* is believed to be a Celtic word meaning "people with designs," because the Pritani were extensively tattooed. When the Anglo-Saxons attacked in the 400s, many Britons fled to the European continent and settled what became known as *Brittany*. To differentiate it from this "lesser" Britain, the island was thereafter called *Great Britain*.

A BIT OBTUSE?: England. After the Roman rule of Britain ended in 406 A.D., it became a battleground for many invaders. The most prominent were the Germanic tribes the Angles and the Saxons. The Angles came from a fishhook-shaped region in northern Germany called Angul (believed to be the origin of the word *angle*—to fish).

WHY DON'T THEY SPEAK GERMAN?: France. The Franks were a Germanic tribe that settled along the Rhine River in Germany during the third and fourth centuries. (Frankfurt is named after them.) They would go on to conquer nearly all of northern Europe, eventually settling in what is now France.

OVERCOATIA: Gabon. In the 15th century, Portuguese traders, the first Europeans to visit this part of Africa, thought the Como River's estuary was shaped like a traditional Portuguese overcoat called a *gabao*. So that's what they called it—which became *Gabon*.

The average human ear grows 0.01 inches in length every year.

UNCLE JOHN'S BATHROOM READER CLASSIC SERIES

Find these and other great titles from the *Uncle John's Bathroom Reader* Classic Series online at **www.bathroomreader.com**. Or contact us at:

Bathroom Readers' Institute
P.O. Box 1117 • Ashland, OR 97520 • (888) 488-4642

THE LAST PAGE

FELLOW BATHROOM READERS:
The fight for good bathroom reading should never be taken loosely—
we must do our duty and sit firmly for what we believe in, even
while the rest of the world is taking potshots at us.

We'll be brief. Now that we've proven we're not simply a flush-in-the-
pan, we invite you to take the plunge: Sit Down and Be Counted! Log
on to *www.bathroomreader.com* and earn a permanent spot on the BRI
honor roll!

If you like reading our books...
VISIT THE BRI'S WEB SITE!
www.bathroomreader.com

- Visit "The Throne Room"—a great place to read!
  - Receive our irregular newsletters via e-mail
    - Order additional *Bathroom Readers*
      - Read our blog

Go with the Flow...

Well, we're out of space, and when you've gotta go, you've gotta go.
Tanks for all your support. Hope to hear from you soon.

Meanwhile, remember...

Keep on flushin'!